A Shell Guide

SUFFOLK

Norman Scarfe

A Shell Guide

SUFFOLK

by Norman Scarfe

Faber & Faber 3 Queen Square London

First published in 1960
Second edition 1966
This new edition published 1976
by Faber and Faber Limited
3 Queen Square London WC1
Printed in Great Britain by
Butler & Tanner Ltd
Frome and London

ISBN 0 571 04901 X

For my parents, with love

Instruments of the Passion on a
bench end at Fressingfield

Preface to the third edition

The *Shell Guides* to counties are essentially personal. Sharing with their readers the discovery of a whole county, the authors soon betray their own pre-occupations as painters or architects, townsmen or countrymen, poets, academics or just addicted observant travellers. My own bias is historical. I like to know how places came to be as they are. I have been much encouraged in this by colleagues and friends, in the 1950s working at Leicester University, more recently working at home here in East Anglia.

In the first Preface to this Guide, in 1960, I spoke darkly of "another book in which I should give reasons for some rather blunt assertions". I am proud that this book, *The Suffolk Landscape*, appeared (first in 1972) in W. G. Hoskins's pioneering county series on "The Making of the English Landscape". Edwin Smith (his death so deeply lamented) and Olive Cook helped immeasurably to clarify my view of Suffolk's face. Among many friends who have helped with the preparation of this 3rd edition of the Guide, I especially want to thank Canon John Fitch, rector of Brandon, and Peter Northeast, headmaster of Rattlesden's school. I am deeply grateful to John and Edward Piper for their expert care in designing the book, and seeing it through the press.

NOTE ON BOUNDARY-CHANGES AND BOOKS

The boundary-changes of 1974 took five Suffolk parishes into Norfolk, ostensibly for the benefit of Yarmouth's expansion. The map in this Guide registers the change, but the five places are still described in the Gazetteer since they remain physically and historically so much a part of Suffolk.

Full lists of the features and contents of the medieval churches appear in H. Munro Cautley's rich tome, *Suffolk Churches and their Treasures* (Ipswich, 4th edn, 1975), and E. Farrer's *Monumental Brasses of Suffolk* (Norwich, 1903). Nikolaus Pevsner's *Suffolk* ("Buildings of England") is very useful for reference. J. H. & J. Parker's *Suffolk* volume, 1855, in their *Ecclesiastical and Architectural Topography of England*, remains valuable.

Norman Scarfe, Shingle Street,
February 1976

Illustrations

Clare inn sign. A swan 'gorged' like this was the heraldic badge of Henry IV and Prince Hal

The New Suffolk Traveller

Suffolk has only in the last two decades begun to be generally affected by modern industrial development. Previously such activity was concentrated in Ipswich and Lowestoft, the two biggest towns. Now its effects are more widely diffused, especially through the southern districts of the county, where the historic landscape is most poignantly beautiful, and the best-known villages lie. Travelling through Suffolk in the seventies, we lament, as the late Nan Fairbrother did in her brilliant, unsentimental, constructive statement of rural England's dilemma, *New Lives, New Landscapes* (1970): "Loving the country now means loving the pre-industrial country, and it is bitter to realise that most of the landscape we enjoy unreservedly is where the twentieth century has not reached."

Southern Suffolk is increasingly seen to be within range of the London commuter. A zone right across the south is affected by the spectacular expansion of Felixstowe's "container" port, alleged to be the biggest in the world. Its success is paid for by the country people of south Suffolk, whose lanes have been pounded, pulverised and generally blighted by steadily growing numbers of juggernaut lorries, humping between the Midlands and Europe loads our half-empty freight-trains were meant for. It is south Suffolk, too, that is straddled by the great pylon-scape from Sizewell's coastal atomic power-station over to Hertfordshire. (The possible blessings of a whole group of atomic power-stations at Orfordness are being considered.) During these last two decades, the plans of the lately extinct West Suffolk County Council produced the astounding result, revealed in the 1971 Census, that *West Suffolk* and *Lancashire* are jointly leading the whole country with the biggest population growth-

rate: and the biggest part of their industrialisation is happening in the south, in Haverhill, and, incredibly, Sudbury and Hadleigh.

So, whereas in 1960 this Guide began rather complacently, it cannot do so now. Yet the rest of this Introduction is substantially unaltered; what served in 1960 is, happily, serviceable still. Only the detail in the Gazetteer has needed correcting. The traveller in Suffolk today still risks being spellbound by the simplest features of its quiet landscape. The proportions of its fields, its houses and its churches are almost wholly the work of those older industrialists, the farmers and clothiers, traders and builders of the Middle Ages. The description of Suffolk in Domesday Book tallies with much that is recognisable today; it helps us more than any other single source to understand the peculiarities of the land itself, so slowly and so little have the essentials changed.

In 1603, Robert Ryece wrote a remarkable *Breviary of Suffolk, Or a plaine and familier description of the Country*,[1] in which the 20th-century landscape is brought very nearly into focus. Three and a half centuries later, Ryece would still find himself at home in his house at Preston, on those cultivated and enchanted slopes, between Kettlebaston and Lavenham, draining down into the streams that made possible the fulling processes of the famous local clothiers of the later Middle Ages. At Preston the medieval church retains a great deal of the character he gave it during the fulfilment of the Elizabethan church settlement: the armorial glass of his own family alliances, and the magnificent arms of the great queen. A moderate himself (and

1. ed. Lord Francis Hervey, 1902. An illuminating study of Ryece's life and work by G. C. Harlow appeared in *Proceedings of the Suffolk Institute*, XXXII, 1970, pp. 43–70.

Moat Farm, **Wilby**

dead in 1638), his friends and neighbours were almost to a man on Parliament's side during the Civil War.[2] His glass was spared by the Puritans, but much that was glorious was smashed.

In George II's reign, John Kirby of Wickham Market published *The Suffolk Traveller*, based on a survey he had made over the years 1732–4. Kirby distinguished three main sorts of Suffolk travelling. "This County", he wrote, "is naturally divided into the Sandlands, the Woodlands, and the Fielding." By the Sandlands, sometimes called Sandlings,

2. A glimpse of some who were not is provided by Clive Holmes, *The Suffolk Committees for Scandalous Ministers, 1644–6*, Suffolk Records Society, 1970.

he meant the light lands running beside the low seashore; he subdivided them further into marshes, arable and heath. They all lie east of A12, the main London–Yarmouth road, which marks a rough boundary with the Woodlands. The Woodlands is the old name for the central two-thirds of Suffolk, stretching across from Haverhill in the south-west to Beccles in the north-east, fertile glacial clay, naturally supporting heavy timber—the oak woods that long made a foundation for Suffolk shipbuilding and in her church-roofs and half-timbered houses still provide for her fame abroad. Never protected by forest law, these woods were cleared over the centuries, and the clays properly worked to make the pastures and,

Elizabethan prospect house: Thorpe Hall, Horham (**Hoxne**) ▷

above all, the cornfields that are now the most characteristic sight. Central Suffolk is the best name for this, since the Woodlands seems no longer appropriate, and High Suffolk, another old name, is vague if not misleading. By the Fielding, Kirby meant the much more open Bury-Newmarket-Mildenhall country, with its longer views, breckland, downland and fenland lying west of the Woodlands and exposed to all the influences of the Midlands: "affording good corn in divers parts", but in fields that had not been enclosed in the Middle Ages (unlike Central Suffolk), and probably acquiring its name thereby.

◁ **Wingfield** Castle

Moat Hall, **Parham**

p14 Tower-mill, **Pakenham** ▷
p15 Post-mill, **Holton**, by Halesworth

Central Suffolk provides the most distinctively "Suffolk" kind of landscape, as peculiar to Suffolk as Broadland is to Norfolk, only more fundamental, since it covers the greater part of the county. Some of its particular features occur elsewhere, but the combination is unique. First, there is an astonishing profusion of old moated farmsteads, five or six hundred of them. Most of the houses go back in part to at least the sixteenth century. Thatched or tiled, half-timbered or brick, they usually have great soaring chimney-stacks. Not all the old houses have survived, and even some of the

abandoned moats have been ploughed in. Some of these moats were designed with a view to military defence (at Wingfield Castle, Letheringham Old Hall, and other manor houses). But they are confined to the Central Suffolk clay. The most important task of a farmer in this district is land-drainage. Where there was no natural drain, no considerable stream (and this applies especially in the northern part), a pond or a moat was dug, as low as possible in relation to the area to be drained. This held the surplus water in the wet months, and stored it as well as possible for use in the summer. A moat not only served a wider drainage-area than a pond, and helped to keep the house walls dry, but it also served to keep the livestock corralled and watered, and defended in the days of wolves and cattle-thieves. It was probably used, too, for keeping the stock-fish that feature in so many medieval menus.

Just as houses were moated, fields were drained by great ditches, kept constantly clean. Their banks glow with the pale light of primroses in the spring. Roads had to skirt these square-cornered ditches, so that in some places modern drivers have to negotiate a sharp bend every hundred yards or so. In wet weather, where the ditches have *not* been cleaned, it is still possible to find one's way barred by a second-class road drowned beneath feet of water. There is a most striking contrast between these crooked Suffolk lanes and the strips of Roman road that have survived, for instance from Bungay to Halesworth or from Otley Bottom to Barham. Other Central Suffolk features are the common grazing lands, sometimes as many as three or four to a parish, often dotted with old cottages, and usually called Greens, but occasionally, between Stowmarket and Sudbury, called Tyes; and the windmills (practically extinguished now) that naturally flourished in cornlands where the wind was always fresh and the water too feeble to drive a wheel. They were usually of the beautiful post-mill variety such as my grandfather

worked, and in which Suffolk specialised: one is being preserved, almost in aspic, at Saxtead: open to the public and enormously popular.

Of Kirby's two other divisions, Sandlands and Fielding, it is enough to say that they each include the most beautiful natural, as distinct from man-made, scenery: especially the deserted heaths. The heaths that lie behind, and a little above, the seashore, have in common with the breckland that lies north-west of Bury extraordinary evidences of prehistoric, British and early English people, the ground still littered with flint tools, and humped with tumuli, of which hundreds must have vanished. One that survived at Sutton Hoo has yielded up relics of a long-ship laden with glittering exotic treasures whose reflection is casting a new light on the whole ancient Anglo-Saxon world. Both Sandlands and Fielding have their marshland or fens, offering occupation alike to the pastoralist and the naturalist. Lastly there are the long shingly sea-boards in the east, and the famous chalkdown landscape of Newmarket, misleadingly called the Heath, in the west on the borders of Cambridgeshire. Newmarket is the best known and least characteristic part of Suffolk, belonging to the great chalk ridge that connects the whole eastern edge of the fens with the Thames Valley and the chalk uplands of Wessex. The seashores, much of them hauntingly desolate and beautiful, are least well known, for they may be travelled only by boat or on foot. Mercifully, coast roads are largely impracticable. Where they exist, as to the north of Lowestoft, the twentieth century has revealed its more hateful forms of unsightliness—bungalow-hutches, exposed caravans, our kind of slumdom.

The decade ending in 1851, the year of the Great Exhibition, marked the climax of the growth of the typical Suffolk country parish. Since then, the parishes of Central Suffolk have dwindled, while the towns, large and small, have grown relentlessly. Before 1851, there had been signs of agricultural distress, but not of decay. In the attempt to deal with rural poverty on the basis of the Hundred, or Union, in place of the single parish, East Suffolk was eighty years ahead of England as a whole, and some handsome workhouses survive (see Onehouse).

William White's *History, Gazetteer and Directory*, first issued in 1844, provides a detailed picture of trades and occupations at the moment when the country parishes were reaching their peak of population. How extraordinarily well-provided those parishes were! Look at Laxfield, for instance, or Stradbroke, with their "Academies" (Church, Nonconformist, non-denominational), shoemakers, tailors, saddlers, grocers, blacksmiths, wheelwrights and carpenters, and corn-millers, as well as the various farmers, the vicar and the Baptist ministers (Particular Baptist as well as Baptist) that one would expect to find. In addition to these, Laxfield had a printer and druggist, a glover and hairdresser, several publicans (Royal Oak and General Wolfe were the principal Laxfield pubs), and an inland revenue officer: Stradbroke had Mr Stephen Smith, bravely entered in 1844 as artist.

Rural Suffolk has been a stronghold of Nonconformity since the Reformation. Most parishes embrace three or four ancient farms, or Halls. The people of these innumerable "scattered" parishes would form a unit only at church, and differences of opinion between the farmers of the parish, which in the early Middle Ages might have led to the formation of a new parish, after the Reformation sometimes led to the establishment of Independent congregations. At Walpole the famous Congregational chapel was converted from a farmhouse in the 1640s. The characteristic Suffolk parish has not only a medieval church, a number of old farmhouses and some cottages, ancient and modern, but also a cubic Nonconformist chapel or two—red or white brick in the east, flint and brick in the west.

The main effect of the industrial developments themselves occurred in the towns: for instance Stowmarket and Halesworth in the Canal Age, Lowestoft in the Railway Age. "Elizabethan" manors or lodges by the Ipswich architect Frederick Barnes distinguish the Ipswich–Bury line of the 1840s. Pathetic little corrugated-iron pavilions that were erected as stations on the Mid-Suffolk Light Railway (1904–52), stand as derelict memorials to that belated attempt to supply good transport facilities to the country people of Central Suffolk.

Nothing could avert the depression and depopulation of the countryside. 1879 stands out as a particularly "black" year. It was not only the labourers who left the villages, but many tenant farmers went too, and even some of the landlords. The country people have taken heart again in our own time, with the artificial stimulus to agriculture provided by two World Wars and by such legislation as the Beet Sugar Subsidy Act of 1925. But the depopulation coupled with the mechanisation of farming has changed the old village communities for ever. The new communities are fostered by the Suffolk Community Council under the County Councils of East and West Suffolk set up in 1888, and reduced to one in 1974. The Suffolk Community Council is concerned with such activities as the provision of village halls, of playing fields, and with the annual competition for the Best Kept Village. Its local history section took a lead in establishing a rural-life museum at Abbots Hall, Stowmarket, of the delightful open-air kind that the Dutch have developed since 1912 at Arnhem. There, reassembled for enjoyment and study, is a growing collection of some of the peculiarly East Anglian buildings, furniture and machinery, that can no longer be preserved on their original sites.

The Suffolk of Gainsborough and Constable, the Suffolk of William Kirby the famous entomologist, and Joseph Hooker the botanist and confidant of Darwin, the Suf-

Minsmere (**Westleton**)

◁ **Westleton** Heath

p20 **Stansfield** (*above*) and **Earl Stonham** ▷
p21 **Kersey**

folk of Crabbe, Robert Bloomfield and, later, of Charles Doughty the Arabian traveller, with its clear lights, its moving clouds, the undramatic objects on its surface, helped them all to make in their various ways that transition from the particular to the universal which seems to English people to be at the basis of all great imaginative achievement. In a way, Gainsborough went on painting the same tree all his life. Constable, who for years had to put up with the smoky light of London, would dream of "the sound of water escaping from mill-dams, etc., willows, old rotten banks, slimy posts, and brickwork, I love such things". We remember Crabbe's Peter Grimes, who "loved to stop beside the opening sluice".

W. H. Hudson got his first love of England from a copy of Bloomfield's *Farmer's Boy*, picked up in Buenos Aires, and when he reached England came on pilgrimage to Sapiston and Troston. Benjamin Britten, reading in the *Listener* E. M. Forster's memorable broadcast about Crabbe, was drawn home across the Atlantic to Suffolk and Crabbe's Aldeburgh. The range and power of Crabbe and Bloomfield (and a number of lesser Suffolk poets) was all that differentiated them. In that less familiar and describable world of the ear, one hears Britten's immediate response to Suffolk. The Deben Valley provokes a spring symphony as directly as the Little Ouse evoked a spring poem. Like Constable, Britten re-creates storm-clouds, and grey ever-murmuring seas, and these he can combine with the harsher moods of Crabbe, and with his own compassion, which he breathes, for instance, into the unearthly beauty of the Moonlight Interlude before Act III of Peter Grimes.

The beauties of the Stour are especially moving in the broad part of the valley near Stoke-by-Nayland, and between Nayland and Wissington. But of course it is no use joining the idiots' procession of cars and Luxury Coaches, blundering about in those enchanted lanes between East Bergholt and Flatford Mill. One should go there, but not unless one goes on foot, and if possible on a mid-week morning in summer. Remember that the subject of one of Constable's most exciting pictures is a mere tree-root, and it was painted at Helmingham, away from all this. Nor is it any use rummaging about in the upper part of the valley for Gainsborough's Cornard Wood. Little Cornard has many delights, but no wood.[3]

An absolute imperative for sightseeing nowadays is to leave every motor vehicle unobtrusively parked as far away as possible from the beauties of the landscape to be enjoyed.

LOCAL BUILDING MATERIALS

The absence of a hard stone-bed in Suffolk is at once suggested by the smooth, unindented coast line, by the way the sea manipulates the shingle as it pleases, working the total destruction of the once-proud city of Dunwich, and indulging in the whim of creating that immense false nose, the eleven-mile spit off Orford. But Suffolk has its resources of stone for building. Flint is plentiful, shiny black and grey, a stone proverbially hard, but dependent, as a building material, on mortar, which is slow to set and subject to frost. So that the flint towers of our churches rarely went up more than ten feet a year. But when they were up, they mostly stayed up, five hundred or so of them, the most familiar feature in the Suffolk landscape. There is nothing uniform about them. Sometimes the flintwork is very ancient and ragged and rough, as in many of the forty-two round towers, some of them 11th-century. Sometimes it is highly finished, as in the front wall of the south porch at Blythburgh, where the flints are squared and close-set, in

3. The late R. B. Beckett's classic edition of *John Constable's Correspondence*, in seven volumes, was published by the Suffolk Records Society. Suffolk features in them all, but the first (1962) covered completely his relations with his family at East Bergholt.

p26 ▷
Eye (*left*)
and **Laxfield**
from west

p27
Kersey (*left*)
and
Earl Stonham
from south,
bell-chamber
louvres
offset by
stair-turrets

Blythburgh

Two masterworks of carpentry: ▷
p30 **Needham Market**
p31 **Grundisburgh**

the manner of gauged brickwork. The beauty of the final effect is not at all commensurate with the degree of "finish" by the flint craftsmen. It depends much upon the weàther—like all old buildings. It depends, too, on the design, on whether an effect of bold simplicity has been aimed at, or whether the flintwork has been deliberately decorated with an admixture of red brick or of freestone. (Flint-and-freestone decoration is called flushwork.) Of course proportion and scale are important too. There is the additional advantage that the interiors of the church walls were left rough, so that Victorian restorers have not scraped the plaster off.

Along that misleading Suffolk shore there are two other building stones. One of them is the Coralline crag, a delightful tobacco-coloured, shelly-textured stone which weathers a rather buff grey in the church-towers of Chillesford and Wantisden that were built of it. The other is more important—an orgillaceous, or clayey, limestone called septaria, that crops out all along the coast from Orford to Walton-on-the-Naze, and best exhibits its remarkable qualities in the keep of the royal castle at Orford, built in the 1160s, and still looking quite composed after eight hundred winters by the North Sea. The baronial opposition were not above using it in the skirting walls at Framlingham. It weathers to anything between warm, soft browns and grey. It occurs in the base of the 13th-century walls of Little Wenham Hall, and was largely used in the 14th-century church-tower at Harkstead. Indeed most of the church-towers between the mouths of the Stour and the Ore have some septaria in them. So, too, have a great many public buildings in the metropolis. For it provided the raw material of the famous Parker's "Roman Cement". Something like a million tons of it were removed for this purpose between 1812 and 1845, but by 1850 the superiority of Portland Cement was beginning to be seen.

"Portland Stone Cement", as distinct from Portland Cement, was the invention of a Southolt man, William Lockwood, working at Woodbridge, who did well with it in the early 19th century. In the last quarter of the century another attempt to produce a substance of this name was made at Waldringfield; then new methods led to the removal of the works to Blakenham, where they remain prominently. Chalk itself has been used quite successfully as a building-stone in the Brandon-Eriswell-Wangford district. "Clay lump" walls are no longer at all common, as they must once have been in Central Suffolk. But clay, straw and hazel-sticks (wattle and daub) is the common wall-filling in the half-timbered buildings that still abound in Suffolk, especially in the clay land that bore the trees, and was called the Woodlands. Examples of exposed wattle are preserved under glass in several old inns, such as Framlingham Crown.

Plaster was found to protect all this clay from the weather; it could be stiffened to receive incised decorations in the Elizabethan and Jacobean periods, and in the later seventeenth century it was the material for an imaginative plastic art. There are several examples of this decorative "pargeting" in Suffolk: the most perfect, an inspired conceit, adorns Ipswich Butter Market. Plaster protected timber as well, a fact ignored by those who strip it off to display the lovely half-timbered effect. The early builders often intended to leave exposed only the brackets and bargeboards which they carved.

Timber is the most truly characteristic of the old Suffolk building materials. The flintwork and the brickwork have close parallels in Norfolk, which boasts nothing comparable with Suffolk's half-timbering. In this medium the chief rival is Essex, whose

◁ Nethergate Street, **Clare**: exuberant pargeting

forests were preserved for hunting. 13th-century houses at Bricett and Stansfield and 14th-century houses from Cornard and Capel to Coddenham and Campsey Ash demonstrate their early use in building. The wonder is that the Suffolk Woodlands lasted so long in view of the demand not only for houses and ships and their furniture, but the elaborate, indeed gorgeous, roofs and fur-

Bench-ends at **Freckenham**
Above: devil dropping supporter into hell
Left: angel

nishings of all the churches. The best of the furnishings are listed in the Gazetteer. They include benches, a few font-covers and, especially, screens. The distinctive beauty of Suffolk screen-work lies in the floreated cusp-mouldings that developed as part of their design, starting at Grundisburgh (so far as the evidence goes) in the late 14th century: it lies equally in the colour decoration that became

Bench-end zoos at **Denston** (*left*) and **Woolpit**

an integral part of the design in the 15th century—the traditional red, green, gold, blue and white; and there is rich gesso work, notably at Bramfield, Southwold and Yaxley.

The fact that so much of the carpentry in Needham nave roof is work of the 1880s detracts nothing from the sublime conception of the original mason and carpenter. Here is a great work, and so there is at Earl Stonham, Grundisburgh, Mildenhall and St Mary's, Bury, and several other places with elaborate open timber roofs such as only Norfolk can rival.

There is no doubt that the building craft in Suffolk reached its richest and most advanced stage in the 15th century. It maintained this position well on into the 16th century, and then declined. Nearly all the church-towers date from the 15th century, and the most characteristic design was "in production" in the middle years of the century—before and after 1450. The most famous of all Suffolk buildings, the churches of "industrial" Long Melford and Lavenham, are works of the end of the century. The body of Long Melford church, the supreme building in Suffolk, was begun, at the east

33

end, in the 1470s. The work at Lavenham lasted from about 1486 to 1525, and was completed just in time for its bells to summon the 4,000 cloth workers of the district to protest about the crisis that marked the beginning of the end of the clothiers' prosperity.

At the end of this greatest period of church building, brick was brought into play: in a large number of warm red porches—of which the finest is at Great Bradley—and in a number of towers (ten in East Suffolk, three in West) of which some are extremely beautiful, laced with diaper work. Their form is essentially "Suffolk", even though the idea is presumably Dutch. They had a small successor, at Brightwell, in the 1650s, and four handsome grandchildren, at Cowlinge, Drinkstone, Grundisburgh and Long Melford early in the 18th century.

Suffolk has been amply compensated for its deficiencies in local building stone by being able to draw on both the ideas and the craftsmen of the neighbouring Netherlands, where builders were more dependent on brick and earlier skilled in its use. Between the building of Mockbeggars Hall, Claydon, in 1621 and that of Huntingfield High House in 1700, at least forty-four houses and farm-buildings were erected in Suffolk with curved Dutch gables. Some are dated on the iron ties with which these exuberant gables are held to the main building. Many of them—as of the dark glazed, or red, pantiled roofs—are found along the coast and in the Waveney valley; which suggests that intercourse with the Low Countries did provide the inspiration to build them. No. 18, Northgate, Beccles, is more like a genuine Dutch house than any house in the county: with its exciting vertical lines it makes wonderful use of a narrow street-frontage. The process of refronting town houses—with new, ornate,

◁ Flemings Hall, **Bedingfield**

Garden-house, **Long Melford** Hall

dated bargeboards in the early 17th century, with pargeting or beautifully leaded and glazed casement-windows in the later 17th century—was redoubled in the 18th century, and extended to farmhouses. The 18th-century alterations involved fixing a brick façade with sash-windows over the front of the old timbered house. One sees examples of this everywhere in Suffolk. And it went on in the 19th century. Late in the 20th, one looks almost in vain for any assured way of improving old buildings by the application of a living style. It usually seems safest to revert to academic reconstruction. Alas.

The great Roman fort of Gariannonum, at Burgh by Lowestoft, reveals not only the full beauty of the age-long local combination of red brick and silver flint in its wall texture, but also the way brick has held its own with flint since the 3rd century. Little Wenham Hall (*c.* 1270–80) is the earliest brick house left in England. The bricks are not red, but the gault variety that have evidently always been popular, because available, in Suffolk. The brickwork of Hengrave Hall (1525–38), starting exactly at the moment where Lavenham stopped, its porch marking the transition from Gothic to Renaissance forms, is white—or rather stone-coloured, if that adjective is not too vague. Not far from Hengrave the brick kilns of Woolpit were celebrated for their white bricks for at least two centuries, and have gone cold only in our own day. By 1692 they had achieved a reputation for being harder and more durable than the common red brick. Much of the white brick with which so many of the houses of Bury are built resembles building in the local stone: that is to say, in some lights and weather conditions, it has something of the look of good flintwork. The sparkle produced by the black and white of flint is occasionally repeated in white brickwork once it has weathered, and when some of the bricks have blackened. One cannot be sure that all "Woolpit" brick came from Woolpit: white bricks have been made in various places.

Pantiles, on the Dutch pattern with double curve and deep trough for running the rains off the roof, were made locally in brick-kilns all over Suffolk from *c.* 1700 to *c.* 1900. The oldest, and the most beautiful roof-covering is undoubtedly thatch, either of reeds or straw: it accounts for the steep pitch of all old Suffolk roofs. The reeds come from the river valleys, and, for example, from Dunwich: they have been known to last seventy years on the roof of Oak Farm, Worlingworth. The favourite wheat-straw is Eclipse, and "should last forty years". One still meets thatchers like Mr G. Whatling, of Wilby Green, who treasure their great-grandfathers' tools, and love their craft so much that they lie awake in the night, longing for it to be morning so that they can get on with the work.

NOTE ON RIBBON WALLS

Ribbon walls, *alias* serpentine walls, or crinkle-crankles, wavy in plan, brick-built, attractive to look at and convenient for fruit-growing in kitchen-gardens, are especially popular in Suffolk. I once listed fifty-eight in the county, mostly late Georgian but five of them late Victorian. I found twenty-six others in England, thinly distributed among twelve counties, mostly in the south-east, away from the building stones. Then Paul Rutledge, the Norfolk and Norwich archivist, unearthed some forty in Yarmouth and Gorleston alone, which suggests that the idea was imported in the course of Yarmouth's 18th-century trade: from the Netherlands?

◁ Brick-nogged warehouse: 80 Fore Street, **Ipswich**

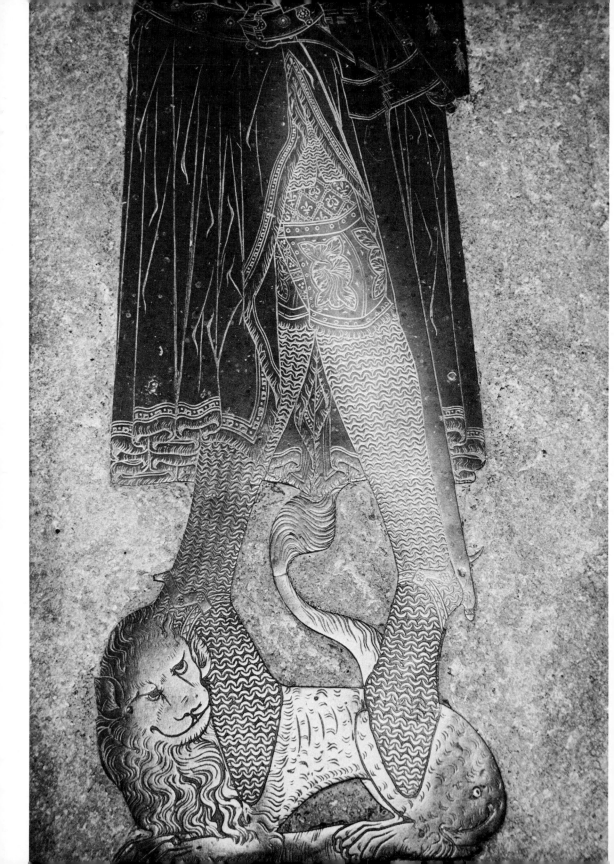

Gazetteer

Places are listed under their substantive names: the Bradleys, Livermeres, etc, are not separated under Great and Little. Great and Little Bradley for instance, began as one, a broad meadow beside the upper Stour, and it seems natural to group their descriptions together.

The numbers in brackets refer to the square where the place-name may be found on the map at the end of the book. The 1:50,000 Ordnance Survey sheets are practically indispensable to the pleasures of sight-seeing in this or any other county.

ACTON [20] divides Lavenham from Melford. Its northern parish boundaries are exactly as they were described in the 10c; and the southern boundaries had been fixed before 1066. Parallel avenues lead up slopes to church and Hall. Cheerfully coloured interior of church houses memorials of the Bures family. That of Sir Robert (1302) is one of the finest military brasses in existence: ample folds of surcoat and intricate decoration suggest rather an exquisite buck. Behind a curtain, Robert Jennens, ADC to Marlborough, reclines in handsome coloured marble, possibly by Green of Camberwell.

AKENHAM [16]. Green and brown undulating farmlands on the very brink of built-up Ipswich. Church, bomb-blasted in World War II, rescued by Friends of Friendless Churches. Tower serves also as S porch, a medieval fashion hereabouts.

ALDEBURGH [18], a small seaside town of strong character: "a bleak little place, not beautiful" observed E. M. Forster, who liked it very much. The long pebble beach, facing east, provides safe bathing, agelong interest of fishermen's boats returning with a fresh catch, and occasional stirs of excitement when the powerful, painted lifeboat plunges to rescue.

Long marshland views to south, where the broad estuary slides down from Snape to former quay here, called Slaughden, the last of whose buildings drowned in our day. The poet Crabbe worked in this landscape. Tang of salt-flats and tarred planks reminds one sharply of his verse-stories in *The Borough* (1810). They included the tale of Peter Grimes that Benjamin Britten used for the first of his operas. *Peter Grimes* has appeared all over the world with stage-sets based on Aldeburgh's Moot Hall. Ben Britten and Peter Pears have their home here, and festivals of marvellous music have been enjoyed in this neighbourhood every summer since 1948.

To the north, another quay, more important in the town's Tudor heyday, flanked a big southward extension of Thorpeness Mere (reclaimed, 19c). The town's main streets still stretch north–south about a mile between its two lost harbours. Its fishermen, as in Crabbe's day and always, are based with huts and nets on the shingle beach.

Alde burh's name, "old fort", indicates pre-English fortification. Defence runs all through its history, against human enemies and the sea. Roman site is lost to sea; so is about half the Tudor town (see Elizabethan map in Moot Hall). At the Slaughden end, northernmost Martello Tower in England flaunts its quatrefoil plan on the sea's brink. The Landmark Trust has bravely restored it.

Outlines and stance of Moot Hall neatly summarise town's history. It seems to be straining to hold up—above the advancing beach—its stormswept walls of flint, timber and red brick. Tall twin Jacobean chimneys added by R. M. Phipson (1854), but the main hulldown structure goes back to Henry VIII's reign: a ground-floor market (now museum) with timbered court-room reached by external stair.

The aisled, symmetrical flint church, too, was rebuilt in Henry VIII's day (when the limp hand of Snape priory was removed); accurately denotes the town's first period of prosperity. It contains small glittering brass effigies of early merchant families. Lord Leicester's actors played in this church, June 1573, two days after performing in Ipswich. There is a good chance Shakespeare himself played here in late summer, 1595, the year after *A Midsummer Night's Dream* was written, and when the Sonnets and *Richard II* were being completed. His company certainly played in Ipswich that year. At that moment a gap in the Aldeburgh records begins!

In the 17c the Dutch wars, sea-erosion, and withdrawal of shipbuilding to the Blackwall yard depressed Aldeburgh. By the time Crabbe's grandfather was Customs Collector, smuggling was probably the most lucrative business left. The latest occupation, as fashionable watering-place, Crabbe recorded in *The Borough*.

Old sandy roads were turnpiked, and tumble-down clay cottages of Tudor streets were rebuilt in brick, often in the eccentric, unbuttoned sea-front styles that characterise the modern town. Occasionally the old outlines survive, in chimneys at Swiss Cottage near the Moot Hall, or fronts and gables at 215–229 High Street.

Aldeburgh's chief Victorian developer, Newson Garrett, also expanded the Maltings at Snape Bridge. Two prominent look-out towers on the shingle are reminders of two rival Beach Companies, Up-towners and Down-towners, who, before the days of the R.N.L.I., competed for the spoils and glory of salvage. Their craft, the legendary beach-yawl, was sailed by a crew of 20–25 men. Not for nothing is the deserted magic path through the heath to Snape called the Sailors' Walk. Pleasant houses of 1920s include Dolphin House in Priors Hill Road, by Oliver Hill, with a very Dutch gable. The Cadbury-Browns' recent house among pines in Church Walk relates nicely to the place. A reasonably planned development of 73 houses (Barefoot & Partners) is rising along Leiston Road.

ALDERTON [23]. Long marsh views to the sea, with Martello towers. Early settlement-pattern in air-photos. Medieval Hall-site west of church, which was splendid in 14c, a mere chapel amid the ruins in the eighteenth. (Nave re-roofed and chancel added, 1864–5.) Robt. Biggs, rector 1723–69, "not distinguished by his activity or literary ability", but honest. His successor, 1769–1813, rebuilt the Old Rectory. Cedar Court is a handsome mid-Georgian house.

ALDHAM [21]. Small round-towered church pleasantly grouped with Hall. Evening sun best reveals texture of tower and, to west, traces of vanished buildings in green pasture with pond.

ALDRINGHAM-WITH-THORPE [18] share setting of heath and woods, great natural beauty threatened by suburban tendencies. Aldringham, the ancient settlement, retains prehistoric barrows. Thorpe, a hamlet that outgrew the parent in Tudor times, became *Thorpeness*, a remarkable seaside "garden suburb" created by Stuart Ogilvy in the age of George V. It began in 1910, with the digging of a pleasure-lake, the Meare, just north of the drained mere that once provided Aldeburgh's main haven. In 1912, the Country Club was opened and best terrace, the Benthills, was built. W. G. Wilson was architect at this period, the houses mostly rather flimsy, clad in dark weather-boarding or cement-panels jointed by quasi "half-timber" planking. The effect here and in The Whinlands, and (inter-war) Lakeside Avenue is pleasant. West Bar Watertower and the Almshouses with 1928 gatehouse are pretentious brick-design by F. Forbes-Glennie, of Selsey, but there is an overall character worth perpetuating. The Ogilvy Working Men's Club, 1925, cost £8,000. The old post-windmill, 1803, brought here from Aldringham, looks very ill at ease in front of "The House in the Clouds", an 85-ft high water-tower on stilts, the tank disguised as a house, the stilts boxed in to form a real four-storey house.

Drive through beech and pine woods to Aldringham church, small, with medieval stones and font, dominated inside by Victorian reredos with Creed, but outside enchanting on edge of valley of "the Hundred River". But west approach to Aldringham crosses Coldfair Green, visually dismal, and dwarfed by Sizewell pylons.

ALNESBOURNE PRIORY [22]. Only a septaria wall remains of a very small Austin priory, and the very name of this ancient parish of Hallowtree has vanished, but the heath and the view over the Orwell continue.

ALPHETON [14]. Church stands among farmbuildings of Hall, remote. Plain box pews. John Shepherd, R. M., wounded 1805 in last campaign of "immortal Nelson".

AMPTON [8] set in woods at edge of Breckland, with "Seven Hills" barrows at northern tip

and on east side a park, "back-to-back" with former Liver-mere Hall, and still sharing the enchanted serpentine mere admired by Repton and Arthur Young. Park now arable. Hall rebuilt step-gabled "Tudor" 1885: fine iron gates from Livermere. Across the street, almshouses (1693) a handsome rusticated gateway inscribed "For everyone's enjoyment" in Latin, Bluecoat school (1705) now cottages, and church set among the gardens.

Most of this is the creation of the Calthorpes, whose story is partly readable in the church monuments; notably Henry and Dorothy (1637, hand-in-hand, by Jn. and Matt. Christmas), her father Wm Whettel (1628, by Nicholas Stone but uninspired), James and his sister Dorothy, founders of school and almshouse, and James, yeoman of Removing Wardrobe to George II and III, who started on this "landskip" in 1736, and whose chaste tablet shows his profile (? by Bacon), 1784.

ASHBOCKING [16]. Tall ash-trees flourish still on small green beside churchyard and hall: added name Bocking from family here 1338–1585. Romano-British families lived beside track from Victorian school to Poplar Farm. Domesday church rebuilt: trim Norman font-bowl, 13c chancel, 14c nave with window-tracery, cusped tomb-canopy (probably of the rebuilder, first of the Bockings) and terrific iron church-chest. Early Tudor red-

Bacton

Badley

brick tower (with diaper-pattern), matches brickwork of Hall. Last Bockings in brass on nave wall. Most evocative, the crude Caroline bench-ends, superior communion-rails, and small, painted Royal Arms of Charles I, dated 1640 and shouting: *God Save the King*. The loyal vicar, Theodore Beale, who must have hoisted them up out of reach, was finally ousted as a "Scandalous Minister" by his godly parishioners, who objected to coming up to the rails for the sacrament.

ASHBY (inset). Bare 13c church in beautiful isolation, approached through farmyard at Ashby Dell, a scene of ancient boat-burial. Base of tower round, top two-thirds octagonal with lancets like work in Friesland and Groningen. Roof-thatch visible inside, as in a barn. Purbeck font on oak supports.

ASHFIELD-WITH-THORPE [10]. Ruined round tower of Thorpe chapel is a romantic landmark. Present parish church at Ashfield, rebuilt in red brick 1853.

ASHFIELD, GREAT [9]. Ash-trees abound, though lopped chestnuts surround church-yard. Headstones. Early Tudor porch combines brick with flint in flushwork. Medieval door. Farriers' tools carved on bench-end (cf. flush work at Little Ashfield). Medieval and Elizabethan chests. Great pulpit, 1619, matching reredos and plinth of holy table, gift of Fyrmage, London merchant. Lord Chancellor Thurlow, son of rector, built Ashfield House and removed to it the carved stone cross serving as churchyard foot-bridge: probably 8c work, uniquely complete for these parts.

ASHFIELD, LITTLE, *see* Badwell Ash.

ASPALL [10]. The ancient Hall, with beautiful 17c plaster ceiling, was refronted and partly remodelled in 1702. The moats form water-gardens and setting for cider house, to which John Chevallier Guild's ancestor, in 1728, brought granite press from Iles Chausey, still occasionally demonstrated. New vats of English oak installed 1972. That ancestor grafted Nonpareil apples from Mr Shulver of Debenham in 1736. Mr Shulver of Debenham is the garage proprietor in the 1970s.

ASSINGTON [21]. Ancient redbrick Hall totally gutted by fire, 1957. Corbets here from 13–16c, Gurdons from 16–20: the last was Gladstone's secretary. The church in the park is a fine building: nave, aisles and windowed south porch enclosing beautiful doors, are 15c: chancel rebuilt 1827, tower 1863, during £3,000 restoration. Brampton Gurdon and his three sons were leading Suffolk Puritans: here he and his two wives are shown on a remarkable monument erected 1648. Willow Tree Farm, with its pleasant Gothick doorway, was formerly Society Farm, one of those in which John Gurdon from 1830 encouraged an experiment in co-operative farming "to raise the condition of agricultural labourers without raising them out of their class". The results, satisfactory, were not widely publicised.

ATHELINGTON [10]. The Hall with its moats looks just as it did in Davy's watercolour of the 1840s. Its lands are "the best in these parts". The wall of an outside shed contains a 17c beam carved with dolphins. The church-tower has lovely texture of red Tudor brick and flint. The well carved bench-ends are not well preserved, and the old benches themselves have been replaced. 16c farmhouse opposite church, with "G.H. 1682" in pargeting.

BACTON [9]. The Manor House, owned by the Pretymans since 1568, is a beautiful rebuilding in red brick, 1738, with their arms on a pediment, and two short wings. Two ground-floor overmantels were painted by Thos. Bardwell, a local pioneer of the conversation piece: one rather crude, 1729, shows Furness Abbey, Lancs.; the other, 1741, in a beautifully panelled room, is an accurate picture of the house from the front, showing further single-storey wings (now removed) and an extensive deer park. Fine staircase. The Grange (pleasant Georgian Old Rectory) now home for the elderly gentle. The church has a splendid and spacious interior, like that at adjacent Cotton: roofs of great beauty. Heaven castellated in lately restored Doom. Wm Morris E window.

BADINGHAM [11]. At heart of scattered parish of moated halls and farmhouses, church slopes uphill and is orientated so that sun rises through E window on John the Baptist's Day, possibly replacing pagan midsummer celebrations. Norman W corners of nave buttress Norman tower-arch. Stone tigress with mirror on porch buttress. Inside, Cautley's "perfect example of single hammer-beam roof" (?1506). Dowsing smashed sixteen of its "cherubim" but some survive among Edwardian replacements. Seven-sacrament font, *c.* 1480, very moving: in Matrimony the bride's face lost, but see wistful head of youth above her. Okenhill, 1562, is Crakenhill of H. W. Freeman's *Joseph and his Brethren*, 1928.

BADLEY [15]. A parish of surprising inaccessibility, the church has been signposted. In 1950 it had all the atmosphere of a rustic scrubbed oak church of the 17 and 18c. A good later restoration has done little to alter the effect, though one misses the red desk-cover, cushion and tassels that adorned the clerk's desk and pulpit. Collection of Poley memorials and well-cut quotable ledger-slabs. Monument to Mrs Henrietta Maria Robins, 1728, on outside south wall. Surrounding deep green fields, rudely straddled by pylons. Hall, late 15c, enlarged mid-16, now reduced to one-third. Carved oak string-course, early 18c fireplaces, and dovecote.

BADWELL ASH (or LITTLE ASHFIELD) [9]. The Hall, romantic with great chimney-stack and step gables, was prob-

ably once quadrangular with towers at the corners of the moat. Tostock builders reconstructed the three finest chimneys after the storm of 16 March 1945. Church stands well in village street, with good flushwork porch. Cf. blacksmith's tools on south-east buttress with Gt Ashfield bench-ends. Woodwork mostly 1868. Flushwork on top of tower has been deciphered: "Pray for the good estate of John Fincham and Margaret hys wyf."

BARDWELL [9]. Hall, a beautiful red-brick and silver-grey timber house, with splendid chimneys and gables, like work at neighbouring Norton. Elizabethan façade on earlier oversailing structure: great hall, chapel and late Elizabethan staircase. The great benefactor of the church was Sir Wm Bardwell (1367–1434): his arms are on the porch, and his bearded and armed figure kneels in a nave window. Too much restoration in 1853. The chancel, lit only by a coloured Victorian window, contains monuments. Annual May Fair takes place. Much recent coarse building.

BARHAM [16]. On steep wooded slope of Gipping Valley. Six Roman roads converged here. Shrubland Hall in this parish presents an Italianate appearance (Sir Chas. Barry, 1850–2) at the head of a cascading stone staircase (also Barry) something like that at the Villa D'Este. The gardens were remodelled by Wm Robinson at the end of the last century, without the Tivoli fountains, but with avenues and vistas that follow some of the lines of original Roman roads.

(Four terracotta windows of a 1530 house survive: one on the spot, and three in nearby churches.) Central block, Jas. Paine (1770–2). Used as hydro with sauna baths and beauty parlour. Barham Manor is an excellent example of Tudor brick-building. Rede Wood lately acquired by County Council to keep in good woodland use. The church, on the ridge, has a clerestory of early Tudor brick, but the rest of the fabric is cased in 1865 flint. Rather a barn. Vast crude Southwell monument, 1640. Wm Kirby the entomologist was rector here: a single cedar marks the site of his house.

BARKING [15]. On slopes above its offspring, Needham Market, Barking's church, rectory (1819 with cedars of 1712) and stables of vanished Hall stand together. To the south, Titley Hill, Priestley Wood and Bonny Wood are all groves and woods identifiable by *name* in a survey of the Bishop of Ely's estates in 1251. (Swingen's Wood, nearby, was Swineside in 1611 and probably Wetheresheg in 1251.) Priestley Wood retains boundary bank and ditch precisely as on map of *c.* 1641, and flora of exceptional botanical interest. Barking church exceptionally rewarding. Late 13c S doorway contains early Tudor carved doors, lamentably decaying, with letters of Sancta Maria's name carved within her initial. In 1644 Dowsing grumbled that "many superstitious pictures were done down afore I came". He, too, noted "There was Marias on the church door." Above it, from the time of the Restoration, is a painted text from Psalm 118, and within,

Royal Arms are painted with heartfelt "God Save King Charles the Second". West doors carved (?1870) with arabesques that go well with terracotta window brought from Old Shrubland Hall.

Noble 14c roof with crownposts and traces of painted celure. East end of both aisles enclosed into chapels by beautiful screen tracery and linked to rood-screen which retains vault-ribs of rood-loft. Enough tracery and colour survives to recreate the whole in the mind's eye: there are birds and a sacred heart. It must not deteriorate. Remarkable 14c outer and inner doors to sacristy. From late Georgian times, two elegant charcoal braziers for warmth, the Lord's Prayer and Commandments for strength, and a serpent, last played *c.* 1830, for joy.

BARNARDISTON [13]. Moated site of old Hall stands beside church. North porch of church contains fine doorway and canopy-work of 14c. Plain Caroline pulpit and hour-glass and altar-rails with candlesticks.

BARNBY [6] has its own diminutive Broad. Small rustic thatched church, extensive faded wall-paintings.

BARNHAM [2]. Breckland village. Dedication of its two churches (to Saints Gregory and Martin) suggests a populous early English settlement. Tall fragment of a tower marks St Martin's, and a completely Victorianised fabric is all that's left in Gregory's lime-framed churchyard: but a piece of carved Anglo-Saxon coffin lid is built into flint cottage north of churchyard. In Water Lane new housing in 1970s for local service families.

BARNINGHAM [3]. More than seventy ponds in this parish. The old Hall of the Cromwellian Maurice Barrow is reduced to one or two cottages near the farmhouse called Barningham Hall. The church has fine tall 14c windows common in this district, and a collection of woodwork as good as that at Fressingfield: the bench-backs (narrow and discouraging to the sleepy) are bratticed, all different, and the ends carved. Gessowork screen still very fine despite the ninnies of 1933 who varnished it. Much 17c carpentry, enough round the west end to re-furnish the chancel whence it probably came.

BARROW [8]. Straight north boundary on Bury–Newmarket road, one of the finest railway embankments in the country running alongside. This is the fringe of the old "Fielding" district: an Elizabethan plan of the open field is preserved in the Bury Record Office. An ancient trackway, marked by firs and hawthorn, is called Shakers Way, a name that refers to robbers, not Quakers. The large Queen Anne rectory burnt out in 1960. Wolf Hall is a Tudor yeoman farmhouse. Several pleasant cottages. Barrow Hall Victorian. Monuments in the church: one by Nicholas Stone's son. Crude overgrowth.

BARSHAM [6]. Waveney-valley situation might be guessed from the combination of 11c round tower, thatched church, curved Dutch gables of late 17c rectory,

and pantiles and Dutch gables of Grange Farm. Odd trellis pattern on the east wall of the church is probably work of Joseph Fleming, rector 1617–36, who installed a new chancel screen and roof in 1633. In the large-scale restoration of 1906–8, F. C. Eden (whose work at Blisland, Cornwall, is better known) preserved the Caroline atmosphere. Much of the stained glass and rebuilding of St Catherine's chapel was by Eden. Perhaps the finest glass-painting here is the west window, south wall, by John Fisher, 1903. Ashman's Hall, distinguished house of *c.* 1817, white brick, with recessed Ionic porch, grand staircase and two circular rooms, perhaps designed by Francis Sandys, stood new and proud in Cotman's drawing for *Excursions Through Suffolk*, 1819: restoration begun, 1976.

BARTON, GREAT [8]. Old buildings mainly of flint and white brick. Much recent suburbanising. Fine church has freestone parapets, flintwork of tower flashing with occasional red bricks and surmounted by flushwork: "new" tower in will, 1440. Monuments. The Hall, which Bunburys of Mildenhall inherited from Sir Thos Hanmer, burnt down 1914.

BARTON MILLS [7] (or LITTLE BARTON) takes usual surname from large corn-mill and wharf on the Lark where A11 (London–Norwich) crosses. Pretty stretch of river, good inn, Forestry Commission picnic place and fine view across fen to Mildenhall. Stark Baptist chapel. Church has some 14c painted glass. Texture of flint

and tile a beautiful blend, biscuit and grey.

BATTISFORD [15]. Church retains Georgian gallery. Small west tower (1841) looks like chimney-stack. Brass to Mary Everton (1506–1608). Two nice monuments (1724) one each side of east window. Small carved head set in 16c chimney-stack of St John's Manor recalls early medieval Preceptory of St John. It came into the hands of Sir Thos Gresham who had the roof of the great Royal Exchange prefabricated here, on the Tye (green) where "Plantation Way" shows modern pink-brick cottages quite out of place.

BAWDSEY [23]. The first radar research station moved here from Orfordness, May 1936, into Sir Cuthbert Quilter's magnificent Manor of 1886, that once housed Holman Hunt's *Scapegoat*, and had the Quilter motto over the door: "Plutôt mourir que changer". The irony! It became the prototype of the radar-chain stations that shared with the pilots the honour of keeping the Germans out in 1940. In Sir Cuthbert's day a car-ferry crossed the Deben by means of chains and a steam engine. There is now a motor-boat for pedestrians. The medieval church has long lost its aisles: tower was reduced by firework display in 1841 but still provides a seamark.

BAYLHAM [16]. Hall stands on high ground at head of a winding approach. Though reduced, remains fine, tall red-brick moated farmhouse of 16c. Bought in 1626 by John Acton, son of rich Ipswich clothier,

who presumably introduced the staircase, the Dutch gable, and perhaps the sixteen royal portraits lately at Shrubland. Church uninteresting. Beautiful weatherboarded watermill on the Gipping: house with medieval core.

BEALINGS, GREAT [16] has long been "residential", a village version of Woodbridge. Bealings House is beautiful Georgian red brick—with a history. Major Moor, author of *Suffolk Woods and Phrases*, bought it on retirement from India, 1806: the curious little folly ("Trimurti") in front of the house is locally held to be the place where he interred his collection of heathen idols, that no ill might come of them. Canon Moor's MS account of his loving restoration of the church, 1842–51, reveals that the bench-ends were almost all carved then, with crests of Bealings families, and not in the 15c as you might suppose from the aptness of the work. Memorials to Seckford and Clench families, and a row of magnificent limes outside. Tower building *c*. 1450. Seckford Hall has one of the most romantic mid-16c façades in England. Rescued in the late 1940s by the late Sir Ralph Harwood who filled it with appropriate fittings and made it a high-class hotel.

BEALINGS, LITTLE [16]. Attractive site in Finn valley. Uninteresting church. Colvin monument.

BECCLES [6] was built on a 50-ft spur jutting northwards

St Peter's House, **Beccles**

above the Waveney. Had it not been given to St Edmund's collegiate church at Bury *c*. 956, it might have become the fortress town its outlines still suggest. The most dominant shape in the view into Beccles is St Michael's church-tower, rich in freestone from its Bury patronage. The 1966 County Planning Appraisal recognised that "the view of the town from the west, rising above Gillingham marshes, must be one of the best of its kind in the country". The west side is steepest, with best views in and out, the best streets (Ballygate and Puddingmoor, which is medieval English for "frog-moor") and the four best individual houses (Roos Hall, down on Barsham Road, Waveney House in Puddingmoor, Leman House in Ballygate and St Peter's House in the Old Market). But the site has confined the town streets on the north and east sides as well. Only to south is town marred by usual commonplace 20c suburban spew.

All the ancient streets are laced together by buildings that got their appearance (rich, red brickwork, strikingly varied pantiles, and occasional curved "Dutch" gables) at end of 17c, after widespread fires. Within the town, main excitement created by these ancient streets meandering from north and south to converge on St Michael's detached bell-tower on cliff-top. The cliff, like old Lowestoft's, is cut by passageways, "scores". St Michael's stands in the (medieval) New Market. Old Market (pre-1066) lies below to the north. The ancient street-names, Ballygate, Hungate, Blyburgate, in the south, Northgate

and Saltgate, Ravensmeer and Smallgate in the north, betray (by Scandinavian *gade* or *gata*, a street) 11c, or earlier, origins.

Admirable 1966 Planning Appraisal recognised west side as "front", east "back" of the town, with industry, the railway, Victorian housing, but also Beccles Common and Boney's Island gloriously redressing the balance.

From the Waveney, Beccles gradually reclaimed this great common marsh (the Fen), subject of endless medieval disputes. In 1086, a salt arm of the sea still reached round Lothingland to the town, which rendered 60,000 herrings a year to Bury abbey. Peter the fisherman was patron of a chapel alongside Old Market. (House on site has medieval glass and Gothick detail perhaps by Chas. Wright who did "Tudor" work at Leman House, 1762.) The move up to New Market beside St Michael's may have marked dwindling of fishery, increase of stock grazing and river-trade: possibly coincided with rebuilding church *c*. 1370. Beautifully designed porch, *c*. 1455, originally painted and gilded. Massive detached campanile, hung with ten bells, is faced with Roche abbey stone and best seen against blue sky. Roos Hall, red brick, *c*. 1583, has pedimented windows in tall front and great step-gabled end. Open by appointment with Mr H. W. N. Suckling. Panelled library, splendid drawing-room, portraits. Waveney House, marvellous, sparkling grey flint front and brick pilastered rear; all pantiled. Leman House, Sir Jn Leman's school foundation, 1631, has rare texture of red brick headers

and flintwork, also pantiled. Benedictine mission returned, 1889: their ambitious "French Romanesque" church designed by a Beccles man, F. E. Banham.

Beccles Fair traditionally starts on St Peter's Day. Returning up Northgate in the dusk after the Regatta, you remember the *Water Frolic* painted by Crome. This is the southern holiday waterway of the Broads. Old-established printers, Wm Clowes.

BEDFIELD [10]. Poplar Farm has notable three-bay oak barn. Church: pleasant features include ingenious Caroline font-cover and monument to Wm Dufton, M.R.C.S., founder of the "Institution for the Relief of Deafness" in Birmingham. Hollow Way, the southern boundary, a public bridle way.

BEDINGFIELD [10] gave its name to family with many branches in East Anglia, main seat now at Oxburgh, Norfolk. Here they lived at Flemings Hall from *c*. 1309 for some three centuries. They evidently rebuilt it *c*. 1586. With great moat, and porch of smouldering brick, and silhouetted Dutch gables, it is one of the most romantically beautiful houses in Suffolk. Later descended to function of yeoman farmhouse. Now home of the photographer of the English theatre. Much 15c timber in church roofs and bench-ends. Some bench-ends fitted 1612. Paten, engraved with Christ's head, survived from *c*. 1520. Sturdy flint tower. Cottage to south-west reed-thatched.

BELSTEAD [22]. Church above steep slopes has fine view, farmhouse floor, rough whitewashed walls, remains of painted saints on screen, with landscape backgrounds suggesting Flemish influence. Ledgers and mural monuments in red-brick chapel to Blosse family 1630–1727.

BELTON (inset, and forcibly joined to Norfolk, 1974). Yarmouth "dormitory" development ill-conceived, 1964. Still, there are windpumps and west view over Waveney. Old Hall has Georgian brick front. Browston Hall, secluded, has remarkable free-style plaster ceilings, one like an early Gainsborough, possibly by Chas Stanley (see Gately and Langley in Norfolk). Church has two fine marbles to the Ives family.

BENACRE [6], seat of Gooch family since 1743. Employed elder Matt. Brettingham, 1763–4, in extension of Queen Anne Hall: totally gutted by fire in 1926. Church, restored 1769, retains spruce Georgian appearance. Gothick chancel screen. Pews not cut down. Fine collection of funeral hatchments. Group of noble (and solid) dames in sculpture by Thurlow of Saxmundham mourn departure of Sir T. S. Gooch, twenty-four years M.P. for Suffolk: provide foil to Pampaloni's graceful marble to Anna Maria Gooch, 1838. Blissful small Broad beside beach.

BENHALL [17], divided by A12. Church thoroughly repaired and refitted 1842, when gallery and north transept (odd in Suffolk) were added. Duke family here 1610–1732, their pedigree on large marble in chancel.

Brass. Old Lodge Farm, adapted from brewhouse of John Johnson's Lodge of c. 1781, down 1952. Benhall Lodge, white-brick 1810, partly burnt and rebuilt 1885. Good example of pargeting (1698) in the street. The beauty of Old School House, 1732 (Dutch gables, inscription over front door) is spoiled by addition. Kiln Cottage, Silverlace Green, part of vanished Kelton, with medieval market.

BENTLEY [22]. Victorianised medieval church in highly coniferous churchyard. Bentley Hall: early Tudor, with cross wings, the hall made 2-storey by Tollemaches in 1582: carved bressumer bears that date and their arms and initials. Handsome studwork-and-red-brick early Tudor range adjacent. All being admirably restored 1974. Across the lane, an equally picturesque brick-and-timber barn. Hubbards Hall, yeoman farm, 1591.

BERGHOLT, EAST [21]. Constable, born here 1776, wrote: "I even love every stile and stump, and every lane in the village." Twenty-one of his pictures of Bergholt are in the Victoria and Albert Museum. His father's house has gone. He began his painting career in the cottage of John Dunthorne (1770–1844), the village plumber, whose tomb, south of the church, is one of many that recall the painter's friends (see *Suffolk Records Society, IV, 1962*). Cottage he bought for studio 1802 now part of petrol-station next to post-office. Reference to market stalls 1459. Many houses from early Elizabethan days when Bergholt clothiers

had a short-lived short-sighted success in export market to Spain. 64-acre "expansion" reduced to $17\frac{1}{2}$ acres, mainly by Suffolk Preservation and Dedham Vale Society pressure, 1963–6. Bergholt Place garden created by C. C. Eley since 1902.

Church, strikingly handsome, early Tudor. Rich flushwork and traceried windows and clerestory on south side look the grander by contrast with incomplete tower, begun 1525. Bergholt made over land for Wolsey's colleges, and that explains insistent legend that tower never finished because he fell. In churchyard bells hang upside down in framed timber cage. Bold rood-turret and stair-turret (with vane and pepper-pot cap) to chambered south porch, give the church its air of distinction. North side shows freestone, red brick and flint. Weathered north doorway had flowers carved on shields in jambs. Both north and west doors have linenfold panels. Interior very well kept, but no match for exterior: restorations too severe. Puritans tore all but one brass from the monuments: the exception a late one, Robt. Alefounder, 1639, whose family were perhaps in a position to prevent it.

North nave aisle has curious remains of tomb featuring camels in bold relief. Epitaph to Edward Lambe, often quoted for quaintness, is a Jacobean monument of rare beauty and the beginnings of baroque feeling. Pleasant monument to Wm. Jones (1561–1636), minister here forty-four years and commentator on St Paul, displaying his books. Beside it a fresco, lately uncovered. Maria Constable's monument is by Alfred, son of Constable's friend Thomas Stothard.

Down by the cool, shadowy Stour, Willy Lott's cottage, one of the best known cottages in the western world, is a typical Suffolk yeoman's house. The idyllic mill bears bears the date 1733: the house was extended by the painter's younger brother, 1819.

BEYTON [9]. Green planted with young ash trees. Truncated round tower of church propped on two great medieval buttresses. Carved benches: bequest of 1480 to "stooling of church".

BILDESTON [15]. Profusion of rich cream plasterwork and dark oak half-timbering of the kind especially concentrated in the late-medieval clothing "towns". Bildeston's great days, when it had an important market and specialised in blue cloth, culminated c. 1524, but even then it had only about one-tenth the size and importance of Hadleigh. Most picturesque row of cottages runs off Square. Baptist chapel, rebuilt 1844, goes back to 1731. Fine very large 15c church involved parishioners in long climb, not so steep as Kersey's and well worth it to see that splendid portal with its original stout, well-carved door. Sacristan's impregnable room above porch, his watching gallery inside above door. Interior proportions recall Southwold: alas, tall rood-screen survived Dowsing, the Puritan iconoclast, only to fall victim to Whitefield's fervour in the eighteenth century. Tablet to Edward Rotherham, Captain of the Royal

Sovereign, leading ship at Trafalgar. Tower fell 1975.

BLAKENHAM, GREAT [16]. Transformed by railway in 1846. "Claydon" station in this parish, hence steel piling company, large firm of electrical engineers and cement works with four tall chimneys exhaling clouds of white dust visible for miles, and beautiful in right weather. "Lunar" quarry landscapes. Church, a dark little fabric, with grisly modern lights. Font retains emblems of Passion, including sacred heart. Tomb with angels kneeling for Richard Swift, London merchant 1645. Caroline pulpit and sounding board.

BLAKENHAM, LITTLE [16]. Chalk quarries and orchards on south slopes. Colour-washed, pargeted old rectory with Dutch gables. Church over-restored, rare James II arms besmirched.

BLAXHALL [17]. Edge of heathland beside the Alde. Tumuli. Nineteen smallholders in 1086. Flushwork on church agreeably repaired with red brick. Beautifully lettered modern headstones to artistic members of Rope family. John Roppe, churchwarden 1711, commemorated in paint, base of tower, beside a 12c carved stone.

BLUNDESTON [inset]. Tallest and thinnest round tower in East Anglia. Plate includes chalice of the Civil War period: 1647. Blundeston House almost Soane's earliest design (1785: intended for Mr Rix at Oulton), never had its brick roughcast as Soane intended. Drawing-room fireplace original.

Blundeston Lodge, rebuilt but in its old setting, is maximum security prison.

BLYFORD [12]. Church has fine Norman doorway. Elizabethan holy table with splendid cushion legs, and monument of 1809. Serpentine House, named after its ribbon wall, has timbered ceiling, with dragon beam.

BLYTHBURGH [12]. Most memorable sight on road from London to Yarmouth: the beautifully designed and weathered great church of the Holy Trinity (its emblem surmounts the east gable), an old couchant animal watching over the deserted marshes of the river that fostered it. Lovely uneven country churchyard disastrously regulated 1973: motor replaced scythe. Body of church dates from middle 15c. Tower, c. 1330, remains from previous building, grafted on to the splendid Perpendicular work by five centuries' weather. Rest of fabric remarkable for unity as well as intrinsic beauty; for the symmetry of plan, with light aisles, and, inside, an unbroken line of roof and arcading from west to east. The richly traceried parapet extends round porch and south aisle, but not north aisle, which contains Norman slit window-heads (cf. Wenhaston) re-used, as rubble. Entry is now by the north chantry-chapel door, which has had to be placed under a flying buttress, so large are the aisle windows. Details are unimportant. The thing you notice inside is light and space, as in a Dutch church. Large north and south chancel windows, as at Southwold, still blocked up from period of dilapidation (east window tracery is good Victorian work); these windows were all full of coloured glass, of which little is left, much of it disappearing in Georgian restorations.

The painted roof, the original background of which was white, has coloured patterns of sacred flowers and monograms partly stencilled, partly freehand, and done in oil-paint. (Urgent roof treatment and repairs, 1973, involve awful discoloration.) Wooden angels with gracefully spread wings were coloured similarly; only half the original number remains, bearing the shields of families connected with the Hoptons. John Hopton (1430–78), lord of the manor throughout the rebuilding, lies buried in the canopied Purbeck marble tomb, stripped of brass effigies, north of the sanctuary. Present choir stalls belonged to his chantry, 1451. Judging by the inscription of Dirck Lowersen van Stockholm, aged twelve, on one of them, the chantry was a schoolroom in 1665.

Bulcamp Workhouse (1765–6: designed by Thomas Fulcher of Debenham) across the river, is now an old people's "hospital". Walberswick was a hamlet of Blythburgh till 1412, when the Prior of Blythburgh was licensed to make a cemetery and parish church there. Coastal changes from 1328 onwards brought the mouth of the Blyth north from Dunwich to the manor of Blythburgh: to Blythburgh's great prosperity and Dunwich's ruin.

Records and finds suggest 7c minster here with East Anglian royal tombs. King owned market in 1066. Remains of small

priory lie behind "The Priory". Opposite was the market-place of the medieval town, with almshouse, Town House and Crown Inn; all vanished. The late medieval "Hart" has Stuart stairs and Elizabethan bedroom panelling. Westwood Lodge, once manor house, has ancient red-brick step-gables, plain white brick front, and marvellous view.

BOTESDALE [9]. Little old "thoroughfare town", like Needham Market, on a main road with surviving Georgian shop-fronts, and grown out of an older parish. Here grammar school 1561–1883 prolongs ancient chapel. Note The Priory, Crown Hill House, and Street Farm (formerly White Hart Inn), also many remarkably "unrestored" cottages and shops. As late as 1844 eight coaches and several carrier's wagons went through daily. Its steeplechase and "Newmarket atmosphere" are described in J. C. Jeaffreson's *A Book of Recollections* (1894).

BOULGE [17]. In park of (demolished) Hall, small Norman church rebuilt unfeelingly by Edward FitzGerald's family: Purbeck font in low brick Tudor tower. At the foot of his grave six roses sent from Naishapur to mark 2,500th year of Persian Empire, 1972, look ill, remind us:

"One thing is certain, and
    the rest is Lies;
    The flower that once has
    blown for ever dies."

BOXFORD [21]. Spellbinding village in valley bottom: first view from Hadleigh road with tip of church "clockbell pin-

nacle" (first made 1465) at eye-level, church and village hidden below. Full of ancient half-timbered houses, often nicely refronted. The Old School House, with great chimney stack, was Tudor Grammar School. Church of beautiful proportions: well lit by Perpendicular windows and clerestory. 14c wooden north porch. 15c south doors and freestone porch roofed 1456. Bequests for north aisle 1468–95 clearly show Lady chapel at east end of it. St John's chapel earlier, in south aisle. Mural painting of Richard II in south chapel. Chancel paved with black ledger-slabs: its lofty modern roof needs colouring. Tablet to woman four-times widowed, "hastened to her end" by a fall in her 113th year, 1738. David Bird, the pastor's baby son, lies asleep in cot, 1606. Ash Street and Fen Street showed (1969) how well new streets can be added to an old village. Since then these models have been sickeningly ignored in Boxford as everywhere else.

BOXTED [14]. John Weller-Poley cultivates lands his Poley ancestors have held here since c. 1400. Yeoman farmhouse unspoilt at Fenstead End. Hall in valley below church a good 16c moated house, much restored sixty years ago: fine oak panelling in hall and series of family portraits beginning with Judith Jermyn, 1575. Several of them are represented in church, notably Wm and Alice, 1587, in effigies of black oak, and their nephew Sir John upright in alabaster. (He died 1638: this fine statue was erected c. 1680.) His widow Abigail died 1652, and has similar monument erected 1725 by devoted grand-

daughter. In Queen Elizabeth's reign Sir John fought the Spaniard "with greatest praise"; later served Christian of Denmark over twenty years.

BOYTON [23]. Coastal marsh and heath, a view over cornfields and Orfordness from Cauldwell Hall. Still a small jetty below Dock Farm. In 18c, probably more seafarers (voluntary and pressed) than farmers. Fine almshouse with sixteen sets of rooms on three sides of a quad, given by Mary Warner, 1736. Book of rules, with forfeits for strolling to Bawdsey Star and tippling, etc, is kept in vestry of uninteresting church.

BRADFIELD COMBUST [14]. Still "Little" Bradfield in 1333, Bradfield Combust 1353. In 1620 came into possession of long series of Arthur Youngs. One planted beautiful lime avenue 1725. His younger son, Arthur, who succeeded him 1785, was this country's most admirable agricultural propagandist, as may be read on his tomb in the churchyard. Twelfth-century nave: St George superbly painted as crusader in 1390s when lord of manor died crusading. Another Arthur Young rebuilt Hall and lodge, 1865, employing Eden Nesfield. Hall "Dutch-gabled" in unattractive flint and red brick.

BRADFIELD ST CLARE [15]. Imagine stables and tiltyard as well as farmyard in 12c when this place held by knightly family from St Clair-sur-Epte. Their Bradfield church presumably first dedicated to him, their old patron. A century later, Clare, St Francis's friend, was canonised, and the Bradfield dedication and allegiance switched to her.

BRADFIELD ST GEORGE [15]. Bradfield Woods Reserve, coppiced since at least the 13c, may be seen on application to the wardens at Felsham. It belongs to the Society for the Promotion of Nature Reserves. 15c tower not large but nobly proportioned: begun (*c.* 1509) by John Bacon according to stonework inscription. Contemporary roofs. Tantalising fragments early Tudor glass; ten medieval oak benches. One would need a *very* clear winter's day to see sixty churches from the tower!

BRADLEY, GREAT [13]. Meadows beside Stour near its source. Church has best brick porch in Suffolk, the bricks said to have been made by "King's own brickmaker". Early 14c tower contains fireplace, possibly for preparation of holy wafers and one of its original bells, made by Richard of Wimbish (Essex). Graceful early 18c pulpit over clerk's desk. Distressing glass in east window.

BRADLEY, LITTLE [13]. Down the valley, 11c aisle-less church of great interest. Tower possibly 10c. Long-and-short work on north-west angle of nave suggests pre-Conquest stone building. Nave and chancel 11c. Sombre little chancel, inside, full of brasses, *c.* 1520–1606. The most interesting, with verse inscription of fourteen lines, commemorates John Daye, the great printer of the Reformation:

Here lies the Daye that
darkness could not blind

When Popish fogs had
overcast the sun ...

Stone monument depicts Richard Lehunt and family, all decapitated except him. Wife later married and had fourteen children by Thos Soame (including Sir Stephen, Little Thurlow).

BRADWELL [inset]. Visually not a very interesting parish but that's no reason to make it join Norfolk in 1974.

BRAISEWORTH [10]. Chancel of early 12c church, still with brass and commandment-boards, serves as mortuary chapel in old churchyard. In 1857, nave taken down, its two Norman doorways (one spectacular) made to serve in neo-Norman conceit by E. B. Lambe. Site allegedly more central, but whole parish no more than 700 acres.

BRAMFIELD [11]. Church with detached round bell-tower contains most beautiful rood-screen in Suffolk. Blissful figure of Dame Elizabeth Coke, lying on her pillow with her babe in her arms, is one of the best pieces of sculptured alabaster by Nicholas Stone. The husband kneels above her in marble. Extraordinary memorial inscriptions on ledger-slabs.

Opposite church, deep ribbon wall at back of Hall, three-storeyed Tudor house remodelled in 18c, with remains of celebrated oak in park. Brook Hall, Cokes' home, down 1805. Holly Farm, beside stream, idyllic.

BRAMFORD [22] (pronounced Braamf'd). Attractive village on the Gipping outside Ipswich, disfigured by Ipswich–Norwich railway, by semi-modern concrete river-bridge, girt with pylons and wires, and by suburban maze. But at Church Green one enters another world. Here and up Bramford Street are traditional 16 and 17c cottages and houses, cream-washed, half-timbered, some over-sailing. Distinguished brick façade of Bramford House (red stretchers, black headers, *c.* 1690) set off by fine porch and wistaria, faces Church Green. Church with its spire presides. Proportion and window-tracery of tower beautiful, texture spoilt in modern restoration. Inside, junction of nave with tower clumsy, but roofs excellent. Angels mutilated: Dowsing claimed to have smashed 841 "superstitious pictures" in 1644. Think of those windows! For compensation, the east window has the best Kempe glass in Suffolk. 14c stone screen (with modern pierced quatrefoils): notable early-Tudor font cover: Elizabethan call to alms cut in south-west pier.

BRAMPTON [6]. Church restored, nave reseated, chancel screened at Susan Leman's expense 1856, the year Wm. Warrington signed the violent stained glass. Three good marble monuments to Leman family, who built great square red-brick hall, *c.* 1794. Brampton Street secluded.

BRANDESTON [17]. Very delightful village. Horses still shod at forge five days a week. Good 15c church tower, west doorway and original door. 1711 altar rails, formerly round three sides of altar. Neglected pieces

of early Henry VIII glass, its design repeated in paint on north wall. Elaborate Charles II monument to Jn. and Alice Revett. Revetts at the Hall 1543–1845. Burnt out and rebuilt on larger scale: now Junior School of Framlingham College. Many Stebbings commemorated at west end of church: their house, Fir Tree Farm, built by Philip and Elizabeth Stebbing 1568 (see also Monewden). Margaret Catchpole really lived here.

BRANDON [2]. A Breckland "thoroughfare town" at crossing of Little Ouse, in primeval country, sandy heaths and chalk, former vast rabbit-warrens (for fur) and deep little mines, like wells, down into rich beds of flint. Old fur and flint industries have given way to state forestry: one approaches by fine drives through the dark forest.

Broad main street climbs south from bridge (rebuilt with three good round arches, 1954) to Market Hill, well terminated by 1878 red-brick school, clock-tower and master's house (archt. John T. Lee). Brandon admirably demonstrates use of local building materials, and nowhere better than round here: see sparkling flint cottages and "Hall" in Stores Street, and the "Bell" and (recent) Meatmarket in High Street. At bottom, some showrooms, and the concrete-branched lamp-standards show how not to treat an old street. Pleasant Georgian houses north and south of bridge: Connaught House (formerly Chequers Inn) and the handsome red-brick Brandon House Hotel (formerly home of leading furrier family, the

Rought-Roughts). The walk west from bridge along tow-path through water-meadows equals in its placid, pastoral way the more famous scenes of Dedham Vale. Brandon Staunch ($\frac{1}{2}$ mile west) is one of seven lock-gates erected by Thetford Corporation in 1829. Before 1652, salt water from the Wash reached Wilton Lode, three miles further west. Some coastal flora and fauna on the heaths. Coulson Lane leads round west side of town, with views.

Market and fairs granted 1319. Fine walk of pollarded limes (Victoria Avenue) leads from High Street to church on pre-Norman site, some distance from Market Hill. North chancel window-tracery suggests prosperous building *c.* 1300. Twin eastern corner-turrets, one leading to roof. View of church from south composed of four handsome Perp. windows. Inside, south aisle arcade and font are late 13c work, the westernmost arch 14c, leading straight on to tower. Good textures survived 1873 restoration, especially 15c oak stall-work in chancel. Two unusual Edwardian windows signed Leonard Walker.

West of church, old Manor Farmhouse lately replaced by housing. Pleasant 1843 school opposite with chalk wall survives as offices. Further west, Brandon Hall, a tall two-storey house, H-plan, of *c.* 1690, has beautiful speckled texture or red-brick headers and black fractured flint, alternating equally. Interior lined with tall pine panelling. Rear wings filled by 1730-ish extension in perfect brickwork, red and white.

Brandon Park (stuccoed house, 1826, with heavy Doric portico) with attractive woodland opened as County Council "Country Park," 1973. G.L.C. "overspill" estates, Knapper's Way, Warren Close, etc, reasonably well laid out with Community Centre next to moribund Edwardian Rought-Rought house. Peldon estate, 140 small bungalows, "might be anywhere", but is, alas, at Brandon.

BRANTHAM [22]. First Suffolk parish seen by passengers crossing Stour estuary on main London–Yarmouth line, inappropriately ugly industrial. Brooklands Farm selected 1887 as convenient site for Xylonite works. Sixty semi-detached cottages built for immigrants from London, good of their sort and date, more or less confined to Cattawade hamlet, which has an 18c bridge over Cattawade Creek. 500 yards northwest of bridge is Braham Hall Farm, the very farm Thos. Tusser was cultivating in 1557 in the manner, and with the implements so widely known through his *Hundred Good Points of Husbandry*, first published that year. Farmhouse incorporates part of 16c house. He introduced the cultivation of barley to this district.

Church known for unexciting reredos Constable painted for it, *c.* 1805–6, in style of Benjamin West. It no longer serves as reredos. The faces are said to be those of Constable's family. Shingled lychgate by E. S. Prior, like 'shaggy parasol' mushroom.

BREDFIELD [17]. Edward Fitz-Gerald born 1809 at White House, a mid-17c building

damaged by troops and a doodle-bug; so that all has been demolished except an orangery, a cottage and a beautiful Dutch-gabled barn. He returned here to stay with George Crabbe, the poet's son and biographer, rector of Bredfield. FitzGerald's letters were mainly addressed from the "rectory" in the years 1853–7. In an early poem he wrote of himself as "one whose youth was buried here". Bredfield High House is a 16c farmhouse with rustic original staircase, all overgrown and dilapidating. A rectangular moated site occupies a commanding position and is known as Bredfield Castle. The church tower, 1452–61, has Tudor brick parapet. Hammerbeam roof has well-carved cornice. Church over-restored 1874 when font, sounding-board and Stuart holy-table were sold to parishioners.

BRETTENHAM [12]. Poplars Farm, very good half-timbering, restored and re-thatched 1957. Church Farm has 16c bargeboards. Church disused 1957, restored and reopened 1962. 14c nave and font. Chancel *c.* 1421. Late Stuart communion-rails: well-preserved black ledger-slabs. Monuments. Hall: projecting wings, late 17c gables, a passing resemblance to Christchurch Mansion, Ipswich. Pleasant Georgian alteration, ugly later additions. In 1956, acquired for a school.

BRICETT, GREAT [15]. A curious village, whistled and shrieked over by Wattisham aircraft. Long barn-like church, partly Norman, founded as

alien priory of Austin canons, *c.* 1114, belonging to St Leonard of Nobiliac, near Limoges. "Leonardus" is carved in interesting south doorway. Fine 14c glass in a south window: the four Evangelists. Tall Norman west tower-arch; late 12c font; marble and alabaster monument to Hy Bright, 1680. The Hall, a farmhouse, but conventual in origin and joined on to the church, has lately been found to be a timber-framed building of *c.* 1250, one partition-wall having four pointed wooden arches, one with wooden dog-tooth ornament: a great rarity. The house has acquired something of the importance of Wenham Hall in the history of building construction.

BRICETT, LITTLE, *see* OFFTON.

BRIGHTWELL [23]. Largely heath, with beautiful small church on wooded slope above pleasant sandy valley. Below the church, a small brick farmhouse, once part of stables, all that is left of a great brick mansion of Charles II's reign. Shown in a Kip engraving in the church. Church tower built with Tuscan columns in reconstruction *c.* 1656. Two unusual alabaster monuments, almost Victorian in feeling: the work of "a German whose ancestors were Italians". Good unsigned east window, 1911. Hall taken down *c.* 1760. Daffodils reappear every April on the site of the great planned garden.

BROCKFORD, *see* WETHERINGSETT.

BROCKLEY [14]. Church, standing beside extensive

moats, is approached through stackyard of Hall. A face watches from the medieval door-handle. Richard Coppyng's tower undated.

BROME [10]. Hall demolished 1959. Its builders, the Cornwallises, have monuments in the church. Church and tombs over-restored 1857–86. Headstone in churchyard to the artist Hy Walton. Oak avenue from Hall to Eye.

BROMESWELL [17]. A watercolour by G. Quinton, 1803, shows the great Napoleonic war camp on the heath above the valley, camp-followers washing and ironing in the foreground, where Sir John Moore had his first sight of mounted artillery, 1797. The yeomanry galloped here in 1914. Nearby lie great airfields. In the church, partly Norman, one of the bells comes from Mechlin. Tower building in 1460. Old textures, oak, brick, stone.

BRUISYARD [11]. Tall, Elizabethan Hall, with three-storeyed porch, and little, delightfully patched-up, never wholly rebuilt, church with low round tower, good 13c doorway and Tudor brick south chapel. Michael Hare, eldest son of successful lawyer-politician, rebuilt Hall, c. 1610, on site of dissolved abbey of Franciscan nuns, itself replacing short-lived college of five unsatisfactory chantry-priests, 1354–64.

BRUNDISH [11]. Church best seen in winter from avenue to Chantry Farm. Square Norman tower, box pews and memorials. Brasses include earliest Suffolk effigy of a par-

son: c. 1360. A ledger-slab records Jn. Wyard, who was Sheriff "at the time of his Majesty's happy return", 1660–1. Memorial to Wm Beckford Miller, the bookseller, of Bungay and Westminster. Royal Arms 1765, delicately painted. New clear glass in fine Perpendicular windows. The Grove and Yewtree Farm are old houses, beautifully kept.

BUCKLESHAM [22]. "Shannon" Inn named after the ship in which the Nacton squire fought the Chesapeake, 1812. Victorian owner of Nacton allowed no pub in that parish. Church beside stream largely rebuilt 1878. Hall on prehistoric settlement and burial site.

BULCAMP, see BLYTHBURGH.

BUNGAY [5]. Except for road traffic, western approach through Waveney meadows is as it was when Cotman drew it for *Excursions through Suffolk:* four tall pinnacles signal St Mary's tower, the castle bastions camouflaged by trees. St Mary's is the focus of all the approaches. The best views *out* of the town are north and west from Castle Hills and the open Outney Common. Pink suburbia is erupting south.

The 12 and 18c were the periods of Bungay's greatest prosperity, when it acquired its present distinction. Between c. 1165 and 1174 Earl Hugh Bigod was erecting his great keep here, seventy feet square and with the thickest walls of any castle in England, racing against the King's builders at Orford. An Act of Parliament, 1670, for the navigation of the Waveney as far as Bungay largely explains

the 18c character of the town: that and the terrible fire which consumed almost every building in 1688.

After the 12c the Bigods made Framlingham their headquarters, though Roger, fifth Earl, was licensed to crenellate his "house" at Bungay in 1294—the date of curtain walls, twin-towered gatehouse, and barbican bailey (with hall and domestic buildings) that stood outside this gatehouse. By 1306 the Bigod power was ended. By 1382 the castle was described as old and ruinous. Repaired 1965. Romantic turret beside river in Castle Lane built 1839 for J. B. Scott. His diaries, *An Englishman at Home and Abroad,* ed. Ethel Mann 1930.

After foundation of Holy Cross nunnery, 1183, the parishioners were accommodated in the Lady Chapel, and kept the dedication of St Mary when priory church became parish church at the Dissolution. St Mary's is distinguished by one of the finest towers in East Anglia, and by one of the most remarkable sets of churchwarden's accounts in England: 1523–1853, a few odd years missing. In them we can watch the whole process of the Reformation as it affected one fairly representative Protestant East Anglian parish. The tower ranks as one of a great 15c series with Redenhall, Eye and Laxfield. Its design is also remarkably like that at Dedham. Yet there is good reason to believe that the major part of it was erected after the fire of 1688, with Redenhall for model. Certainly the flushwork stops abruptly with the second stage, and the upper stage, with splendid belfry louvres, is vastly taller

Burgh Castle, looking west over the Waveney

than those of the churches named above. It is as if the top two stages of Redenhall have been combined, and the effect is most striking. St Mary's has signed monuments to the Browne families. Oval tablet to Thos Bardwell, the painter, who died here 1767, outside by west door. Holy Trinity's early round tower beautifully made: its Georgian monuments commemorate General Robt Kelso, who served under Rodney in the American War of Indepen-

dence, and Matthias Kerrison, who made his fortune at Bungay staith; the father of General Sir Edward Kerrison of Hoxne. William Lamb's monument (mercer and draper, d 1768) is one of many signs of Bungay's Georgian prosperity. Others are provided by streets of red-brick façades—often with Dutch gable-ends, as at Beccles, and wonderfully handsome doorcases. Great fire of 1688 missed one house, with conspicuous carved woodwork (*c.*

1540, with arms of Drapers and Mercers Companies), opposite St Mary's. Present Butter Cross erected 1689, surmounted by an elegant lead statue of Justice (without a blindfold), acquired by the town in 1754. John King, Bungay apothecary, established baths on the pleasant elevations of the Earsham side of the valley, *c.* 1730, and published his *Essay on Hot and Cold Bathing* in 1737. Baths removed late 19c, but 16c building used to accommodate some of the bathers remains. The Bungay Theatre opened 1773; its first stage-carpenter, David Fisher, became manager and owner of fifteen theatres in Suffolk and Norfolk. A new theatre, opened in Broad Street 1828, became Corn Exchange twenty years later; now a textile warehouse. Assembly Rooms were established at the Three Tuns Inn. Bungay's best-known activity since the 18c has been printing. Messrs Clay and Son came here in 1876. Bridge Street, threatened with road-widening, must be saved. Chateaubriand stayed at Bridge House.

BURES ST MARY [20]. St Edmund crowned here, Christmas Day, 855. St Stephen's chapel is on undulating slopes above village. Dedicated 1218 by Archbishop Stephen Langton, restored by late Miss I. B. Badcock, it houses magnificent tombs of three Earls of Oxford. (1) ? Robt de Vere, 5th Earl, stone effigy c. 1296 on tomb chest of c. 1340. (2) Large alabaster tomb, ? Richard, 11th Earl, commander at Agincourt, with wife Alice in heart-shaped hat and beautifully draped dress. (3) Alabaster tomb ? Thos, 8th Earl, 1371, six canopied niches either side, each with two male weepers. Smallbridge Hall, down by river, home of Waldegrave family c. 1380–1700, was large new house when the Queen visited it in 1561 and 1579; now much restored, a school. Cottage in village with splendidly carved bargeboards was presumably a Waldegrave house "the Ferriers". Church has 14c wooden north porch and elaborate Tudor red-brick south porch on Essex model. Red-brick south chapel: tombs include a comical Waldegrave pile, 1613. Chancel once fine.

BURGATE [10]. The delightful painter Henry Walton (1745–1813) lived and worked at Oak Tree Farm much of his life: oak-shaded pasture still called Painting-room Meadow. Church, mutilated by Victorians, perhaps by same 14c architect-builder as Redgrave. Great Purbeck table-tomb surmounted by brass effigies of Sir Wm de Burgate and wife (1409: fringe round the skirt of his hauberk was the fashion: cf. Eighth Army pullovers below battle-dress tunics). Church chest painted with knights tilting has lost colour since Murray recorded it 1892. Gruesome memorial of 1914–18 War.

BURGH [16] pronounced Burg, to distinguish from Burgh Castle. St Botolph's church stands on edge of ramped Roman villa-site that stretches towards Clopton churchyard. His body apparently lay in chapel here from 680 till Bury monks took it over. Small pleasant old rectory of Queen Anne brick.

BURGH CASTLE [inset] was ripped from Suffolk in 1974. Three massive walls of Gariannonum, probably erected in the 290s, look westward over marshes that were once an estuary. Traditional flint and brick. With fine crops of corn growing inside and out, the fort now looks ruefully unwarlike. Its nine acres were probably fairly full of Roman buildings. Irish St Fursey set up Christian mission here in 7c. Motte of Norman castle occupied south-west corner. Church has round tower and Victorianised interior. Ledger-slab marks Thos Greenwood, 1677, a local Royalist. Village institute contains beam with quaint Tudor note.

BURSTALL [22]. Beautifully traceried windows and moulded arcade in 14c north aisle.

BURY ST EDMUNDS [8]. After Norwich, Cambridge, and perhaps Lynn, Bury offers the richest experience of an historic East Anglian town. Yet it must be savoured soon, for the extraordinary decision to double the town, from 20,000 to 40,000, is relentlessly changing both its heart and its country setting.

A town of the early East Anglian kings lay along the west bank of the river Lark, its minster church of St Mary later making way for St Edmund's abbey. Under a French abbot, Baldwin (1065–98), the town was re-established to the west of the abbey and designed to serve the abbey and its shire (St Edmund's "Liberty", later the county of West Suffolk, extinguished without a murmur in 1974). Later expansion, in Victorian times and our own, has kept to the west and north, so that till now one of Bury's greatest visual delights has always been views of green countryside from the heart of the town across to the east beyond the abbey and to the south over the meadows of the Lark's tributary, the Linnet. Our blurred suburbanised vision, incapable of distinguishing merit or meaning in either "urban" or "rural" environs, is now ready for the concrete and neon by-pass (opened 1973) right across the slopes of former medieval vineyard in the east, with (against all planning principles) acres of housing and light industry immediately beyond that, cut off from the town by the motorway.

Let us be grateful for bustle and prosperity in the old town, and for the defeat of a proposal for Comprehensive Redevelopment north of the great marketplace, in the St John's Street area. Each one of the old streets and urban open spaces (Chequer Square, St Mary's Square, above all Angel Hill and the Market Place, which includes the whole area between Corn Hill and the Butter Market) is worth a slow, appreciative, exploratory walk.

Room here only for basic outlines, working-parts of a town laid out in the 1060s and 70s on the grid-pattern running west from west front of abbey church—the present Churchgate Street. This was the first attempt in Suffolk at anything like the old Roman urban "civilisation", a town that was more than just a place of industry and trade, though they were always prominent. St Edmund, last king of East Anglia, slain by Danes in 869, acquired a posthumous reputation as a sort of national Resistance leader, so that his shrine and great endowments at Bury were respected not only by King Cnut, but also by William the Conqueror. His mummified corpse made Bury a great centre

Churchgate Street, **Bury**.
Looking through the Norman Tower to houses built into west front of former great abbey church

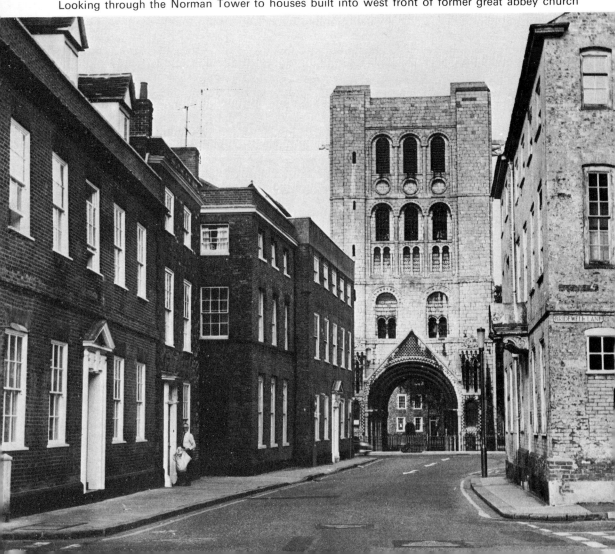

of medieval pilgrimage, before Canterbury, an English rival of St James of Compostella. The superb Norman tower, leading triumphally through from Churchgate Street to the romantic house-studded west front of the ruined abbey-church, was built to serve also as bell-tower to his new church of St James by Abbot Anselm (1121–48), when he was prevented from going to Compostella. At the far end of Churchgate Street, No. 79 Guildhall Street (with Norman window and two doorways) marks west end of Norman street-grid. Its northern extent is shown by Moyses Hall, c. 1180, in the Market-place. Over-restored by Gilbert Scott, 1858, still a marvellous antiquity, housing the Borough Museum.

Another glorious, massive stone gateway, delicately carved, leads from Abbeygate Street and Angel Hill into Abbey Gardens—courtyard of (ruined) abbot's palace. Ruins of the abbey, one of the greatest in Europe, are mostly filched away, right down to the foundations—but these are intelligibly laid out by the Inspectorate of Ancient Monuments: their detailed *Guidebook*, by A. B. Whittingham, excellent. The best *town* guide, Victorian, by S. Tymms, long out of print. Despite great fires, as in 1608, streets of old town never wholly rebuilt since Norman times. Bury Fair, on Angel Hill, a great commercial and fashionable attraction throughout the Middle Ages and down to 19c. The town kept up with fashions by changing the detail: while main framework of houses and streets continue serviceable, so Norman stone and later timber-

and-plaster ones have been given new façades. The Guildhall a good example: 13c main entrance and walls set behind early Tudor porch and early 19c outer walls. Even Robert Adam's designs for the "Town Hall", now handsome Exhibition Gallery, essentially four new façades on old Market Hall. One wholly new building was Cupola House, now a wine merchant's. When Celia Fiennes saw it new, in 1698, it was house and shop of Thomas Macro, apothecary: "new

mode of building, 4 roomes of a floore, pretty sizeable and high" with lanthorn "at least sixty steps up from the ground and gives a pleasing prospect of the whole town".

Countless instances of Georgian delight in building. On Angel Hill, Angel Hotel itself (with 13c undercroft) and No. 8 (with borough offices, and a fine collection of clocks) and Athenaeum (by Francis Sandys, architect of Ickworth, etc). Northgate Street has several town houses of local

The Abbey Gate, **Bury**, built after 1327

landed gentry, a function Bury already serving when Domesday Book compiled. Lloyds Bank has beautiful front on Buttermarket. Soane remodelled for banker 81–82a Guildhall Street. Pentecostal Chapel, Churchgate Street, erected for Presbyterians, 1710, red-brick, exuberant and fine. No. 36 Churchgate Street is perfect example of modest Georgian town dwelling. Abbeygate Street has best Georgian shopfronts. In 1740s, scarcely one of these shops was protected against weather: by 1782 "there is but one, which belongs to a cooper, that is not enclosed with sash-windows". Whiting Street retains pleasantest mixture of houses and shops. Theatre Royal, Westgate Street, 1819, had great advantage of being designed by Wm Wilkins (architect of National Gallery), who knew needs of playhouse, having inherited management of Norwich Theatre Royal. In Southgate suburb, "rusticated blind arches" of G. Byfield's gaol, 1816, now "The Fort", have a look of old Newgate. In St Andrew's Street, St Andrew's Castle, convent on site of medieval watch-tower, is proper local Gothick.

Victorian Bury expanded steadily. Railway from Ipswich opened 1846, crosses low north end of town on embankment and handsome skew-arch white-brick bridge: waiting-rooms consequently on first floor of Sancton Wood's fanciful station-house with cupola-

Bury Market Cross, by Robert Adam (*above*) and former Presbyterian meeting-house, Churchgate Street

The Norman Tower ▷

turrets. In 1841 this Norman suburb became new parish of St John, with church (by W. Ranger) whose 178-ft spire ("ignorant"—Pevsner) and flying buttresses and pinnacles like outer-space probes, signals charming homely neighbourhood of Brackland. High Church interior contrasts with unassuming contemplative quiet of 1750 Friends' Meeting House opposite. 1837 R.C. church of St Edmund, good Greek revival building in Westgate Street. Victorian suburb beyond Westgate by St Peter's, 1858, a Gothic design by one of the Hakewills: displays admirable appreciation of local building materials, so does adjacent primary school. In latest suburbs south of Linnet, fine new hospital complex. East from Westgate Street, St Mary's Square (the pre-Norman market-place) is idyllic; and east again debonair new Shire Hall buildings completed for West Suffolk County Council just in time to preside over its own passive extinction.

From here the lime-walk through the grass and tombstones of the great medieval churchyard to the Norman gate-tower is the best of all Bury's enchantments. Glorious hulk of St Mary's church crouches on its rise, flanking Honey Hill. Rebuilt mainly 1424–33, successor to Anglo-Saxon minster-church displaced by Norman abbey. Details of nave and chancel roofs and whole conception equally rewarding. Monuments. Suffolk Regiment chapel in north aisle (decorated by Comper).

In this same marvellous cemetery, Abbot Anselm's church of St James was also rebuilt (except its bell-tower) in late Gothic, almost certainly John Wastell's design. Its light, spacious nave, re-roofed by Gilbert Scott 1862, and its Victorian chancel, lately replaced by lofty new Gothic building by S. Dykes Bower, brightly painted and cheerful. St James's has been cathedral of diocese of St Edmundsbury and Ipswich since 1914. The extension insensitively ignores, instead of relating to, the ruined west front of St Edmund's abbey, once the broadest and most superb of all the great church portals of Europe.

BUTLEY [17]. Exciting coastal marshland. New school, 1959: Lindsay Morgan, with county architect. Daffodils among beech-woods. Ancient tract of oak forest: Staverton Park. Early 14c priory gatehouse, "one of the noblest monuments of English monasticism". Founded 1171 for Austin canons, priory became best-endowed convent in Suffolk after Bury, with one of the largest churches. As at Bury, little survives but gatehouse with beautifully carved stone frieze of shields in flint setting, with arms of Christian countries, officers of state, baronial families, East Anglian families, Suffolk families, a row each. Successful Hadleigh clothier established his seat here 1544: converted again 1738, but 14c fabric survives, including tall, brick-vaulted rooms, each domed so that no brick cutting needed. Nearby little parish church exhibits septaria, crag, flint, plaster and rugged thatch. For first thirty years of Victoria's reign, Thos Crisp, greatest English stockbreeder after Robt Bakewell, sent trainloads of fine beasts abroad from Abbey Farm, centre of one of the finest Suffolk farming estates today. Avenue of quincunxes planted by Georgian peer, who had perhaps been reading Sir Thomas Browne's *Garden of Cyrus*.

BUXHALL [15]. Copinger family held manor 1428–1948. Too many ugly Council cottages of the 1930s, and pylons. Coles Farmhouse, named after the 1733 owner, late medieval "2 up 2 down", timber-framed, plastered, thatched, perfect. Maypole Farm, part of pleasant group of cottages and farmbuildings, has Tudor chimney-stacks and old windows. Church c. 1320: window tracery uniformly beautiful, but interior a disappointment since 1877 restoration. Ancient rectory of many squarson Copingers has restored red Tudor chimney and white-brick façade, 1852, with fine bow of 1890!

CAMPSEY ASH [17]. Magnificent 14c timbered hall survives, as private house, from days of fashionable nunnery. 16c water-mill alongside, and some medieval stonework in farmbuildings, and a great reedy, tree-sheltered fishpond across lane. Flintwork of churchtower sprinkled with brick in upper stage. Disappointing interior: no trace of extensive restoration and rebuilding, 1788–92. Peninsular War monument. Brass. Deserted park and gardens.

CAPEL ST ANDREW [17]. Largely occupied by coniferous Tangham State Forest, with cottages in glade on site of Tangham Manor-house. Capel church standing as late as 1529. Home Farm opposite site incorporates septaria from its fabric.

CAPEL ST MARY [22]. Traversed by A12 and by mill-stream falling into Stour. Boynton Hall, Domesday manor-house associated with Capel church, retains 14c timber aisled structure. 14c window-tracery in chancel: good glass (F. C. Eden) in south nave aisle. New Ipswich dormitory of 560 dwellings has changed village of 600 people into suburb of 1,700.

CARLTON. See KELSALE.

CARLTON COLVILLE [6]. Over-Victorianised church in pleasant churchyard. At north-east corner, old red-brick and pantiled farmhouse shows textures that might have made Lowestoft dormitory (Woodlands Avenue, The Firs, etc) south of churchyard acceptable. So does pantiled rectory with ribbon walls on two sides of garden.

CAVENDISH [14] has had thirteen different manors at various times: its attractive heart lies beside the upper Stour. Green, crowned by church, with 1480ish flushwork clerestory and prominent stair-turret above tower: old thatched cottages ("Hyde Park Corner") nestling beneath. Decayed in 1956, these cottages were saved by an appeal, burnt down and again rebuilt. Pleasant buildings of all periods include white-brick Hall, Regency with pretty lodge, Blacklands Hall with Tudor chimneys and Regency

Gothick front to north wing, and, standing in the orchard of Overhall, a solitary gable-end of the 16c home of the Cavendishes, now an apple store and poultry roost. Sir Jn. Cavendish, royal official, reduced to putting his valuables in the belfry in 1381. The rebels got them, and caught and beheaded him. He left £40 for the making of this chancel. 15c eagle lectern as well as Jacobean one. Sunday School held here as early as 1787. Old Rectory, home of philanthropist Sue Ryder.

CAVENHAM [8]. Roman *Camboricum* must be in this neighbourhood. Breckland and downland landscape utilised for ancient defences, the Black Ditches. Medieval packhorse bridge rebricked in 18c stands beside present idyllic course of Icknield Way. Church tower had west porch with chamber over. Late 17c brass, found since Farrer published *Suffolk Brasses* (1903), notable for its rudeness, the predominant quality of this 13–14c church, especially the font (undateable).

CHARSFIELD [17]. Diapered brick church-tower and south porch, both on earlier flint bases. Leman monuments. Ronald Blythe's *Akenfield* is based on this and neighbouring villages.

CHATTISHAM [22]. White-brick Georgian rectory, Tudor carving in porch. Agreeable old church with vastly thick walls, sloping like ship's sides in chancel: nicely cream-washed, has seen better days: traces of large 13c chancel-arch and fine Perpendicular west window. Crude

monuments. Poor-box cut out of solid block. Oil lamplight.

CHEDBURGH [14]. Reticulated 14c east window with beautiful glass of 1926, incorporating medieval fragments. White-brick tower and spire, 1842: simple altar rails, same date.

CHEDISTON [11] (often "Cheston"). 14c south porch and door. Notable early Stuart altar rails. Pulpit 1637, from Cookley church. Excellent nave roof and traceried cornice. Georgian Commandments with Moses and Aaron on west wall. Hall 1830ish "Elizabethan"; down 1954. Site of Roman building just east of church. Ash Farm has step-gable and old tiled roof.

CHELMONDISTON [22] (often "Chempton"). Church unimaginatively rebuilt: old one destroyed by Nazis. Creditable new council houses (architects: Johns, Slater and Haward, Ipswich). *Pin Mill* lies down at shallow edge of Orwell estuary, where the "Butt and Oyster", going back to 16c, is associated with smugglers, the stories of Arthur Ransome, and innumerable sailing holidays.

CHELSWORTH [15]. Very pretty Brett-valley village: chestnut trees, well-kept cats, picturesque houses. Carved corner-post on No. 91, Old Farm. Church humped-up: lofty and wide, very short east to west. Fine 14c canopied tomb. Vivid remains of coloured medieval doom. South porch and traceried doors no longer used, worth seeing. Tablet to a Pocklington (1840).

Clare churchyard islanded between Norman market-place to south, and Callis Street (probably pre-Norman market-place) to north

CHEVINGTON [14]. Like Hargrave, still has a more feudal appearance than its neighbours. Church, a real beauty, stands up behind the half-dozen village buildings. Abbots of Bury had house north of church, on ancient, irregular ditched and ramped site where 17c Hall Farm stands. A green way leads towards Bury. 13c chancel and east end of battlemented nave: 15c west end and upper tower. Decayed flush-work of tower shows through crumbling plaster. 14c wooden porch spoilt by rough-cast. Transitional doorway has foliated capitals. Whole interior washed white. Chancel seen to perfection in Lent, with purple frontal, dark rear-curtains and "debased" 1697 east window: all very strikingly framed by a seven-ft wide chancel arch and subsidiary pointed apertures north and south (four ft). 15c pews at west end: figures playing sackbut, lute, cymbals, etc. 14c chest in chancel, and tablets to military White family. Tan Office Green Methodists have thatched flint-and-brick chapel.

CHILLESFORD [17]. Church tower of coralline crag, which may be seen in pit off Mill Lane. Chillesford sands and clay were later deposited by tributary of Rhine up which swam the 60-ft whale whose skeleton was

66

Clare: Chilton Street, traditional rural terrace beside tributary of Stour. Dereliction complete, 1975

found in the old brickyard. Short nave and chancel divided by curious arch, probably Norman, altered 15c, with canopied opening either side. Victorian plaster arms. Rich blues in 1865 window. Old Froize Inn (Suffolk for pancake) now Decoy House. Decoy disused but wild duck still settle at sunset. Street now concrete-kerbed!

CHILTON [20]. Hall, tall-sided

Tudor brick building standing inside stone-bridged moat, is only the east wing of the Cranes' great house, *c.* 1430–1643. Church, admirably restored 1972, remote in cornfields. Fine brick tower. Cranes' brick chapel has excellent roof. Only base of screen survives: roodloft and pews ("stools") willed by Robt Crane, 1500. Alabaster figures of Cranes lost canopies 1868. Triple wall monument by Gerard Christmas, 1626, shows

Sir Robert, who died 1643, between his childless Hobart wife and Susan Alington, great grand-daughter of Burleigh, by whom he had five daughters and coheirs, one a grandmother of Walpole. Sudbury factories close in.

CHIMNEY MILLS, *see* CULFORD.

CLARE [20]. Beautiful little town, an important seignorial

67

Cotton: the clerestory proclaims the splendid roof it lights within

borough in 13c, now manages well with a parish council. Large area school lately built. Distinction of some of the ancient houses preserves its residential character. Prehistoric camp, double-banked, an astonishing earthwork, has cottages built into one bank. Jagged splinter of 13c shell keep stands on great motte against sky:

centre of widespread Norman "Honour of Clare", outside works finally raped when railway station built within the bailey: all now part of an admirable "Country Park". Fine remains of celebrated Austin Friary, inhabited as "Clare Priory" since Dissolution. Prior's house and cellarer's hall, long a secular dwelling, are

once more an Augustinian concern. The original infirmary is kept roofed. Chilton chapel is now a cottage with late Norman doorway.

Parish church of singular beauty crouches above the market-place, east wall rearing straight out of street, like Poitiers cathedral, great choir and aisle windows sparkling, flintwork flushed with sprinkling of bricks, and twin roodstair turrets, capped and crocketed, projecting above junction of choir and nave-like clipped wings of heraldic dragon, or trunnions of piece of heavy artillery. Watchful sundial over south porch says "Go about your business." Within, arcading fine (main rebuilding *c.* 1460–1520). Chancel repaired 1617, when heraldic glass put into east window. (Dowsing smashed over 1,000 "superstitious pictures" here: thought heraldry not superstitious.) Modern glass by F. C. Eden. 17c gallery in south aisle with marble memorials. Rich chalice given by 18c naval captain—not by Elizabeth from Armada salvage. Fine ringers' pitcher, 1729. Beauties of Clare include Nethergate House, 16c, transformed 1644, the date of one of the staircases; nearby White House; various examples of pargeting. Here one sees pedestrian funeral processions and immemorial faces: Non-conformity prevails and swans nest on the Stour bank beside the castle goods yard.

CLAYDON [16]. "Thoroughfare" village in Gipping Valley undergoing vast new roadworks at main road-junction. West wall of nave pre-Norman: much of fabric rebuilt 1851. Chancel designed by rector, Rev. George Drury, who also executed stained glass and much of the carving, and presumably designed the Gothick folly over the churchyard wall with the spoils. Transepts designed by diocesan architect Phipson: the south one now provides perfect setting for distinguished Madonna by Hy Moore. Clay-

don was the scene of Father Ignatius's early (unwelcome) endeavours in the Victorian Anglo-Catholic revival. Brass inscription to Samuel Aylmer (1635), who probably built Mockbeggars Hall, charming house of 1621, three of its five Dutch gables gone.

CLOPTON [16]. Manor House with screens passage. Hammerbeam roof of church (modern angels) well seen from altar rails. Bad restoration 1883. Tower stands nobly over south porch. Churchyard beautifully sited on side of little valley, cornfields alongside. Railed tomb, Jn. Page, Crabbe's master.

COCKFIELD [14] has nine hamlets, eight of them called Greens. Church recalls Hitcham in its beautiful proportions and way east buttresses of tower stand in nave. External appearance of tower buttresses very fine. East window by Kempe, restored canopied tomb of 14c knight, and skilfully designed classical monument. Long early Tudor brick-and-timber cottage adjoins churchyard. Fine Georgian rectory.

CODDENHAM [16]. Site of Roman Combretonium beside the Gipping. Present village lies between trio of 200-ft hills. Post Office has late-medieval frame, pargeted. Gryffon House was inn licensed *c.* 1620. Choppins Hill Farm handsome, with aisled medieval frame. Former rectory, 1770, looks east across park to church and cluster of old cottages where water is still well-drawn. Slope governed offset of tower and porch: nave

and chancel climb east to alter. Remains of roodscreen, late, 1534, removed for treatment. Grave-slab of Rev. Matt. Candler, 1604–63, eroding on south wall. Monument to Huguenot rector, 1739. Painting: Christ shown to multitude.

COMBS [15]. Ebbs Farm has carved wooden window-corbel. Old thatched cottages at Little London, unsophisticated as an African kraal. 14c church, approached over open meadow, has processional way under tower and 15c glass. The St Margaret scenes are particularly vivid: she is depicted tending sheep; thrust into prison, in prison birching the devil, and stepping into boiling oil. Also scenes of charity, with inscriptions, and baptismal scene. Notable bench-end with triple head, and engraved Danzig flagons of Orlando Bridgman, 1731, of Combs Hall, M.P. for Ipswich.

CONEY WESTON [3]. Despite proximity of Breckland coneys, name means king's town. Towerless church interesting early Dec. but thrice restored by Victorians. Ribbon wall at Hall.

COOKLEY [11]. Walnut Tree Farm of outlying Elizabethan yeoman, Hill Farm and Buck's Farm Dutch gabled. Church hopelessly restored 1894.

COPDOCK [22]. Great diapered red-brick barn in field beside church. Church exterior Cotmanesque. Interior unhappily "improved" in loyal and thankful remembrance of Queen Victoria, 1901. Good modern glass east window.

CORNARD, GREAT [20] ("corn land"). Old Essex-type wooden church-spire slated in Victorian restoration. 14c tower has Tudor brick external turret. Elizabethan wall-paintings and horrible stained glass. Medieval aisled interior at Abbas Hall.

CORNARD, LITTLE [20]. Costens Hall, early 17c, with good chimney-stacks and view, dilapidating. Peacock's Hall, charming Queen Anne building next to church. There is a Sharpfight Meadow and a Killingdown Hill: old swords were found at "Dane's Hole". Little Cornard's men had fine record in 1914–18 War.

CORTON [inset]. Corton Wood is the first natural beauty seen on leaving North Lowestoft: yet that borough is bent on having caravans alongside, at Dip Farm, impossible to screen. Further north, village, then holiday camps, early, 1924. On cliff, remains of St Bartholomew's great church: fragmentary magnificence as at Covehithe, Walberswick. 92-ft tower finished c. 1486. Rest a rebuild of c. 1375 (see carved crucifix in chancel, brought inside from east gable, 1891). Early Tudor wills show glittering interior. All in ruins late 17c: chancel patched up and re-roofed 1694, again 1768, and finally 1846, when it was extended westward into ruined nave—possible solution to some late 20c problems of "redundant churches".

COTTON [9]. Extensive moats: Hempnalls Hall striking with its tall brick Elizabethan gable-end, stepped, and crowned by twin chimneys: empty and decaying like its adjacent pastures. Church has very fine 14c doorway, richly carved and with traces of colouring: inside is a lovely, clean, large building, arcades c. 1300, flowing window-tracery. A soft, clear green pond-watery light seeps in through east window. Excellent nave roof, referred to in will 1471. Good stout benches on brick floor. Cotton Lodge, 16c, being handsomely restored 1974–5.

COVE, NORTH [6] (pronounced Koov). Long, narrow, trimly-thatched church has Norman south doorway: tower quoins of flat bricks, perhaps Roman. 17c texts on nave walls, 14c painted scenes in chancel, repainted since uncovered 1874. Hall has fine George II brick front with parapet, pediment, pantiled roofs and skirting walls. Good staircase: decorative plaster ceiling on first floor.

COVE, SOUTH [6]. Thatched church with rare painted rood-door: shows St Michael as large as life but a shade worn out since conception in 15c.

COVEHITHE [6]. The church must have been one of Suffolk's finest. "Town" and church decayed in 17c, and Dowsing "brake down 200 pictures". Church dismantled 1672, massive tower preserved as sea-mark, and present little Charles II building put up inside ruins. The melancholy splendour of these ruins captured in water-colour by Cotman.

COWLINGE [13] (pronounced Coolinge). Early 14c church of septaria and brick incorporates 12c fragments. Early altar. Medieval painting over chancel arch: St Michael in feathers weighing souls. Interior wonderfully unspoilt (1969). Medieval graffiti on pillars of both aisles include carrack of c. 1300 and reminder to Hail Mary. 15c screens. Brasses. Georgian brick tower (1733) and monuments including Scheemakers sculpture of lawyer, Fras Dickins, seated in Roman dress, who rebuilt tower. Royal arms and Commandment-boards, 1731. Capability Brown worked on Branches Park 1763 but probably stopped in '64 after row about payment.

CRANSFORD [11]. Well-built rectory, 1848; Wm Pattisson. Church Victorianised. Borrett monuments. Fiddlers Hall has splendid Elizabethan chimney stack and 14c name, Visdelou.

CRATFIELD [11]. Here as at Bungay and Melford we can see in parish records the detailed development of the Reformation. Perhaps the richest of all the East Anglian seven-sacrament fonts: mutilated, but still full of grace and movement in its carved panels and niches. Clock-bell in oak frame, c. 1400, given by Wm Aleys. Freestone parapet of tower built 1547 from sale of chalices, censers, and crucifix. Town House adjoins churchyard.

CREETING ST MARY [16] now includes All Saints and St Olave and has one of the finest situations of any Suffolk church, commanding miles of the Gipping valley to the west, and a tributary valley to the south. All Saints stood in same churchyard till 1803. Typical East Anglian font under 14c window, and black-and-white marble monument of 1808. Five windows by Kempe and beautiful late-Elizabethan silver-gilt steeple cup. Rector left £20 to tower, 1378. Old Rectory (now school) rebuilt *c.* 1863: a work of Henry Woodyer.

CREETING ST PETER [16]. Church in sight of main road, but approached by grass way and screened by limes. Upper part of splendid St Christopher. Enormously thick Norman nave walls and crude north doorway. North side of churchyard full of cowslips and primroses is not fenced off from pleasant fields and view to Stowupland. Roydon Hall, built by Capt. Robt Flicke, 1590s, with well-cut beams, a beautiful coved and moulded bedroom ceiling and other plasterwork. Splendid barn: queenposts.

CRETINGHAM [16]. Church nicely plastered outside (except flint tower and porch). Inside of fresh dairy cream, nave and chancel continuous, walls thickening out at bottom. Dark-stained box-pews and rails on three sides of altar. Double-decker pulpit with pendant acorns. Royal arms of Charles II. 17c wall monuments. Moat Farm 1602. Ancient thatched cottages, Kittle's corner.

CROWFIELD [16]. Hall, a George II brick building, now down in the world, was built for Sir Hy Harwood. Large pigeonhouse 1731. Church has the only half-timbered chancel in Suffolk, but restored Thorpeness style. The "village" runs along Stone Street, the Coddenham–Peasenhall Roman

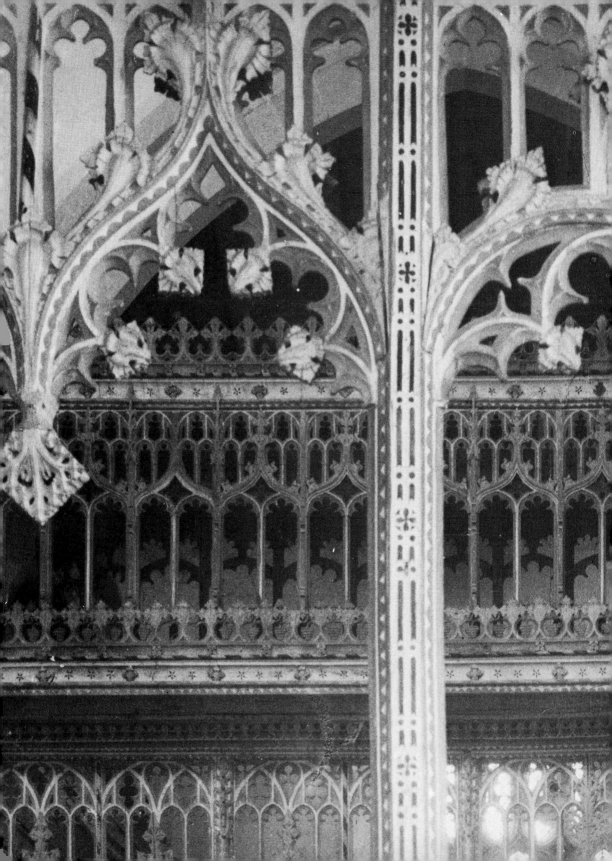

road. Tollgate Farm marks Debenham–Ipswich turnpike which forked off here to Gosbeck.

CULFORD [8]. Hall, now a Methodist boarding-school, was built for the distinguished Marquess Cornwallis in 1796, by Robt de Carle the younger, of Bury. Sir Nathaniel Bacon's bust, with painter's palette, lurks in gloomy base of church-tower (1627). Sedentary effigy, erected 1654, is a fine work of Thos Stanton. Church rebuilt 1856, except Georgian tower which was unsuitably flint-encased. It stands in Repton-ised park full of seedy Wellingtonias. Modern school by County Architect at edge of parish. Chimney Mills, on the Lark, used steam as well as water: hence graceful chimney.

CULPHO [16]. Small church with tower over south porch and doorway of *c*. 1280, when it was given to Leiston Abbey: hence "Abbey Farm", now only a moated site. Unrestored nave, bare and oil-lit. Stuart holy-table in children's corner. No pulpit. Odd chancel-arch of 1883.

DALHAM [7]. Thatched 'estate' cottages set back in gardens along either side of stream (the Kennet). Through woods at north end of village you climb escarpment to tall plum-red brick Hall, built by Bishop Symon Patrick of Ely in Anne's reign, with flint-grey church standing respectfully by. In-

Dennington: the parclose screen and loft

scription round top of tower and paintings within describe how steeple was re-edified in 1625. It had a spire that toppled down in storm at time of Cromwell's death. Sir Martin Stuteville's monument with bust of himself and two wives says he "saw the new world with Francis Drake". He may have been on the last voyage, when Drake and Hawkins perished. North side of church has specially attractive texture, and monuments to faithful servants of Afflecks, including "punctual poultrywoman". Cecil Rhodes bought Dalham but died before he could reach it. His horse was brought here by his brother, who erected village hall in his memory. Hawson Hills superbly wooded. Smock Mill.

DALLINGHOO [17]. Church tower once central before chancel disappeared. Tudor, Stuart, Georgian and Victorian woodwork inside: fine pulpit with back and sounding-board incorporates exquisite Tudor shield-of-arms with rose and Katherine of Aragon's pomegranate. Moat Farm Tudor, on magnificent site, and lately modernised with skill.

DARSHAM [12]. Church yellow-plastered on south side. Narrow 13c chancel. Fine monument of streaked pink and white marble with black columns and small recumbent females to Sir Thos Bedingfield, 1660; Judge of Common Pleas under Charles

Denston

I, "upon whose murder" he "retired himself to this town". Hall, step-gabled, still bears his mantled arms in stone. Font given in 1404.

DEBACH [17] (pronounced Debitch). Airfield now a mushroom factory. Its making by U.S. engineers is subject of moving chapter in Robt Arbib's *Here We Are Together* (1946). Church, towerless and barnlike, rebuilt 1853 by diocesan architect Phipson. Exterior already venerable. Curious little log-steeple for one bell in churchyard. Osborne Reynolds (1842–1912), distinguished professor of engineering, came of three generations of Debach rectors.

DEBENHAM [10] (pronounced Debb'n'm, though river that starts here as a number of large ditches is pronounced Deeb'n). Fritillaries grow near "the gulls". Church on hill at apex of village street. Lower stages of square tower presumably pre-Norman: it has porch to west, with Lady Chapel over. Beautiful 1420ish nave arcade. Descent into chancel suggests early origin. Monuments.

Despite fire of 1744 which destroyed thirty-eight houses there are interesting old buildings all down the main street, a few of them nicely shaded by pollarded trees. Crows Hall an historic beauty, much moated.

DENHAM [8] by Bury. Earthworks of ancient castle just across Gazeley boundary presumably represent "Desning", a military outpost of Clare. Extensive orchards. Hall, early 19c in middle of large moated platform, is divided among local workers. Ivied corner-

tower of earlier house hangs over water. Church contains two most remarkable monuments to Puritan Lewkenor family: one, 1605, shows Sir Edward and Lady Susan kneeling in effigy with two rows of children under canopy and heavy strapwork pediment: colour once splendid—black, gold, terracotta, imitation marble. Double row of figures extraordinarily lifelike. The other, their grandson, died at twenty in 1634, who lies under a monument as beautifully carved as the other is crude: a first class work in white Italian marble on a black slab, with alabaster: J. & M. Christmas, 1638.

DENHAM [10] by Eye. Church may have been collegiate, connected with Hoxne priory: hence miserere seats in chancel. Bedingfield monuments in north chapel: pleasant stone effigy of recumbent woman probably one of them. Fine arms of Charles I dated 1637.

DENNINGTON [11]. Church intensely exciting. Nave and aisles full of richly carved medieval benches (some being carved in 1525) and plain Georgian box-pews. Double-decker pulpit and reading-desk by Robt. Wightman, 1625–8. Then highly elaborate painted wooden parclose screens, surmounted by their original lofts (for access to candle-beam and for musicians). On south, these screens enclose Lord Bardolph's majestic alabaster tomb. Wm. Philipp, Lord Bardolph, founded chantry for two priests, 1437. He fought at Agincourt. As Treasurer to Henry V's household he is said to have managed the great king's

funeral. His will forbids funeral pomp for himself—only twenty burning torches when his corpse entered cities or towns. He died 1441, his wife 1447. Their tomb and glorious screens are of that time.

Beyond, even grander, a long stone chancel with much decorative carving, alive with light from clear-glass east window: probably built for Sir Wm Wingfield (nephew of founder of Wingfield College), patron here 1349–98, the empty matrix of whose brass has been moved from position before high altar. Over windows, the sculpture is largely leafy, with birds and wimpled ladies, but over south doorway, clothed lady and naked man recline back to back. Some 14c glass survives: unusual blue-and-white glazing by Constantine Woolnough of Framlingham, 1858.

DENSTON [14]. Collegiate church: clear affinities with Melford. Externally it looks like great nave of seven bays and no chancel: inside detached candle-beam still marks division. Whole rebuilding shortly before 1475, when chantry college founded by will of Jn Denston, with Master and two co-brethren to say masses for living and souls of dead, and to minister to needs of inhabitants. Interior unspoilt. Fan-vaulting in south porch. Jumble of medieval glass in east window: one pane has comic strutting bird that goes well with crocodiles and other beasts on roof cornice. Complete nave benches also carved with animals and grotesques. 18c box-pews in aisles. Chancel stalls very fine. Medieval glazed tiles. Beautiful window signed

M.T. (Martin Travers—who restored the church), 1932. Chantry Farm-house has lavishly carved oak ceilings. Hall, which once had great gatehouse of Wingfield kind, has broad two-storey early 18c front and early Tudor rear range.

DEPDEN [14] has highest point in Suffolk: Elms Farm. Church has number of 17c features. Nearby council buildings unfitting.

DRINKSTONE [9]. James Cartemey left residue of goods to tiling of church 1519. The "minister of the parish" gave £400 towards the red-brick steeple, 1694: also presumably built splendid stables next to later 18c rectory. Good 14c church with beautiful remains of 15c screen. Memorials. "Ticehurst", dated 1599, has splendid malting in rear. Drinkstone mill, dated 1689, one of three dated 17c post-mills in Suffolk is still in good order.

DUNWICH [12]. A small village now nestles behind a fatally sandy cliff. Tracks of Roman roads lead to it, across the heaths. It occupies the western suburbs of a gated, ramparted town that, in King John's day, was only slightly smaller than Ipswich. Of its eight (possibly nine) parish churches, none survives. All lie wave-battered and tide-mauled, mere lumps of masonry lost in the sea-bed. There would always have been time for bells and other valuables to be removed, but the legend of the distant sound of their ringing is treasured by the romantic.

Present main street runs east from site of St James's leper-

Drinkstone mill, 1689. Mr W Clover's family has worked it since the 1750s

hospital, with fine 12c ruins and Victorian parish church beside it, past excellent new museum, and Ship Inn, to the corner where the Bridge Gates led on into the town. To the left, main car-park occupies site of another medieval suburban hospital (Maison Dieu). To right, footpath follows line of town ramparts, into west side of which Greyfriars Priory built its eastern flint skirting wall in 13c (wall and gateways survive). Immediately east, inside the old town, All Saints parish church finally went under the sea in our own day: west side of graveyard still on cliff-top, with headstone of young man buried 1826, whom the sea will disinter when it is time. Cliff path leads on beyond Greyfriars to site of the town's Middle Gate. Here a wooded path follows line of Midgate Street west, and another path to right leads to St James's and the Museum. Here, and in Gardiner's famous History of Dunwich, 1754, and Henry James's *English Hours* and Charles Keene's drawings, and thoughts of the implacable sea-monster in Mozart's *Idomeneo*, so alarmingly presented on the opera-stage at Snape, we become acutely aware of the unending conflict between the men of coastal Suffolk and the sea.

EASTON [17]. In river meadows, James Kerr is turning Model Farm into living farm-museum with old breeds, to demonstrate farm-life to town-dwellers. Whole "estate village" character derives from 19c ownership of Earls of Rochford and Dukes of Hamilton. Their house, ultimately Edwardian, was enclosed by the longest ribbon wall in the world: alas it has now been breached to allow building of usual "Sunningdale" bungaloid development. But several *cottages ornées* survive: and Easton Harriers. Plain church full of good dark-stained woodwork: enclosed

low box-pews of 1816, and two Elizabethan Wingfield family pews with canopies, alongside the altar: very grand and funny. Monuments to Wingfields, Rochfords and others.

EASTON BAVENTS [12]. Reduced to a narrow strip along seashore north of Southwold: includes a small "broad" for benefit of wildfowl. Church went under water late 17c.

EDWARDSTONE [21]. Old Hall down 1952. Lynns Hall belonged to Waldingfield clothiers 16c. Church has brasses and monuments. Notable 15c roof. Aisle "new" 1462, vestry 1506. Stuart pulpit. Parts of Father Smith organ: case by Bodley.

ELEIGH, BRENT [15]. Hall and church nobly sited together on hill above village and stream. Hall, William-and-Mary, with bay windows, cupola, and notable staircase with plaster ceiling having oval painted centrepiece with shield of arms of Colman. Main gate brought from Holland *c.* 1919. Well-kept church of much beauty. Medieval crucifixion on east wall. Box-pews. East end of south aisle screened by rustic parclose with painted shields. Two-decker early Stuart pulpit. Walls cream. Broad, open chancel has Charles II altar rails. Decorated tracery with ugly glass, and most affecting monument to "that good man, Mr Edward Colman", 1739, by Thos Dunn: semi-recumbent in winding-sheet with heavenly cherub in cloud above. Dr Colman, Fellow of Trinity Cambridge *c.* 1700, built fine parochial library, where M. R. James made a famous discovery.

ELEIGH, MONKS [15]. Church-tower (bequest to it, 1434) standing above cottage and small green (complete with parish pump) was one of the most familiar railway-poster scenes of Suffolk. Medieval south doors and pulpit: early 17c poor-box and holy table. Highlands (or Higlins) Farm has carved oak stringcourse and arms of Robt and Eliz. Munnings, 1594. Fenn Farm has black-and-red brick front, 1742. "Meadowbank" in the Street was probably Gildhall, with kingpost perhaps *c.* 1400. Ingenious house near Highlands with traditional steep-pitched roof: by Philip Dowson, 1959.

ELLOUGH [6] (pronounced Ella, from *elgr*, Old Norse for heathen temple). Christian church, with well-built square tower and appropriately stark grey frame stands boldly above narrow valley. Churchyard invaded by thickets of young oaks. Threatened with redundancy: stripped of furniture. Brasses include effigy of Margt Chewt, 1607, aged eighty-five, in headdress half as big as herself. Small medallion profile of Rev. R. A. Arnold, rector here over sixty years, died 1877. Georgian rectory opposite being renovated 1973.

ELMHAM, SOUTH [5], now nominally six parishes, formerly ten (including Homersfield and Flixton) and forming a deanery. Appears to go back to 680s, when the second bishopric of the East Angles was established. In South Elmham St Cross is a ruin known as the Old Minster. On available evidence (which two excavations

Monks Eleigh, former water-mill

have not resolved) this seems to have been built *c.* 1050 on site of the bishop's seat of 680s replaced, probably about 750, by the church at North Elmham, Norfolk. Arguments summarised in my *Suffolk Landscape* and recent articles in *Norfolk Archaeology*.

Late-enclosed greens, primrose verges, gated roads, moats and unexciting churches. (*Flixton* and *Homersfield*, properly part of South Elmham, are treated alphabetically.) *South Elmham All Saints - cum - St Nicholas*. Stone cross, buried in brambles, marks site of St Nicholas. All Saints nave early Norman: 11c round tower. SS Ursula and Dorothy in glass. Church Farm mostly Tudor with pond and moats, beautifully restored by Michael and Sheila Gooch. The Elms, across a field to the west, contains 14c timbered upper aisles. *St Cross* (originally called Sancroft St George) parish church dedicated to St George. St Cross is a corruption of the word Sancroft. Church has tall clerestoried nave, east end stepgabled. Hall has, on first floor, remains of timber-framed great hall of a palace of Bishops of Norwich. Brick and flint ruins, perhaps those of bishops' steward's house. Home Farm has Tudor brick gable. *St James*, north nave wall has early flintwork. Tudor brasses, Stuart pulpit and holy table. *St Margaret* the church porch has a room over, with ruined barrel organ, reached by 15c brick newel. Old hourglass stands before pulpit. *St Michael* has very good Norman south doorway. Post-mill. Iron fount on Green. *St Peter* has wide-moated

Lynns Hall, **Edwardstone**

Hall, with 15c stone-mullioned traceried windows, probably from Flixton nunnery. Like all others in South Elmham, church has Norman doorway.

ELMSETT [15]. Red House Farm above a brook and a rookery has great chimney stack, so have Poplar Farm and, in village, the rectory on its large moated site. Gently undulating cornland. Tall lavatory-brick grain silo. Ugly little concrete memorial of tithe war, 1935, opposite church, which is beautifully kept, with broad ship-like nave, plastered ceiling, gallery and organ properly at west end. Altar railed three sides. Monuments.

ELMSWELL [9]. A manor of Bury abbey, who housed Henry VI here, 1433. Flushwork of tower and porch exceptionally fine (despite periods of neglect). Tower, building 1476, displays lily: John Lyly's will, 1477, lists his tools (shaves, chisels, planes, etc, themselves shown in flint-work at neighbouring Badwell Ash). Monument to Sir Robt Gardener, Elizabethan pro-consul. His 1614 almshouses, trim, adjacent; a small thatched cottage unaccount-ably neglected below. Vast nearby "dormitory" develop-ment, inexcusably unrural in lay-out and texture. North of railway, The Street shows acceptable older suburban development lining edges of former Button Haugh Green: group near Willow Farm especially attractive.

ELVEDEN [2]. Breckland scene in 1916 of earliest, formative training in tank warfare.

81

Forest village. Remains of original modest East Anglian church may be seen in present south aisle, with Kempe east window. The Edwardian age re-shaped this church in a way most distasteful to our own. Unredeemed by later additions, including stained glass. Georgian Hall reconstructed 1870 for Prince Duleep Singh, East Anglian antiquary, with interior designs in the Indian style by Wm Norton of London. It was more than doubled 1899–1904 from the plans of Wm Young for the Earl of Iveagh with white marble hall based on Taj Mahal. One wing now converted to workmen's flats. Lord Iveagh understandably prefers a cottage. His estate is a model of productive large-scale large-cycle light-land farming. Capability Brown received £1,460 from General Keppel for work done 1765–9: it may have been done here, Miss Stroud thinks.

ERISWELL [1]. 14c church simple, Victorianised, was chapel of St Laurence. Took dedication of St Peter's ruined church, now part of a dovehouse with ancient chalk wall. Tiny square doll's house of a flint chapel labelled *Wesley Doctrine*. Victoria Place, a terrace of cottages erected 1852 by New England Co. for Propagating the Gospel in Foreign Parts!

ERWARTON [22]. Hall has rich red-brick Jacobean fantasy gateway with round arches and pinnacles like chimneys. Hall itself c. 1575 with later moulded ceiling and "robust" staircase of later 17c remodelling. Stair-hall painted with *grisaille* but either not finished or covered with Victorian wallpaper.

Reconstruction 1858 left much unspoilt. Church interior spoilt 1836. Monuments suffered extraordinary fates.

EUSTON [2]. Famous noble seat since Arlington acquired Elizabethan house in 1666. In 1750–6 Kent's pupil Brettingham redesigned north side; this wing luckily survived fire of 1902 and provides main body of Duke and Duchess of Grafton's house since 1951 remodelling. At right-angles, a section of the old main wing (rebuilt in 1902) is retained as dining-room and wall-space for some of the larger family-portraits, a superb collection going back to James I. House stands calmly beside a tributary of the Little Ouse, despite Kent's plans for a higher site on the "downland" slopes that did receive his domed, octagonal "temple" (now a cottage). Delectably wooded park had nearly £1,000 worth of Capability Brown's attention. Miss Stroud shows that it probably went into lowering the level of the lake: quotes "formerly the great lake was above a foot higher than the floor of the mansion, but that now the water appears to as great advantage, yet the whole place was rendered dry and comfortable". Where drive crosses bridge an old mill has been disguised as church. Medieval church in park stuccoed and remodelled in 17 and 18c. Interior has very delicate wood-carving in Grinling Gibbons manner: the frame of the altar-piece is surely by the master: also very pretty ornamental plasterwork. Neighbouring landscape described in Robt Bloomfield's poetry. Present Duke has 8,000 acres of this

light land productive, an endeavour ranking with better-known neighbouring enterprise. Hall Farmhouse sparkling combination of flint and red brick.

EXNING. *See* NEWMARKET.

EYE [10]. Small, sleepy market town away from main roads, its castle, like Clare's, the centre of a great honour: it managed to become a borough in 1408, a parliamentary borough in Elizabeth I's time and now gives its name to an electoral division. Wm Malet, one of the Conqueror's magnates, built simple motte-and-bailey castle at junction of River Dove and tributary: started market in castle on Saturdays, market-day on the bishop's manor of Hoxne near by: Hoxne's trade ruined. Blunt ellipse of bailey running west from motte imposed itself on shape of present town. Malet's son founded Eye priory. In Henry VIII's reign castle followed priory into disuse, though not entirely, for a windmill stood on the motte from before 1690 till early 19c, when present folly built. The great splendour of Eye today is its church. Noble flushwork tower and south porch were being raised in 1460s and 70s. (Porch said to be "shockingly restored with brick in the flint panels": this contrast of colour and texture of course provides one of its main beauties.) Over £40 collected in 1470 alone, "partly of the plough, partly of church ales ... but chiefly of the frank and devout hearts of the people". Two days after Elizabeth's accession there was a bequest of twenty ounces of

Erwarton Hall

silver towards a new cross, "if the laws of the realm will permit and suffer the same". The rood, with its crudely painted medieval lower panels, was magnificently restored by Sir Ninian Comper, 1929, best seen perhaps from west gallery. Font-cover also Comper's. Interesting monuments. Kerrison memorial, Gothic, in Broad Street, exhibits a bust of that excellent baronet (1821–86) by F. Giuntini. Linden House, a beautiful two-storey early 18c building with gauged brick-work. Stayer House, 16c timber-framed, has handsome Georgian staircase front added. There are ribbon walls, Dutch gables and a 17c gazebo in the town, but also a hideously unsightly poultry factory.

EYKE [17]. Old Scandinavian for oak. Church has broad Norman crossing with tower-base, very Cotmanesque. Headless effigies of Jn Staverton and wife. Staverton Park, mainly in Butley parish, has notable ancient oaks, the Thicks, shown to be primitive oak forest. Lovely water meadows.

FAKENHAM, GREAT [2 and 3]. Largely occupied by Honington airfield. Field Farm has splendid Elizabethan chimney stacks. Quoins of pre-Conquest church at each end of nave. Rushford Hall, beside Little Ouse, white-brick Georgian house, seven bays lately extended to twelve, behind gorgeous wrought-iron gates.

FALKENHAM [23]. Splendid west doorway of church (St Ethelbert) bears arms of England, Warwick, and Mowbray Duke of Norfolk: beautiful tower screened by limes. 1806 white-brick nave and apsidal chancel. Tablet commemorates Geo. Roddam, naval physician to George IV and (?fatally) to the poor Princess Charlotte.

FARNHAM [17]. Church on side of valley looking across upper Alde and A12 to Stratford St Andrew. Nave full of dark-stained Georgian box-pews. Much exterior buttressing and restored red-brick tower. Roman villa-site north of Langham Bridge.

FELIXSTOWE [23]. Municipal Edwardian seaside resort facing south round a wide shingly bay with safe and delightful bathing, the beach divided into innumerable sections by groynes and breakwaters, backed by some hundreds of wooden huts hired for the swim or the season, ranged along a 20-ft wide concrete promenade begun in 1902 and reaching two miles from Cobbolds Point to the Manor House. At the mid-point is the pier, built out half-a-mile in 1904 with electric tram and shelters for fishermen: from the end Belle steamers took you to Yarmouth, Walton-on-the-Naze, even London. No Belle steamers now: pier reduced to a stump after the last war. The grandest hotels, Felix and Cliff, have become offices: Fisons unsuccessful in bid to replace the Felix by great tower of offices at edge of cliff! But the town can never wholly lose its character of resort, its convenience for the people of Ipswich. Surviving engravings of picture Gainsborough painted of the fort from Bull's Cliff show the essential foundation of the modern town: the craggy cliff on top of

which the shopping and residential area was built up from the mid-19c onwards, and the long low spit stretching to Landguard Point, covered now by private hotels and lodging-houses, dominated by gigantic cranes of new gigantic roll-on-roll-off container port. Manor House and all this commercial, port end of the town, was part of the determined creation of Col George Tomline of Orwell Park. In 1867 he acquired manorial rights from the Duke of Hamilton (after whom the main shopping street is named. It is dignified by Lloyds Bank.) His railway from Ipswich to Beach and Pier stations opened ten years later: to Town Station 1898. He built Pier Hotel (now "Little Ships" in honour of the motor gunboats that operated from here in World War II) and the Manor Hotel (now "Manor House", threatened with sea-erosion). A. J. Balfour was captain of the Golf Club 1889. German Empress stayed with her children in 1891. St John's, a large red-brick church of 1894–1895, designed by Sir Arthur Blomfield and Son; spire nicely (but probably unintentionally) balances Harwich's as one approaches that harbour from the sea. Early service was in progress one Sunday in 1917 when a force of fifteen to twenty-one German planes killed and wounded several visitors and inhabitants. St Andrew's church (architect: the late Hilda Mason with Raymond Erith) has external defects of appearance of any bare concrete structure, and still lacks tower, but the material is skilfully handled and displays inside excellent proportions of traditional East

Anglian church. (Built in "humble thanksgiving for answered prayer" in rejection of 1927 prayer-book measures.) Also two ancient parish churches: *Walton* (merged with Felixstowe in U.D.C. 1895), largely rebuilt 1860s and '90s, has a medieval brass, 1459: 17c lock-up cage recently re-erected as agreeable bus-shelter beside churchyard. "Old" Felixstowe church has picturesque buttressed tower with septaria: a mainly 14c building, has some monuments and much poor Victorian workmanship inside. Remains of submerged great Roman fort visible nearby at lowest tides: some scholars now think it the site of *Domnoc*, where St Felix established the East Anglian bishopric. Felixstowe Ferry was an agreeable collection of holiday shacks and "informal" buildings opposite Bawdsey: appearance finally spoilt by sea-defence works since great tide of January 1953 that drowned forty people in the Langer Road area. Several notable examples of Felixstowe's seaside architecture survive the barbarities of our times: Harvest House (the Felix), Lloyds Bank and Cobbold's Point Lodge, all by T. W. Cotman, the painter's nephew; High Beach terrace, by Wm. Brown (London).

FELSHAM [15]. Over-restored church has beautiful flushwork north porch, c. 1470. Flint and white-brick well combined in village. Hill Farm notable, half-timbered. Remains of brick mausoleum of Jn Reynolds, sheriff, 1735, "who thought differently from all men while he lived". Bradfield Woods reserve includes Felsham Hall wood.

FINBOROUGH, GREAT [15]. Woolpit-brick Hall 1795 designed by Francis Sandys stands on slight eminence with projecting bow and baroque statues on lawn: seat of the Eastern Electricity Board. Blissful remote old farmhouse called The Butterfly. Pettiwards rebuilt church with hot-water system 1874–5 (Phipson). Prominently striped spire and interesting monuments to Wollastons and Pettiwards, the last killed in Dieppe raid 1942, leading commando troop.

FINBOROUGH, LITTLE [15]. Little church with no steeple, mainly 1856.

FINNINGHAM [9]. Eleven freemen, owing customary duties to Bury abbey which they performed at Rickinghall, had a church here in 1066. Much restored 1880s, but south porch, *c.* 1463, retains medieval door. Good medieval Suffolk roof and font with curiously designed cover and bench-ends, one carved with watchman on a tower. Frere family monuments: they lived at Green Farm, beside Church Green. North of church, beautiful pargeting of figtree (17c) and vine (mid-18c). Marvellous mature avenue at Finningham Lodge.

FLEMPTON [8]. Early Flemings settled beside Lark, which waters the Breckland here, and whose willows and freshness offset suburban growth. Golf course. Church with truly fine

Bridge Street, **Framlingham**. (Mr Allen's successor's tame lettering is *sans serif*)

85

piscina, good plain pulpit and altar rails.

FLIXTON [15] by Bungay. Church mostly rebuilt by Salvin, 1861, said to have copied original faithfully. Arch of Margery de Creke's Austin nunnery embodied in "The Abbey" farmhouse.

FLIXTON [inset] by Lowestoft, originally included Oulton. Church ruin on ridge of field beside Old Hall farmhouse. Decoy, a small broad, belongs to Flixton House.

FLOWTON [16]. Attractive little church. Square truncated tower topped with old red bricks. Nave has large "debased" Tudor window: great roof beams and king-posts, same period.

FORNHAM ALL SAINTS [8]. When Lark navigable (endpaper old edn) Bury freight unloaded here. "Priory" originally Babwell friary, Franciscan, with lively history. Long flint wall now encloses house (fine red-brick gable and chimney) of Boldero family, 1557–1610. Church with early Tudor porch and aisles. Monuments.

FORNHAM ST GENEVIEVE [8]. Scene of battle between rebel Earl of Leicester and Henry II's men, who won, 17 October 1173. Fornham Hall sold to the demolition men 1950. Park used for infantry training. Church burnt down 1782.

FORNHAM ST MARTIN [8]. Looks across Lark to new Bury housing estate. Church has Tudor red-brick porch with step-gable. Victorian interior gloom relieved by two gilt

cherubs. Two fine misericords built into ugly lecterns. Village institute erected 1886 by Sultan of Johore in memory of his friend, Major-General Ord.

FOXHALL [22]. One of the surprisingly unpopulous parishes about Ipswich, nevertheless conceals in its healthy birchwoods a motor speedway. Church now almost unrecognisable, concealed in outhouse of Hall. Obelisk (1831) in small fir plantation.

FRAMLINGHAM [11]. Little old market town on side of low hill to which it owes its former greatness, the site of one the chief English baronial castles. Observe at leisure the mellow beauty in all the ancient houses and shops of the town, their red pantiled roofs climbing one above another from the millbrook at the bottom to group themselves round the triangle of the market-place.

The fine castle-walls with flanking towers, presumably a rebuilding in 1190s by Bigod, Earl of Norfolk, failed to withstand King John's siege in March 1216. Framlingham continued to go with Norfolk title, and seems to have been done up c. 1483, when Jn. Howard of Stoke-by-Nayland became Duke. Something of the Howards' Tudor magnificence may be seen from their tombs in the church: their unsympathetic characters are revealed by Holbein. Their main memorials in castle are bridge and shield of arms at gate and eight delightful brick chimneys erected round the old battlements, to make themselves feel at home: five of them for purely ornamental purposes. Third duke

saved from axe by death of Henry VIII: it had already fallen on his son, the poet Earl of Surrey. Edward VI granted the castle to his sister Mary, here at the dangerous moment of her accession. Park extended a mile to north, included Little Lodge and Great Lodge to which owners could retire from publicity of castle-court. Sir Robt. Hitcham bought it all, 1635, leaving it to use of his college, Pembroke, Cambridge. He ordered all save stone buildings to be pulled down and workhouse, almshouses and school to be set up. All that one now sees within shell-keep, of any substance, is poor-house of 1729, used as such till 1837, when fitted up as public hall, with Georgian west gallery from church. Gallery back in church, and this hall restored; provides ascent to wall-walk and best view of Lower Court, earthworks, and outer bailey. Notice stone chimneys and remains of hall and chapel of c. 1150 embedded in north-east side of inner court, opposite poorhouse.

Church, between castle and market, a Tudor rebuilding (embodying supports of 12c chancel arch)—late 15 and 16c. Almost royal grandeur. Tower very noble. Big key to castle in church porch.

Over the threshold, effect immediate and marvellous. Rich nave roof, hammerbeams encased in wooden vaulting. Opposite south entrance, poignant wall-painting of Trinity shows Christ robed in ermine, recalls custom (as recorded at Southwold) of real clothes to cover the hanging Christ. West arch now perfectly contains famous organ, made in 1674 by

◁ **Framlingham** church: the 3rd duke's tomb, 1554

Thos Thamar for Pembroke College, Cambridge (Framlingham's patron). Thamar re-used parts of earlier instrument and built it into earlier case that has stamp and beauty of Laudian church of 1630s: case one of only eight that survived Cromwellian lunacy. Sound of this organ's Great Chorus has been described as "the rough authentic voice of the late seventeenth century, at watershed between conservative English and new ideas from abroad". Here in 1708, it was mounted superbly on new gallery: once the roods were down, western galleries for organ and choir were natural sequel. Now the eyes turn east to singularly beautiful reredos (perhaps made about the middle of the 18c), whose central painting of the heavens also goes back in mood to the Laudian church. On either side, carved stonework of Howard tombs well seen in soft blue-green Victorian light. Chancel rebuilt for them by third Howard duke. He was careful to have tomb (1536) of son-in-law, Duke of Richmond, Henry VIII's bastard, brought here from Thetford Priory, and set up immediately north of altar. His own (1554) shows him old, with a beard like a dagger, and his second wife, Eliz. Stafford, 1558, surrounded by classical niches with figures. These tombs have been rated "the last and perhaps most distinguished example of the abortive sculptural Renaissance of the early sixteenth century, before contacts were destroyed". They combine French and English, Renaissance and Gothic influences. Of its kind, the duke's tomb "bears comparison with

anything in northern Europe". Tomb in north-east corner has effigies of first two wives of fourth duke, rightly executed 1572. Small tomb of his daughter adjoins. His father, the poet Earl of Surrey, executed by Henry VIII, was commemorated here much later; his large coloured tomb, perhaps by James I's master mason, William Cure. South of Howards, restrained tomb of Sir Robt Hitcham, 1638, who willed Framlingham to Pembroke College.

In town, Hitcham's alms-houses largely Victorianised, but those of Thos Mills, 1709, in excellent order, handsome red and black brickwork. Mills started as wheelwright and, as Kirby put it, "in the times of late disorder turned Holder-forth among the Anabaptists at Saxted". He lies buried in little building in own front garden near almshouses. Unitarians have pleasant little brick box, with dove over-balancing behind preacher. Good 17, 18 and 19c fronts on Market Hill: No. 34 especially attractive behind pollard tree-screen. In Castle Street, No. 38 is delightful, and No. 7, once printers' now stationers', has front of distinction, with central bow, balcony, twin doorcases and empty niches above. Not useful to particularise further in a town of so much attraction. Bookshop in Castle Street.

FRAMSDEN [16]. Beautiful post-mill in working order, thanks to Chris Hullcoop. Hall basically the Radcliffes' 15c moated house, with remarkable carved truss, altered by a Tollemache in Elizabeth's reign: timbered and brick barn. Boundary

Farm, one of the places in Suffolk where fritillaries grow, is early Elizabethan with decorated ceilings, good attics for former farm-hands and external bead-courses with initials of Wythe family who built it. Nearby brick building resembling gatehouse with curved Dutch gables was elaborate stable and grooms' quarters: fine hay-racks, like altar-rails, destroyed during the installation of a grain machine. Church with good tower and typical Suffolk porch is well roofed and lighted. Six stalls with well-carved misericords.

FRECKENHAM [7] looks west from Suffolk over the low fens. "Castle", a great chalk motte 40 ft high, Norman. Handsome red-brick Tudor manor house faces motte. Church, spoilt by Victorians, contains remarkable group of windows in south chancel wall, and poppy-heads with smooth, darkened figures, well carved. Panel of Nottingham alabaster depicts patron of blacksmiths, St Eligius, with horse's leg.

FRESSINGFIELD [11]. Archbishop Sancroft's family had lived at Ufford's Hall, one of several Fressingfield manors, several generations. The old house preserves double flight of stairs and cock's-head hinges. His tomb is beside the stone-panelled church porch. Inside, beneath the carved oak roof, is a nave full of oak benches carved to an overall design: one of the benches, which are the church's great treasure, bears initials of Alice de la Pole, Chaucer's grand-daughter, who married Wm de la Pole, Duke of Suffolk. St Dorothy sits

Frostenden

on another bench, with her basket of roses. Along the back of one bench shields with seven emblems of passion include the diceboard. Former marketplace opposite the Swan. Cowhouse at Church Farm contains timbers of former aisled hall. Fox and Goose stands, like Pettistree Greyhound, south of churchyard: formerly guildhouse. St Margaret of Antioch on a corner-post stamps on the dragon. Queen Anne vicarage with original windows and pantiles. Whittingham Hall, home of the Thos Baker whose bust by Bernini is in the Victoria and Albert Museum, stood in the field beside the present house which stands framed in tree-lined walks called The Gallops.

FRESTON [22]. Diapered redbrick Tudor tower stands in beautiful park of oaks and full-grown copper beeches beside shore of Orwell estuary. Designed in four stages externally, it contains six rooms one above another. Probably built by Thos Gooding, prominent Ipswich merchant, who succeeded the Latimers here 1553. Church drastically restored 1875.

FRISTON [18]. Huge post-mill bought 1972 for restoration. Church has plain modern furnishings and Victorian paintings in chancel. Very fine carved arms of James I. Baptist chapel 1831. Meres at Moor Farm. Early 18c fragment of old Hall built into 19c farmhouse at head of stately avenue. Vernon-Wentworths moved to Victorian house on Blackheath beside Alde estuary, with handsome new Georgian river front by Raymond Erith.

FRITTON [inset]. Incomprehensibly and reluctantly went to Norfolk, 1974. One of the most remarkable small churches in East Anglia, dedicated to St Edmund, and above the altar in the low apse his martyrdom is still to be seen in early Norman paint. It looks exactly like an episode from the Bayeux Tapestry. Nave extended west (see north wall) and round tower added, 13c. Rest of wall-paintings done when nave widened to south in early fourteenth century, at about the time when Fritton Lake was reaching its present form—the result of early medieval peat-cutting. (76 per cent of total income of manor in 1318 came from turbary—the extraction of various grades of peat.) Tower repaired 1518. At Old Hall, by the lake, fishing and gardens open Easter–October.

FROSTENDEN [6]. Church stands beautifully beside farmhouse-Hall above little valley—one of the pleasantest views along A12.

◁ **Fressingfield** porch. Sacristan's upper chamber surmounted by eroded Wingfield/De la Pole shield.

GAZELEY [7]. Desning Hall (1845) beside great moat represents *Deseling* of Domesday, which had two well endowed churches, one the present parish church, with curious east window above village green. Old flint-and-panelled smithy needs rescue. 1830s flint terrace opposite sensibly renewed. Great charm of church in unrestored interior. Splendours of chancel, *c.* 1300, still seen, especially (with binoculars) its panelled wooden roof. Remains of sedilia and 14c glass. Medieval pulpit almost wholly renewed. Demonstration of tracery motifs (EE/Dec) in the font panels. Ancient carved wood benches, some with traceried backs. Good Victorian glass E windows. Enormous painting by Jaques Stella, Poussin's friend. Flinty bridleway leads over dry flinty fields from Desning Hall to earthworks of Earl of Clare's castle.

GEDDING [15]. Hall, red-brick, moated, designed in Henry VIII's reign as gatehouse, like small version of Layer Marney. Monstrous corner tower 1897 designed by mayor of Leicester. Church owes pleasant appearance to red-brick top of tower (?willed 1469).

GEDGRAVE [18]. Marshland with secret line of cliffs on Butley river and a very Dutch-looking wind-pump. Hall, Queen Anne red-and-black brickwork with later sash windows. Coralline cragpit.

GIPPING [10] was a chapelry of Thorney (Stowmarket), part of ancient "New Town" development embracing Old Newton and Stowupland. So Tyrell family, here from Henry VI's

Gipping chapel from site of hall

reign to Victoria's, went to Stowmarket for burial. Their chantry chapel here, *c.* 1484, adjoins site of Hall (still marked by well). Approached through a farm gate and seen through silvery willows it is among the most perfect examples of Perpendicular architecture in Suffolk, with great windows occupying most of the space between wall-buttresses, so that the doorways had to be accommodated within the window-frames. Buttresses and walls rival the most brilliant examples of decorative flint-work anywhere, and the exterior of priest's chamber north of chancel is especially notable. Initials of founder's wife, Anne Morley Lanherne Arundel, repeated six times in stonework. Roof and small brick tower are later additions. Jumble of original glass in east window. Local constable's truncheon inscribed "G.II.R. Gippen."

GISLEHAM [6] (pronounced Gizzle'm). Chancel, blue-washed, has very nice 14c window-cases. Brass to Adam Bland, Sergeant to her Majesty, 1593. Tablets include E. B. and M. P. Pugh, two brothers who died prisoners of war: "Their graves lie amid the forests of Siam."

GISLINGHAM [10]. Splendid unspoilt church: its interior redolent of oil-stoves and Cotman. Red-brick steeple 1639 replaces one that fell 1600. Late 15c north porch given by Chapmans, its roof renewed 1661. Low-pitched double hammer-beam nave roof. Three-decker pulpit set amidst box-pews of the congregation: some medieval pews on the brick floor at the west end. Arms of George III well placed in tower arch. Note phonetic spelling of Georgian bell-ringers. Large mid-17c wall monument with Anthony Bedingfield kneeling. Blue Columbine, depicted in three lights of 15c glass, grows at Yaxley nearby.

GLEMHAM, GREAT [17]. Crabbe's home 1796–1801 pulled down soon after. Glemham House, 1814, in Repton Park. Grove has perfect *cottage ornée*. Church: one-armed Georgian clock on its tower, and well-preserved seven-sacrament font inside: man at penance in Henry IV hat, robes of Mass-priest well chiselled: best of all, Unction with christmatories. Beautiful roof. South aisle a copy of Marlesford's. Service books include early Prayer Book from Chiswick Press (1801). Monument to Saml Kilderbee, Town Clerk of Ipswich and Gainsborough's lifelong friend.

GLEMHAM, LITTLE [17]. Acquired by Christopher Glemham of Farnham shortly before his death, 1549, "in prime of all his years". His father, self and son have notable brass inscriptions in church. Grandson married a Lord Treasurer's daughter and presumably built the Hall, originally a great house like Blickling, with wall and gazebos like Melford, entered through elaborate fantasy gatehouse. Their son distinguished royalist general in Civil War: grandson sold to one of the famous North brothers, Dudley, economist and leading Turkey merchant, with very fine marble monument in church. Son married Elihu Yale's daughter and gave the Hall its unsatisfactory appearance, neither Elizabethan nor Palladian, *c.* 1722, by stripping away brick-decoration of old house and throwing walls up higher to include dull attic storey and conceal roof. Other beautiful North monuments in striking north chapel, of Soanesque design, coloured French grey, not least the noble sedentary statue of Dudley Long North (1748–1829) by Gibson, in Rome, 1833. Moat Farm, with Tudor brick gable-end, is the former Pistree Hall.

GLEMSFORD [14]. Large village on flat-topped spur, a strange mixture of late medieval and late Victorian. Made own contribution to local cloth industry by 1460s: Gleynforths were white, while characteristic "Suffolks" were dyed in the wool, usually blue. 15c wood-carving of Michael on corner-post serves as sign for Angel pub. Designs of church windows, porch and flushwork panelling suggested by Long Melford (or by same craftsman), likewise externally inscribed nave roof high-pitched with kingposts. Jacobean pulpit. Silk-throwing mill 1824 followed by horse-hair seating factory employing nearly 500 people by 1855. Startling red-brick school for 500, 1871. Flax, horse-hair and silk still worked.

GOSBECK [16], lying east of earlier Coddenham, started as Easton and became Easton Gosbeck *c.* 1174 to avoid confusion, then dropped first name. Nave of small church retains complete Anglo-Saxon walls. Victorian reredos well painted.

GROTON [21]. Hall and church stand side by side, a familiar memory to Jn Winthrop, the Moses who organised the main local exodus to New England in the days of Charles I, and became first governor of Massachusetts. Hall unpretentious Elizabethan farmhouse, where horse still ridden as means of getting about. Church memorable for rich texture of grey unfractured flints. East window has beautiful flowing tracery. A

Hadleigh church and Deanery Towers

proud chestnut tree stands by. Tablet to Alex. Hogg, a Berwick purser who served on Cook's last voyage and under Nelson at the Nile, Copenhagen, etc.

GRUNDISBURGH [16] (pronounced Grundsbra). Central green with stream and watersplashes, now concrete-kerbed. Many surrounding roofs 17c, but red-brick church-tower the most handsome presiding object, serving as south-west porch: 1732, with ornate south face, marred by insertion of modern clock. Distinguished church: splendid "false" hammer-beam roof; late 14c screen, rather crusted with gilt, but with notable naturalism; fine font; articulate St Christopher. Among many

monuments notice brass to Jn Awall, 1501, in south aisle. He lived east of church, at Basts, rebuilt by son Thos, member of London Salters' Company *c.* 1515 (see salt-cellar on north-west and south-west corbels): a most remarkable half-timbered house, designed with one-storey hall and dining-room. Thos married Alice, daughter of Langston (master cook to Edward IV *and* Henry VII) and they built south chancel aisle. Hall, Jacobean, with charming Victorian front, being restored and remodelled (Ronald Geary) for Lord Cranworth.

GUNTON. *See* LOWESTOFT.

HACHESTON [17]. Church well kept: Nottingham alabaster, Kempe windows. South wall-

posts of nave roof absurdly transferred to aisle. Glevering Hall by elder Jn White 1792–4 and Decimus Burton 1834–5: one of the best Georgian houses in Suffolk but ill-cared-for; park by Repton. Wistaria Cottage *c.* 1541 by client of Sir Anthony Wingfield, K.G.

HADLEIGH [21]. Antique market-town, once famous clothing town, lying along delightful tributary of Stour. Badly exposed to depression in 1630s and 1879–1914, its life in 1914 seen in Simon Dewes' *Suffolk Childhood* (1959). Now exposed to peril of London overspill. Heights to north already lined with factories. Yet for physical beauty Hadleigh rivals any Cotswold town. High Street runs north–south, parallel with river, other streets at right angles, all rewarding. Church Street terminates in most remarkable group of late medieval buildings in contrasting materials: 14c flint and freestone church, the tip of whose tapering lead-covered spire appears engagingly at eye-level on the descent into the valley: distinguished half-timbered Town Hall, Cloth Hall or Guild Hall with both first and second floors oversailing, *c.* 1430s: Deanery "gateway" or "towers", 1495, of red brick with elaborate diapering, a smaller replica of Oxburgh, Norfolk (1483). Town Hall runs back to Market Street, to which it shows red-brick Italianate face, 1851, next to little Doric corn-exchange, 1813. Very fine medieval river bridge at bottom of street. At top, in High Street, No. 44 is pargeted saddlery established 1774 now selling sports gear. Richardson &

Preece's shop has vivid Renaissance wall-paintings. Nos. 62–66 (restored and handsomely pink-washed, 1957) are made from fine Charles II house with many original fittings; best glazing of its kind in East Anglia, and notable rear gables. No. 33 is a Georgian beauty. No. 89 has doorcase. No. 99 has 1618 gables. Nos. 108–110 dated 1649 is symmetrical with central courtyard, and so one could go on all through Hadleigh. Queen Street commemorates Victoria's accession, Angel Street, George Street and Benton Street are lined with interesting houses of all periods. 92 Benton Street has fine wood carving of 1655, and the street ends perfectly with a farmhouse.

HALESWORTH [11]. Thriving small town on winding thoroughfare. Two pleasant precincts at its heart: the churchyard, which has 1686 almshouses along its south side (now gallery and county library); and the market-place, interestingly wedged between churchyard and Chediston Street. Market granted 1222. Social Club, on west side, a large timber-framed late Tudor building echoed by similar, slightly more ornamental, Gothic House facing east end of church. North from market place pleasant public footpath to Old Rectory is lined by (rebuilt) Serpentine wall, parallel to main thoroughfare which winds past Angel Hotel and shop with strikingly carved bressumer (Gannymede, eagle, lions, etc), crosses the river into Bridge Street, and forks: north to Broadway and Stone Street, the Roman road to Bungay,

and east into Quay Street. The river joins the Blyth just below Halesworth and was made navigable to quay here, 1756. Chance to preserve fine maltings and brewery missed, but Brewery House saved, 1970, reduced to handsome proportions of years soon after it was Wm Jackson Hooker's home (1809–21). Here the great botanists of the day visited him, and his equally famous son, Joseph Dalton Hooker, was born. Their garden here was bulldozed, but Kew is their memorial garden. Wedgwood medallions (1930) commemorate them in the church. Park being developed between river and new relief road might include botanic garden.

Heavily restored church has good tower and weathercock. Monuments include nice marble to a tame Chief Justice, 1687, who lived in Gothic House, opposite. Pulpit. Rare Georgian holy-table: woodworm in beautiful cabriole legs. Dramatic stone fragments, perhaps c. 1050, now interpreted to show hands suspending leafy canopies from above: striking comparison with Nunburnholme Cross reminds us of neighbouring Rumburgh's link with York.

HARDWICK [8]. House pulled down c. 1924: notable painted closet c. 1613 removed to Christchurch Mansion, Ipswich. Suburbia.

HARGRAVE [8]. Pleasant white-washed church with Tudor brick tower. Crude screen.

HARKSTEAD [22]. Wonderfully situated above Stour estuary.

Fine church largely built of local septaria, including south aisle, erected in this century. Tower has superb great 14c window and makes excellent baptistry.

HARLESTON [15]. Hall, red-and-white brick building of 1850, with Dutch gables and prosperous quadrangular barns. Little thatched towerless church, looking like Victorian illustration, retains medieval features and its pre-Norman dedication to Augustine. 16c cottages on Green, and brash pink new council estate.

HARTEST [14]. In steep cleft of tributary of Stour: most buildings grouped pleasantly about Green, including a curious Nonconformist chapel. Church has pretty carved scroll pattern on aisle roofs. 16c north porch, with original church door, has pyx and wafer carved in one spandrel. Complete Jacobean pulpit. Monument to Lieut Harrington (1812) is by Sir Richard Westmacott's brother.

HASKETON [17]. Distinguished church with round tower (octagonal top) and steeply splayed windows. Good Victorian glass and 15c fragment, but not the small glass crucifix that infuriated Seth Chapman's parishioners, 1644. Memorials include "A man in manners though in years a boy", 1635; two brothers who died in Smyrna, 1660s; and two who died at Jutland and the Somme. The medieval Hundred met by the present post office. Hall Farm moated and idyllic.

HAUGHLEY [9]. Fields dominated by uncompromising

grain silo in last decade, dominated for century after Norman conquest by French motte-and-bailey castle, most formidable earthwork of its type in Suffolk, but unable to withstand Leicester's Flemings in 1173 when Walton, Orford, Dunwich and Eye frightened them off. Then destroyed and replaced by a royal manor and park; in hands of Sulyard family 1538–1811. They built the present mellow red-brick house about 1625, with two front window-bays like the porch of New House, Pakenham, stone-pedimented windows, step gables, and a room of later handsome panelling: gutted by fire January 1961, but now rebuilt and beautifully restored and landscaped; spirited modern poultry and egg-packing station in park. Church entered beneath 1725 fire appliances, south aisle giving impressive view of very wide nave. Sixty-ton parish coal-house on green, 1861, and very pleasant old cottages in village street. Dial Farm (with striking early-Tudor carved porch, brought from another village a generation ago) has massive internal timbers. New Bells Farm, brick, plaster and half-timbered scene of Lady Eve Balfour's experiments with "soil as the basis of civilisation". A company of soldiers on their way to Harwich to embark for the Peninsular War manned the guy-ropes for the erection of the weather-boarded post-mill that stood beside Station Road till World War II.

HAVERGATE ISLAND [23]. Principal inhabitants several pairs of avocets. Godwits, curlew-sandpipers and other rare birds are encouraged to reside here. A more vulgar species gave its name to the northern tip of the island: Cuckold's Point. For permit to visit, apply R.S.P.B., The Lodge, Sandy, Bedfordshire.

HAVERHILL [19] (pronounced Hayveril) owed its severe late-Victorian character chiefly to revival of coarse-clothing manufacture, horse-hair goods, etc, by Messrs Gurteen and Sons, employing some thousands of hands here and in neighbourhood. There is a rope-walk, something almost extinct in England. Weavers Row should be noted as pre-factory industrial buildings now that counterparts in Sudbury are coming down. Gurteens personally contributed Town Hall (E. Sharman, Wellingborough) and tower and spire of prominent red-brick Congregational Chapel (Searl and Son, London). Tradition goes back to celebrated 17c Puritans: both Natl Ward and Saml Fairclough were from here. Church (heavily restored 1867, 1904) has monuments. A jeweller's shop survives miraculously from age of Jane Austen. Former vicarage has splendid Tudor chimneys and queer Cockney Gothick plaster front: decaying disgracefully. High Street on major Roman road provided linear pattern of little town to 1950. 1955 agreement with G.L.C. to expand to 10,000, then to 18,500, now to 30,000. "Why stop at 30,000?" asks 1971 Master Plan (Frederick Gibberd, consultants) and says "The answer is in the character of Haverhill." A frivolous answer. If Haverhill's character counted, it would have suggested a London New Town elsewhere: the old town centre is quite unequal to its new functions. That is what is wrong with Haverhill, not the bold new estates climbing the slopes to south and north, designed by G.L.C. architect, and despised for their high density by uninformed local critics. Clements Estate (to south) occasionally achieves massed roof-lines of traditional hill-top town, but contains terrible features, like the "Suffolk Punch" pub. Best aspect of Chalkstone Estate, on opposite ridge, is its use of natural features—as at Linton Place and Kirtling Place, where pleasant open terraces line steep gully.

HAWKEDON [14] has two remarkable ancient red-brick and timber houses, modified and refronted in Jacobean times: Thurston Hall and Swan's Hall. Langley's Farm has Tudor moulded chimney and painted plaster fireplaces with unusual vineleaf patterns. Jn Langley rector 1546. 15c church retains atmosphere notably "unrestored", the colours and textures of old timber and ancient paint and glass. Bench-ends spirited. Elaborate, delightful wall-monument to Richard and Dorothy Everard (1670, 1678). Western gallery. Roman gladiator's helmet found, 1965.

HAWSTEAD [14]. In 1784 Rev. Sir Jn Cullum published a classic *History of Hawsted and Hardwick* (second edition 1813), and hoped that it would lead his readers to set "a proper value upon being born in the eighteenth century, distinguished above all that preceded it ..."

The book inspired Gilbert White's *Selborne:* its author is buried outside north door of this church. Last remnant of Hawstead Place pulled down 1827. Overgrown moat and bridge remain, and two fine piers of gateway in garden of adjacent house. Statue of wild man, 1578, moved by Drurys to Hardwick, where destroyed by wild children of new suburbs. Gothick alms-terrace beside the Green, erected by Philip Metcalfe, 1811. Hammonds Farm, partly *c.* 1580. Church oppressively rich in monuments: the finest to Sir Robt Drury, 1617, by Nicholas Stone, a black sarcophagus under a twin-arched canopy, surmounted by oval niche with bust of his father, Sir Wm, in plate armour. It is wonderfully finished, the first important example of Stone's break with Elizabethan and Jacobean forms. Sir Robt's widow moved to Hardwick: their only children Elizabeth (fifteen) and Dorothy (four) are buried here: Elizabeth's tomb, with inscription probably by Donne and incomparable cherubs, is by Gerard Christmas. Wrecked in 1926 earthquake, and restored by Mrs Esdaile, it is again in need. The authorship of twelve other monuments is known, three by Bury sculptors. Delightful Victorian "Elizabethan" school.

HELMINGHAM [16]. Hall, ensconced in park of red and fallow deer, retains unusually defensive appearance for house largely of Henry VIII's reign, a sort of Azay-le-Rideau without that fantastic French skyline. Basically a half-timbered building, faced in Georgian, in diapered early Victorian, and

in modern red-brick that is acquiring a mellow texture, and battlemented by Nash: an uncompromising quadrangle occupying whole of its ancient moated platform. Drawbridge raised and lowered night and morning. Step gables and brick finials but little further external decoration. First Lord Tollemache's barony created 1876. Model cottages still stand well in their gardens all over this neighbourhood. One son had the good sense to found a brewery, so that Helmingham Tudor is a common local inn-style. House in splendid order since family came to live in it again, 1953. Interior much Salvinised. Rich Palladian work in "boudoir", 4th Earl of Dysart's library which contains many treasures. Full collection of 16c family portraits in excellent condition, among other notable pictures and objects. The most beautiful of the Tollemache monuments in the church commemorate third Earl of Dysart, 1727, and Gen. Thos Tollemache who fought gallantly under William III. Church tower parapeted 1543, a worthy ornament in park and village (*see* my *Suffolk Landscape*).

HEMINGSTONE [16]. St Gregory's rustic church fabric suggests 15c rebuilding of pre-Conquest square tower like that at Debenham. Beautiful red-brick Hall with Dutch gables over wings and porch, early 17c, long empty, lately (1957) reoccupied. Stonewall Farm restored half-timbered home of Cantrells in Elizabethan days. Church has altar tomb with nice inscription to Wm Cantrell, henchman of Duke of Norfolk. Beautiful font.

HEMLEY [23] has Hard on the Deben, a landing-place leading to village and vanished Haspley. Church has fine red-brick tower, lovely remote situation.

HENGRAVE [8]. Beautiful little church of *c.* 1419 with pre-Conquest round tower standing in park and almost under the tranquil walls of the freestone and white-brick Hall rebuilt for "Kytson the Merchant" 1525–38. Jn Eastawe was commissioned to "make" the house according to a "frame" he had seen at Combey Park, the Duke of Buckingham's estate in Gazeley and Denham—probably a plan or model of his great new Gloucestershire house, Thornbury Castle. That the frame incorporated the very latest adornments of great houses may be seen in the result—a superb quadrangular house, late Gothic with one magnificent exception: the rich Renaissance carving (shields supported by pairs of *putti* in Roman armour) on the celebrated triple baywindow over the main entrance. Of notable glass-painting, that in the chapel represents twenty-one scenes from Creation to Crucifixion and may be mentioned in the same breath as Fairford and King's College Chapel. The house is now run by nuns as Catholic ecumenical centre. Internal structure-timbers and plaster—much Edwardianised. In 1575 the grounds were laid out in "true Dutch style". In 1578 the Queen and Leicester and the entire court were here. On that August day they were treated to a spectacle "representing the fayries, as well it might be": it is not recorded that Bottom the Weaver per-

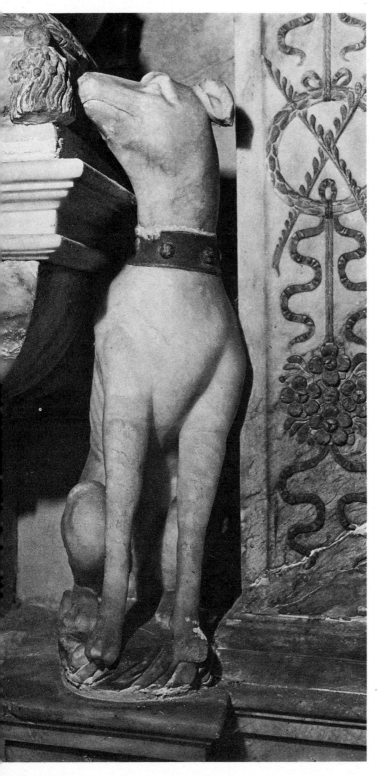

formed. Jn Wilbye (1574–1638), most versatile and possibly greatest of English madrigal-writers, lived here in a room looking out on the church, 1593–1628. The church contains a beautiful arcade and a profusion of monuments. Apart from the well-known Kytson and Gage monuments there is a Thos Gage Craufurd who fell cheering on his men in the orchard of Hougoumont during the battle of Waterloo. Hengrave has an ancient greengage tree, presumably related to that which was introduced from France by Sir Wm Gage (1657–1727), after whom the fruit took its English name.

HENHAM [12]. Roads either side of park vaulted with magnificent oaks. Hall pulled down 1953. Fine ornamental gateway and lodge (Jas Wyatt, modified by E. M. Barry) remain at south end of great park, which has matured substantially as Humphry Repton ordained. Small obelisk beside road south through park: "London 100 miles." Weeping larch of unrivalled spread in Hall gardens. Cork tree.

HENLEY [16]. Dull exterior of great tithe-barn misleading: internal timber-work superb. Terra-cotta window from old Shrubland Hall set in nave of church.

HENSTEAD [6]. Church with elaborately thatched roof and gargoyles has splendid Norman doorway and some monuments: till 1906 restoration it had box-pews and fine three-decker pulpit. Henstead Grange has nice red-and-black brickwork and glazed pan-

Hawstead: heraldic greyhound at head of Elizabeth Drury's tomb

tiles. *Hulver Street*, charming neglected hamlet in Hundred River valley, owes name to holly-copses being cultivated here as early as 1267 (for winter browse). Only about a dozen hollies now dotted about the hamlet.

HEPWORTH [9]. Well-proportioned church suffered from fire 1898. New double-hammerbeam roof looks well. Very remarkable carved late-medieval font-cover, over 12 ft high, seems to have suffered more from 1872 restoration than from fire. Truncated tower, and church tiled too fiery a red.

HERRINGFLEET [inset]. Flagrant suburban and "holiday chalet" sprawl over portentous recent road-bridge spoils precious natural marshland and riverside feel of the place that "Broads" sailors come here to enjoy. More trees would help. Old smock draining mill still works. Bell Inn picturesque red-brick and timber. Of *St. Olave's Priory* of Austin canons, rare early 14c brick vaulting survives. Manor House Farm has Dutch gables, 1655. Large thatched barn of Tudor brickwork at Abbey Farm. Hall, in park designed by Norton Nicholls, is middle and late Georgian congeries with small orangery. Church in very good care. Roof thatched (wheatstraw) 1952. Superbly built round tower of at least two periods (the top ?c. 1090–1100). Crowded Victorian benches and stone west gallery. Georgian pulpit almost on top of altar. Chancel windows have kaleidoscope of window-glass brought from Cologne. Medieval English glass includes

patroness, St Margaret, with crestfallen dragon.

HERRINGSWELL [7]. Icenian territory with tumuli. St Ethelbert's church burnt out 1869 and rebuilt for £1,250.

HESSETT [9]. St Ethelbert's Church is one of the most beautiful late-medieval buildings in Suffolk, with something of the feel of a contemporary Somerset church, Ilminster for instance. The splendid but rather rigid stone parapets suggest the builders of Lavenham: so does the slightly mechanical arcading. Here, unlike Lavenham, the glass is memorable for its beauty: remarkable medieval scenes. The rarest of all the medieval survivals, the pyx cloth and corporal case, have been handed on permanent loan to the British Museum. 15c screen, repainted, external walls disagreeably stuccoed.

HEVENINGHAM [11] (usually abbreviated to "Henning'm"). The Hall is the one first-class Palladian building in Suffolk: designed for Sir Gerard Vanneck, son of a rich London merchant, by Sir Robt Taylor, long connected with Bank and City. For his central block, Taylor gutted previous house of 1710. Wings either side end in subordinate *pavillons*. Composition deeply impressive from front, where stream widened into irregular lake when Capability Brown landscaped park in 1782. At rear, kitchen gardens contain serpentine walls (1796), and there is an orangery by James Wyatt. Wyatt's designs for the interior created at least one of the most handsome

rooms in Europe: the great entrance-hall with fan-spandrelled barrel vault, marble floor, and open screens supported on yellow-brown scagliola columns. Dining-room, library, and Etruscan room, all remarkable. More homely, an oval "print room", a series of prints stuck straight on to wallpaper, where Sir Gerard dined when alone. But the Vannecks have gone to Australia, and how to use and maintain all this is still unresolved.

Church has early Tudor brick clerestory and roof. Family pew of Heveninghams, with woodwork from former screen. One wooden effigy survives from 1400-ish tomb of theirs. Gothic Farm delightful.

HIGHAM [7] near Bury, formerly hamlet of Gazeley, became parish 1894. Church built 1861, one of the few entirely Victorian churches in Suffolk, by Sir Gilbert Scott, who presumably had Little Saxham in mind when he designed exterior of tower. Its base contains the baptistry, covered by beautiful groined vault. Pier arcade of north aisle admirable. Flint schools, 1861. Flint smithy near toll-house on A45.

HIGHAM [21]. Fine situation and agreeable houses: most prominent, looking south across wide Stour valley, Higham Lodge, early 19c Woolpit brick. Most attractive, Barham's Manor, with early 18c pedimented front, plastered and cream-washed, with two bows, shallow slate roof, old timber-work at back. Hall, down by church, has beautiful Georgian front of Woolpit brick. Church has an altogether

unsuitable tiled reredos, with Ten Commandments, glazed: redeemed by beauty of stone north aisle arcade.

HINDERCLAY [9]. Church has nice rustic cream-washed interior, its low, plastered barrel ceilings in aisle and nave giving it a slightly Cornish feeling. Some box-pews. Edmund Farrer, distinguished indefatigable local antiquary, was rector in earlier part of this century.

HINTLESHAM [22]. Park lends whole village a sort of sylvan shade. Hall built by recusant Thos Timperley in Elizabeth's reign. Superb plaster ceiling bears initials of H. Timperley who fled the country in sympathy with James II, 1688. Between 1725–40 house given charming Palladian façade well forward of the old one, to provide entrance hall and gallery above, with view of farmlands and Hintlesham Great Wood, probably aboriginal woodland. The house, rescued and magnificently restored by Robert Carrier in 1972, is cheerful scene of revived summer festival, exhibitions, chamber concerts and opera; above all it has become a centre for the enjoyment of his incomparable cooking all the year round. Church, pleasantly set in tree-shaded village, retains old brick floors, timbered roofs, monuments. Late incised slab shows cavalier Capt. Timperley, 1629, with staff, sword and love: "There's a true heart entomb'd him."

HITCHAM [15]. Noble church in well-kept churchyard. Tablet in choir (which is five steps up from nave) comme-morates Rev. Professor J. S. Henslow (1796–1861), devoted rector from 1837. Despite protests of farmers he established schools in this area with voluntary botany on the syllabus (a great success), started benefit clubs, cricket and athletic clubs, parish outings to the local towns and Great Exhibition. He delivered lecturettes at the half-yearly flower shows, and took an active part in founding Ipswich Museum. Bust by Woolner 'at Kew. He was buried at Hitcham and welcomed in heaven by Arthur Young. Chancel in poor state before 1878 restoration. Monument to Sir Geo. Waldegrave, 1637: this branch lived at Wetherden Hall, one of the most impressive moated sites in Suffolk, though only the old servants' and outhouse range survives—occupying an entire side of the great platform. Brick House Farm, Tudor, near site of Roman villa, has black flint flushwork unusual in houses.

HOLBROOK [22]. Royal Hospital School for sons of officers and men of Royal Navy and Royal Marines, moved from Greenwich 1933. There they had the Queen's House. Here the architecture is not the work of genius, but it is serviceable and the effect of the whole campus, dominated by tall clock-tower and embraced by long arms of main block, is impressive from the Stour estuary below. Architects: Herbt T. Buckland, Wm Haywood. Sculpture on portico between gymnasium and swimming-bath by Hermon Cawthra, large mosaic by Eric Newton in neo-Romanesque chapel.

Parish church has good monument to Judge Jn Clenche and family, 1607. Pleasant water-walks near mill-dam and beneath great new reservoir dam. Cinder-built house here.

HOLLESLEY [23] (pronounced Hozeley). Marsh, heath and small fertile valley: to get the hang of the parish one must leave the village street, take to public footpaths and follow the little stream up from church and Church Farm, nicely grouped where the ancient shore-line dips into the marsh. Church has ugly late-Victorian north aisle, but is redeemed by fine craftsmanship of mid-20c carved benches. They are as accomplished as good 15c work. 14c incised slab from tomb of Wm de Geyton, prior of Butley when gatehouse was building. Church tower good example of the 1450-ish class and familiar sea-mark has eight bells rung by team of Borstal boys. Hollesley Bay Labour Colony established under Act of 1905. When juvenile delinquency became a "growth industry", the Colony became an open Borstal institution, and 280 new dwellings are about to house its staff. New main buildings, red-brick, horizontal, admirably designed for both function and landscape by Brewer, Smith & Brewer. Small nature reserve on heath. *Shingle Street* has been sea-bathing and fishing hamlet along ridge of beach since 1810, a year or two after erection of Martello Towers.

HOLTON ST PETER [11] by Halesworth, has a picturesque post-mill with a fan-tail and no shutters: still in fairly good order. On windmill side of Blyford Road a pretty house with an acacia tree displays excellent modern pargeting. "Gavelcroft Farmhouse" takes its name from its curved Dutch gables. Cottages have Dutch-looking pantiled roofs. Church has tall slim Norman round tower: Norman doorway rudely carved with couchant dragon.

HOLTON ST MARY [21]. Small parish above floor of blissful Stour valley. Lark Hall is a good old house, well named. Vast truncated church tower contains nice early Perpendicular window: tablet to Rev. Stephen White, by whose exertions a charity school was founded, 1748: painted panel shows man with spade and document and says: "Not slothful in business—serving the Lord."

HOMERSFIELD [5] (pronounced Hummersfield: *see* Elmham, South). Church stands on definite platform above Waveney, looking across to splendid tower of Redenhall. Interior restored out of recognition, but beautiful 14c cross survives on nave gable. 1920s almshouses by Maurice Chesterton.

HONINGTON [9]. Cottage where Robt Bloomfield was born 1766 stands near church, behind blacksmith's shop: redbrick front added, and much rebuilding. From here he went to work at Sapiston. The village now gives its name to a large airfield. Church has fine Norman doorway and narrow Norman chancel arch. Beautiful 14c font has crucifixion scene in its east panel, sun and moon in background.

HOO [17]. Broad limpid moat of Godwin's Place said to mark site of 1430 house of John Godwin, London grocer, replaced *c.* 1620 by present small farmhouse. But *c.* 977, another Godwin gave Ely a big estate here including, in 1086, a small church. Dedicated to Andrew *and* Eustachius (a Norman preference) it survives, with beautiful rustic interior and narrow rich-red Tudor brick tower, looking down into Deben valley. Rails round three sides of altar. Large pepper-pot font-cover. Formidable iron-locked chest of poplar and oak, probably 15c.

HOPTON [3]. 18c top stage of 14c tower shows beautiful combination of flint and freestone, with generous proportion of freestone for East Anglia. Early Tudor brick clerestory. Hammerbeam roof, very striking: repainted by five remarkable daughters of Victorian vicar. Monument to Thos Raymond "first sole keeper of the Papers of State to Charles II".

HOPTON [inset] by Lowestoft, with falling sandy cliffs and probes for oil offshore, is holiday-camp village. 14c church burnt down 1865 and kept as ruin in mown lawn, walls complete, enclosing large Irish yew. New church beside main road, 1866, by S. S. Teulon, with fat central squinched tower and ironstone decoration above crude windows. Interior decoration limited to bands of red in the white brick. Nice blues in Burne-Jones east window. Window to Sir Thos Troubridge, wounded at Inkerman.

HORHAM [10] (first syllable short as in horror). Church tower, nobly proportioned and "new" in 1512, has twin louvres at bell-chamber level, like Mendlesham and Eye. Double-decker pulpit of 1631 has lost sounding-board. Stained glass in one window includes arms of Edward III and Black Prince. 16c brick-gabled house now Horham Post Office.

HORRINGER [8] (still sometimes spelt in its old form Horningsheath). Church on green beside main entrance to Ickworth Park: restored under Cottingham's direction 1867, and given new chancel except perhaps for east window with restored reticulated tracery. Neatly kept. Pretty monument to Valentine Mumbee, "a person of great good sense", by Thos Singleton of Bury. Green surrounded by variety of neat cottages in plastered timber, flintwork and white brick, tiled or thatched. The Hopleys was "gothicised", *c.* 1833, for a London publisher. Before that it belonged to Peter Gedge, editor of the *Bury Post*.

HOXNE [4] (pronounced to rhyme with oxen) was spelt exactly the same way as early as *c.* 950, eighty years after St Edmund's martyrdom at a place called Haegelisdun. Some 150 years elapsed before the current tenaciously held tradition was fostered that Hoxne was Haegelisdun. In the 10c the East Anglian bishop established his south seat in St Ethelbert's church at Hoxne. Here was one of the two East Anglian cathedrals (the other at North Elmham, Norfolk) for over a century till 1078, when the bishop moved strategically along to Thetford. In the 13c a cell of monks of Norwich cathedral priory moved into the vicinity of St Edmund's chapel here, and the cult of Haegelisdun began—Norwich's belated attempt to break the Bury monopoly in St Edmund. Marble cross marks site of oak to which people still half-believe Edmund was tied for execution. Hoxne Priory, half-timbering and herring-bone brickwork, was built after the Dissolution. Another notable brick-and-timber house stands on South Green. Pre-Conquest and medieval market south of church (SS Peter and Paul), which has fine tower. Chancel rebuilt 1879 contains frightful Victorian glass. A rather clumsy classical monument to Thos Maynard, 1742, with life-sized statue, is signed by Chas Stanly. Original west door. Beautiful Georgian headstones. Swan Inn preserves its medieval name and functions. To the west, quadrangular baroque stables on bishop's ancient hall-site. Thorpe Hall (five miles away in a corner of the parish) is a Tudor red-brick house, with tall rooms on two storeys on either side of great four-stage projecting porches back and front—one large pedimented window lights each room north and south. Another notable brick and timber house stands on South Green.

HUNDON [13]. Beautiful broad rolling fields. Brockley Green cottages well restored beside the Plough. Main settlement on slopes of tributary of Stour. "The Thatchers", a timber-framed house going back to mid-15c, has a fresco of the Paschal Lamb painted on the chimney breast at a time when

the hall occupied both storeys. Old School House was new c. 1700. Pinhoe Hall incorporates Tudor gatehouse. Church burnt out 1914 retains impressive frame, with south nave parapet traceried as at Blythburgh: rebuilt by Detmar Blow. Georgian headstones by Soane family of carvers.

HUNSTON [9]. All the detached cottages of the village go back at least to 17c. One, dated 1619, has original porches front and rear. Hunston Cottage has great chimneys. Church unusual in these parts in having transept and being mainly 13c, though much character lost in crude Victorian clean-up.

HUNTINGFIELD [11]. High House, a trimly symmetrical red-and-blue brick farmhouse, moated all round, with Dutch gables at each end, and smaller twin gables in front bearing date 1700. Huntingfield Hall is a striking square early 19c Gothick building in brick, designed to represent gateway to castle or nunnery, a valid East Anglian theme for a house, but front door betrays Turkish influence. Between 1859 and 1882 just over £2,000 spent on the church, the rector's wife magnificently bedizening with her paints both chancel and nave roofs. Interesting monuments and inscriptions.

ICKLINGHAM [8] has two parish churches. St James's is remarkable for splendid Victorian external display of grey and black flintwork, but interior increases one's disrespect for the insensitive Victorian restorers. All Saints is one of the great examples left in England of a beautiful unrestored church.

Lofty chancel and south aisle early 14c, with superb window tracery, especially in the aisle. Top of tall square tower is of chalky flints. Roof rush-thatched. Approach over a disused grass path from village street and find an interior radiantly light and clear of superfluous furniture: late-Victorian harmonium almost the only recent addition. Restorers confined themselves to east window where the glass they inserted is unnaturally pink. On chancel floor lie 14c tiles, the arrangement somewhat Victorian. Nave contains ancient solid reed tussock-stools, rustic medieval chest and a magnificent early 14c chest, bound with wrought ironwork. Church mainly used by swallows and martins but parish has managed first-aid repairs. The Breckland wind tries the south door. One cannot doubt that the place-name perpetuates the Iceni: the Icknield Way traverses the parish. Roman finds include lead fonts bearing the Christian monogram, and remains of probable baptistry.

ICKWORTH [8]. Park, 1,800 acres, eleven miles round, with astonishing great house two-thirds of which acquired by National Trust 1956 from Hervey family, Earls and Marquesses of Bristol, living here since late 15c. Open Weds, Thurs, Sats, Suns, April to October, 2–6 p.m. Park open daily. Present house begun c. 1794 by Fredk Earl of Bristol and Bishop of Derry, a son of the author of the justly celebrated *Memoirs of the Reign of King George II*. It is a portentous building of brick, stuccoed on a front of over 200 yards, with domed almost circular rotunda at the centre, a long curved arm either side, each ending in an oblong block that would alone seem a large country house. Geometrical plan cited as illustration of the earl-bishop's "Enlightenment". It was modelled by Francis Sandys from plans of the Roman architect Asprucci. Of the two friezes round the rotunda, based on designs by Flaxman and Caroline Wharncliffe, part of the upper was executed by Coade, the rest by the brothers Casimiro and Donato Carabelli of Milan. Rotunda originally meant for habitation, wings for assembly hall and temple of art, but when Napoleon entered Italy, Lord Bristol's collection was confiscated: he died 1803 without seeing his building. It long stood unfinished, wings three or four ft above ground and cupola a mere shell: resumed *c*. 1822 according to a modified plan, the east wing to be the family's self-contained house, the corridor arms and rotunda decorated and furnished in late-Regency manner as staterooms. Bills with the great furniture-making firm of Banting amounted to over £5,000 by 1830. There are notable pictures and silver, beautifully shown. The mass of the house is now seen at its best, Victorian formal gardens and arbours having reached maturity. To south-west lies site of earlier house (and village). Church much rebuilt has interesting foreign glass and Horace Walpole's charming epitaph on Molly Lepel. Present walled garden and fine red-brick greenhouse date from *c*. 1718, when Vanbrugh visited the Herveys.

IKEN [18]. Beautifully remote and silent beside the head of the Alde estuary, as it must have been when St Botolph established his model abbey in the 7c. Yarn Hill, an impressive eminence now in full cultivation. So, under new reclamation schemes, is much surrounding heath. Church, dedicated to Botolph, and perhaps on the scene of his exemplary monastery. (Excavations in 1974 under Hadstock church, Essex, showed it had rival claims to be thought Botolph's famous site.) Here in 1968, fire destroyed nave. Victorian chancel of Kentish ragstone. Good 15c dark flint west tower. Chancel, at least, should be restored and maintained on this proud, calm, timeless spur above the tidal waters.

ILKETSHALL [5] like adjacent South Elmham, is a collection of parishes that does much to provoke and little to satisfy an enquiry into its origins. There are four Ilketshall parishes: with Mettingham and two Bungay churches they were known as "the Seven Parishes". *St Andrew*. Green commons. Tudor-brick manor house. Church bench has accomplished renaissance carving. Two gartered shields of Howard arms. *St John*. Church at point where Roman Stone Street has become disused. Elaborate traceried remains of canopy of honour. "The Mount" perhaps bore original Ulfketil's hall. *St Lawrence* church stands well upon ancient raised platform. *St Margaret* has Norman round tower.

INGHAM [8]. Church rebuilt 1861. The plain-glass windows

seem to be in 15c mullions. Two monuments record longevity and long service of a vicar and a master of Bury School. Massive 17c barn, eleven bays.

IPSWICH [22]. A thriving port and market-town, a dozen miles from the sea at the head of a beautiful estuary, the top corner of which presumably suggested the old name Gipeswic (*wic*, a town: *gip*, corner of the mouth). Before April 1974 it was the county town of Suffolk in a limited sense, for Bury was then the ancient county town of West Suffolk, and Ipswich was a borough with separate "county" status. But since the 1974 reorganisation of local government, Ipswich has been the administrative centre for the whole county, despite its peripheral situation. It is one of the oldest and most interesting towns in England, with a complex character of its own. Its role as a capital of one of the "new" counties may help it to find a new distinction.

In the 1960s Ipswich took its own character too much for granted, and let many historic buildings, whole sections of its streets, make way for multi-storey "comprehensive redevelopment" schemes, and "high-rise" office blocks. Its very identity is now in peril. The New Towns Act 1965 envisaged revolutionary expansion, from 120,000 people to a quarter of a million: for Ipswich "New Town" Messrs Shankland, Cox produced an imaginative scheme, the Exchequer would finance the indispensable major road-structure. In June 1969, Exchequer found wanting, the whole grand design (like Wolsey's for a great Euro-

pean College here in 1529) collapsed. Ipswich County Borough Council was left with an old development plan unrevised for a decade. After four more years a subdued, uninspiring plan emerged for "the sub-region" (Stowmarket–Felixstowe) but *nothing* for urban Ipswich. The dangers of haphazard growth, with inadequately financed traffic structure, still menace the town.

Yet the distinctive urban shape of the large Anglo-Saxon borough survives. Revealed in delightful detail on the old maps (Speed 1610, Ogilby 1672, Pennington 1778), the pattern of town streets is Ipswich's most remarkable historic possession, for it is purely Anglo-Saxon. Bury inherits a grid of streets from the Normans. Ipswich's layout was virtually complete by about 991–1010, when the defensive ditches were dug. And the main elements go back to the 7c.

The Victorian Town Hall occupies the site of St Mildred's church, probably founded *c.* 700 alongside a hall of the East Anglian kings. In front of the Town Hall, Corn Hill represents the Anglo-Saxon market-place that in the Middle Ages occupied the whole tight-built oblong between Tavern Street and the Buttermarket, flanked by the brook that ran down Brook Street from springs in the woods where Christchurch came to succeed Trinity Priory, itself on the site of a Domesday church. Line of Tavern Street marks boundary between easily inhabited sands-and-gravels (on which town-centre grew) and more heavily wooded clay slopes of Christchurch Park.

Brook Street and Tavern Street thus form an aboriginal cross-roads where Great White Horse stands. Tavern Street's continuation east (Carr Street, made ridiculous by crude grey high-rise "comprehensive development" grossly out of proportion with rest of street) ran past industrial pottery, in production from 7 to 12c. Another early Anglo-Saxon way presumably ran down Queen Street from market-place to St Peter's church and across to Stoke, at the "corner of the mouth" that gave Ipswich its name. Here freshwater Gipping joins salt estuary and a bridge was recorded in 970.

Despite devastation detailed in Domesday Book, this uncommonly big Anglo-Saxon town survived with at least ten churches, with many of its early customs (chartered in 1200), and boundaries (four miles by five, as they still are). New parishes grew: St Clements *c.* 1200, St Helens, St Mary Quay. The Normans had only a temporary castle here: one at Walton-Felixstowe was more use to them. Nor did Ipswich have cathedral or abbey to create physical focus. Two 12c priories of Austin canons were the main religious houses: that of Trinity left most mark, being replaced by Christchurch mansion and park after Dissolution: that of SS Peter and Paul, down by Quay, was doubly dissolved, first *for* Wolsey's college, then *as* Wolsey's college. Nothing left but reeling red-brick college gateway and great church of St Peter, with big flint tower and Tournai marble font and the thought that the formidable Edward I stayed here in 1296 to marry his daughter in this

Ipswich ▷
p110 above The docks: old maltings at Stoke
below The Custom House

p111 Warehouses and tower of St Clement, seafarers' patron, first to greet them at the old quay

church to the Count of Holland, in jewellery and clothes whose very buttons are described. St Peter's now overshadowed by quayside granaries and about to be islanded by motor-traffic..

Three flourishing friaries had also lost all their local popularity by Wolsey's time: Greyfriars have given name to Ipswich byword for fiasco since multi-storey flats, offices, shops and car-park built on site, 1965, most remaining empty in 1974. Erected when town's whole centre of gravity tipped west from Corn Hill to new roadside "Civic Centre", sharing delights of dual carriageway ("Civic Drive") with grandiose new cliff-face insurance blocks. In 1974, new office complex for Willis, Faber & Dumas promises to be enormously better conceived, and actually takes into account its neighbour, Friars Street Unitarian Meeting-house, timber-framed for Presbyterians 1699–1700 by house-carpenter Joseph Clarke and one of the half-dozen best surviving buildings in Ipswich.

In 1524, Ipswich ranked as sixth or seventh richest English town. Clevely's big panorama (in Christchurch mansion) painted in Gainsborough's day, shows an essentially medieval and Tudor complex of timber buildings. Best survivors in Fore Street, especially No. 80, the merchant's house and ware-

◁ **Ipswich**; St Lawrence's tower and the Ancient House. The pargeted figures are a shepherd and a traveller, and Atlas brought to his knees by the globe

109

St Matthew's, **Ipswich**, 1884 flintwork and battlements

St Margaret's, freestone clerestory signals spectacular double hammerbeam roof within

houses backing on to the quay, the merchant, Miss Lord, still in residence. Other good groups: 18–20 St Nicholas Street, and St Mary Elms churchyard. Walk that best reveals town's character starts at quay-side, where Custom House (1843–5, by J. M. Clark, who may have had Georgian model of Lancaster in mind) followed construction of new Wet Dock, 1839–42, and led to arrival of railway—the two events that most trans-

formed Ipswich. From Custom House, past grimy secularised fine 15c church of St Mary Quay, turn up Foundation Street (where Gainsborough lived in 1740s), turn again, at site of recent desecration of old Half Moon Inn, into Lower Brook Street, past E. Anglian D. Times offices (Johns, Slater and Haward) and some of the most characteristic surviving houses new in Gainsborough's day, their former setting of

orchards and bowling-greens revealed in Pennington's map. On into Upper Brook Street, past new Sainsburys and C&A (redbrick and right scale) past end of Butter Market (which contains Ancient House Bookshop, the most sensational Ipswich building, 15c timber-framed with boldly projecting upper floor, full of heavily moulded 17c ceilings, and outside decorated with carved timbers and pargeting—swags,

St Margaret's. Charles II's arms gloriously framed. Late-Stuart baroque painting in late-medieval roof beautifully echoes adjacent Christchurch Mansion's Italianate symmetry and Flemish baroque gables

arms of Charles II, and sculpted scenes showing the Four Continents—rich unparalleled extravaganza, *c.* 1670), and past the Great White Horse, celebrated in Pickwick Papers (saved by the Corporation when Trust Houses tried to sell for yet more offices), and up Northgate Street, past Sketch-leys (embedded in Assembly Rooms of 1821), and house with Tudor corner-post, and Pyken-ham's Gateway, *c.* 1471, its brick step-gable lately rebuilt.

Here we reach site of North Gate and line of Anglo-Saxon defences and cross into Soane Street, to front gate of Christchurch Park. No town in England has so venerable and splendid a park and mansion open and available so near its heart. In Napoleonic Wars it was "crowded as Kensington Gardens" on fine summer evenings: it was so in Defoe's day, as it is today. The main "E" built 1548–50. Elizabeth stayed six days, 1561, displeased with tactless clergy and admonitory performance of Bilious Bale's *King John*. Dutch gables and porch added 1675, when hall took present character. Full of old furniture and local relics and pictures, including works of Gainsborough and Constable.

Churches and chapels. Twelve medieval churches still stand, almost all worth a visit; so are a few of the later ones. First the old ones, alphabetically. *St Clement*. Its tower welcomes shipping at quayside, its churchyard is now picturesque centre of one-way traffic system. Thos Eldred, who sailed round world with Cavendish, lies buried here. So does Sir Thos Slade, who designed Nelson's *Victory*. *St Helen*. Rebuilt 1835 and given transepts. Rev. Richard Can-ning (1708–75), reviser of Kirby's *Suffolk Traveller*, whose portrait by Gainsborough is in Christchurch mansion, commemorated here: also Richard Canning, naval commander in wars of William III and Anne, who "through the resentment of party and through misreported facts died a private Captain, 1734, aged 67". *St Lawrence*. Chancel rebuilt by a draper, John Baldwin, 1449 (*see* outside east window) and tower begun by John Bottold, 1431, largely rebuilt 1882 by Fredk Barnes (Ipswich architect of railway stations on Bury line) with elaborate fancy flushwork. Gains-

Ipswich: Unitarian meeting-house, timber-framed by house-carpenter Joseph Clarke, 1699–1700

Ipswich. Headquarters of Willis, Faber & Dumas, 1975. Foster Associates' brilliant solution to office needs of worldwide marine insurance in congested heart of town. Dark glazed walls reflect sky and tower of St Nicholas

borough's daughters christened here. (Usually kept locked.) *St Margaret*. The finest-looking Ipswich church, flanking north side of St Margaret's Plain, nearest equivalent to Norwich's St Peter Mancroft. Splendid late 15c roof, painted in reign of William III. Prince of Wales' feathers, 1660, perplexing. Arms of Charles II handsome. *St Mary Elms*. Ripe red early Tudor tower. Ironwork on south door possibly Norman. Hamby monuments beautiful. North aisle window by Comper, 1907. *St Mary Quay*. 13c foundation, rebuilt mid-15, with elaborate timbered roofs on best Suffolk pattern. Damaged in World War II, rescued by Friends of Friendless Churches but secularised. Famous Pownder memorial brass in Christchurch mansion. *St Mary Stoke*. Ancient church much rebuilt by Butterfield, 1870. *St Mary Tower*. Chief civic church, rebuilt in disastrously un-East Anglian Gothic 1860–8 by a banker (and diocesan architect, Phipson). Its sunny Dutch atmosphere extinguished by Victorian gloom. Brass to notary, 1475, shows his writing materials. Monument to Wm Smart, benefactor of town's library, shows town panorama painted in 1599. Fine pulpit, up to standard of Unitarian chapel. *St Matthew*. Pleasant exterior beside "Civic Drive". Much Victorian enlargement. Carvings of Christ's early life on font. Kneeling figures of donors on remains of screen. *St Nicholas*. Churchyard rather municipalised to conform with Grey Friars scheme. Well moulded 14c arcade. Painting, 1807, by Ipswich drawing-master John Smart. Brasses and ledger-slabs. Studied and re-set in chancel in 1966, extra-ordinary carved stones, now thought as late as *c.* 1120, despite undoubted early 11c Scandinavian influences: St Michael fighting dragon (Caen stone), tympanum with boar and dedication to All Saints (Barnack stone), and figure panels of Apostles (Barnack). *St Peter*.

115

Sturdy tower (93 ft: *c*. 1463–76). 12c font of Tournai marble with prowling beasts. Evangelical revival in Ipswich began here, 1801. Victorian enlargement and gloom. *St Stephen*. Churchyard now public garden. Tower of nice patchy flint-and-brick. Monument with figures of Robt Leman and wife, died same day, 1637. Prince of Wales' feathers, 1661, cf. St Margaret's.

Nonconformist chapels, that of the *Unitarians* is outstanding. Built for the Presbyterians a decade after 1689 Toleration Act, it has most in common with best churches of New England, such as Hingham, Massachusetts, set up by East Anglians of 1630s who dared to believe a church no more sacred than any other building, and who liked long sermons. This building focuses on pulpit, set up on tulip base and ascended by beautiful stair. Arched windows, lunettes, box-pews, gallery and great brass chandelier. Studwork walls by house-carpenter: it was a meeting-*house*.

Clevely shows fields and windmills coming almost to town-centre, which experienced some good Victorian remodelling—notably up Museum Street and about Christchurch Park and parts of Stoke. Town Hall, 1867, and Post Office dignified. But suburbs sprawled out over all surrounding hills, providing good views down over old town, but little else to interest visitors. Before 1940, main spread east up Woodbridge and Felixstowe roads, and here High Anglican interior of *St Bartholomew* (1896–1900 by Chas Spooner) well worth seeing: east end with pale *art-nouveau* glass in "rose win-dow" beautifully composed. To north, between Norwich and Bramford roads, *All Saints* presents glowing red west face to setting sun, with moulded-brick window-tracery: by S. Wright, 1892. Further out, *St Thomas's*, Bramford Lane, 1937, by Cachemaille Day, has pleasant exterior, grey brick, flint panelling and well-proportioned tower.

Since the war, apart from the office complexes mentioned, the only notable buildings are Cliff Quay Power Station (Farmer & Dark), Telephone Exchange, robust Civic College (Johns, Slater & Haward, 1961) looking much better set now that trees are taller, and schools by same firm: St Johns (near Woodbridge Road), St Matthews (Civic Drive) and Gusford Primary, near Belstead Brook, where post-war estate has sprawled lamentably.

Hamlets, etc, in the Borough
Westerfield Hall, dated 1683 on downpipe, Dutch gabled, warm brickwork, formal front garden. Mill Farm, too, Dutch gabled. Small church's beautiful oak hammerbean roof houses thirty-six well-carved angels. Monuments record accidental deaths of Deborah Whitefoord and her son, who had been wounded at Waterloo.

Whitton-cum-Thurleston Church, at rural brink of suburban ocean, totally rebuilt 1850 by Fredk Barnes. Dutch gabled Caroline barns at Sparrowe's Nest.

Ixworth [9]. Medieval village on Peddar's Way, whose modern heavy traffic is destroying the town's life. Commister Lane, cross-link to Thetford road, its potential attractions lately bungled: and uneasy *flats above garages* at Thorpe end! Otherwise delightful houses of all periods in village. Most remarkable, "The Abbey", whose Georgian sash-windowed walls contain very considerable remains of Priory of Austin canons founded 1170. Present owners, Dr and Mrs Rowe, are steadily revealing and restoring remains, including massive piers of cruciform Romanesque church, and stone-vaulted rooms (clunch) embedded in their well panelled post-Reformation house. Renaissance tomb of Sir Richd Codington in parish church relates that he swapped Nonsuch for this priory with Henry VIII. Church tower, building 1470s, bears name of Robt Schot of Ixworth, 28th Abbot of Bury. Well-kept ledger slabs and memorials. Step-gabled Pickerel Inn a landmark in Kirby's *Suffolk Traveller*.

IXWORTH THORPE [9]. Rustic church might have sat for Cotman's watercolour of Clippesby in Broadland. Restoration 1972, a model how it can be done. Thatched roof, wooden bellcote on top of small red-brick tower, south porch of weathered Tudor brick, decorated with flint, diaper-work, and step gables. Carved bench-ends: delightful interior.

KEDINGTON [13] (sometimes pronounced Kitton). As suburb of Haverhill, village grossly over-inflated in 1960–2. Church among the first a visitor to

Kedington. Grissel Barnardiston kneels beyond her father's tomb

THOMAS BARNARDISTO
VI THOMAS OBIIT A°

Suffolk should see. Here, almost more than anywhere in England, crossing the threshold is like stepping back at least two centuries, though the great collection of funeral monuments ends just inside the door with C. R. Rowlinson, killed in a bomber raid on Essen. From the road one sees the flicker of old flushwork patterns in the tower's east face, and the glow of red brick, possibly Roman. Under pews, floorboards lift to reveal Roman building. A crucifixion of *c*. 900 now inside east window. Interior beautifully light as one crosses the cobbles of the porch, steps on to the uneven brick floor, taking one's first impression of woodwork and monuments. Aisled nave, low-pitched Tudor roof with 19c skylights Georgian singing-gallery and children's step-pews at west end, and box-pews in aisles, and painted fluting to make the nave piers look classical, and the communicants' stalls in chancel. The most prominent woodwork early 17c: mellow canopied Barnardiston pew with separate compartments for men and women was formed then out of old rood-screen: new (folding) screen bears date 1619 which would roughly serve for the focal three-decker pulpit with panelled back and canopy, wig-pole and hourglass, and for the two holy tables, which were railed on three sides in 1707 by Sir Saml Barnardiston. His was the leading family of Suffolk Puritans in the previous century, and here they all lie.

above: **Kedington** church: looking east: 3-decker pulpit and Barnardiston pew
below: looking west

Beside the screen, to the south, table-tomb of Sir Thos (the great Puritan Sir Nathaniel's grandfather). This monument was put up before his death in 1619. His daughter Grissel is shown nearby in stomacher, farthingale and frame-supported coiffure. Her eldest brother lies in adjacent remarkable tomb, with coffin-cover protruding and two wives kneeling above under twin arches. His son and heir, the Puritan Sir Nathaniel, leans out of opposite aisle, one hand on his wife's, their disengaged hands propping their heads uneasily. This line died out 1745: present one descends from Sir Nathaniel's youngest brother Thos, whose eldest son Thos is described in the chancel as having "travelled to Jerusalem and the most remarkable places of Syria and Palestine and the seven churches in the Lesser Asia". Their house behind the church was pulled down *c*. 1780.

KELSALE-CUM-CARLTON [11]. Kelsale guildhall, *c.* 1495, half-timbered and worth seeing, adapted as parochial school by Rev. G. I. Davies, who built Church House 1891 at own expense as club for his parishioners: now useful E. Suffolk teachers' centre. Large church crowning hill has early Tudor nave sloping up to chancel: earlier church now serves as broad south aisle. Old Norman door rebuilt in north wall. 1620-ish pulpit, with bracketed book-board (Aldeburgh's pulpit was made here). Splendid marble table-tomb with trophies to Thos Russell (1669–1730). Standing effigy of Saml Clouting (1765–1852) by Thurlow of Saxmundham. Flourishing vineyard adjoins churchyard below Manor House. Pleasant 1851 Methodist church below that. Serpentine walls at Kelsale Hall (Regency) and also at By-the-Crossways. Diapered Tudor brick barn with terracotta lions of ? Mow-

brays at Kelsale Lodge. *Carlton* Church, in grounds of Carlton Hall, has beautiful Tudor red-brick tower. Pulpit 1626: altar table 1630.

KENTFORD [7]. Icknield Way crosses Kennet amid Newmarket paddocks. 14c church tower patched with white brick. Nice flint walls, carved headstones, box pews, faint wall paintings.

KENTON [10]. Front of middle-Tudor red-brick Hall built by Garneys family has four pairs of pedimented windows on ground floor, matched by four pairs of square-headed ones above. Church contains their brick chapel, as well as 13c chancel, given an admirable new arch and east window by Victorian restorer.

KERSEY [21] has one of the most famous Suffolk village streets, running down both sides of steep valley to water-splash, essential running water for

Kersey church from north, with village below

manufacture of "Kerseys" in later Middle Ages. Cottages mainly half-timbered and over-sailing, with one notable middle-Tudor red-brick house beside the ford. Stallion's tail, professional sign of vet., hangs from eaves of one house. Sampson's Hall on Boxford road preserves name of owner in 1381, Sampson of Harkstead, a leader of that year's revolt in the Ipswich area. Ruins of Lady chapel of Austin priory in grounds of Priory Farmhouse, which embodies remains of 14c aisled hall, perhaps the Priors Lodging. (Not shown.) Parish church occupies spectacular site above village. Distinguished west tower, "new" in 1430, battlemented 1445. Interior has suffered abominably from Reformers and restorers, but some of the carpentry has been well restored, notably the traceried ceiling of south porch, found rotting behind plaster, 1927. Broad aisle built out toward village in 14c: interruption of carving on splendid arcade attributed to Black Death. Rich stone carving above, almost hopelessly mutilated, probably represented works of mercy! Two plastered bays of the roof bear Sampson arms. Monuments to Thorrowgoods.

KESGRAVE [22]. Down to 1924, a church, a house or two, and some tumuli on the heath: since then an appalling ribbon of bungalows has appeared. Church, shaded by cedars, has beautiful Tudor brick tower, repaired 1702. Early 13c chancel with lancets. Font by J. Smythe, Woodbridge, 1843. Gipsy grave just inside churchyard. At west edge of Kesgrave

Wood, reedy mere beside rubbish tip and gravel quarry: fading figure of St Francis painted realistically on pump-house by Irvin Smith, an American serviceman, 1944.

KESSINGLAND [6]. At south end of coast-road, messy looking village. Small zoo attractive. Grove House has ribbon wall. Rider Haggard lived some time at Grange. Church has most noble seamark of a tower, 96 ft. without brick parapet, convincingly dated c. 1439–49 and attributed to Richard Russell of Dunwich, a stouter version of Walberswick. Handsome west doorway, niches and window—the pattern of many Suffolk towers c. 1450, but grander. Beautiful font by same hand as west doorway. Nave thatched. Ugly broad chancel 1908 has glass by Kempe. Kessingland lifeboat saved 144 lives 1869–1936.

KETTLEBASTON [15]. Remote, enclosed, sloping lands. Rustic church ("High"), beautifully kept. Men in 1384 remembered 1363 as year when church "built anew". This must refer to chancel, tower and nave roof, for nave walls are Norman, with scroll-painting in window-splay, and square font perhaps by same late 12c mason who made south doorway. White sloping walls, brick floors, crown-post roof, screened sanctuary: a model for all parishes, how to make the most of an ordinary ancient church.

KETTLEBURGH [17]. Hall has Elizabethan bay added to earlier gable-end: unique in Suffolk houses, effect perfectly Victorian! Church and Church Cottages make pleasant group.

Set of Commandments contemporary with Queen Anne's arms.

KIRKLEY, See LOWESTOFT.

KIRTON [23]. Guston, Strewston and Croxton were the more important places here till 16c. Kirton was merely "the settlement beside the church", a building of no architectural interest, though tower, c. 1520, has good texture of brick and septaria. The other settlements have vanished, though Croxton lives on as name of several local families.

KNETTISHALL [3]. Church and churchyard abandoned to coney and cuckoo. Church furniture in neighbouring Riddlesworth, Norfolk. Delightful heathy Country Park for picnics and walks.

KNODISHALL-CUM-BUXLOE [18]. Buxloe is practically deserted: ruined base of round church tower stands beside two cottages, where paths still converge. Red House Farm (formerly "Ghosts' Hole") beautiful brick house dated 1678, E-plan, with three Dutch gables, and niches in porch-front. Knodishall church tower erected in time of Edward Jenney, son of a judge and grandson of John, whose amusing brass, 1460, remains in the much-restored church. Georgian red-brick rectory with additions. Hunts Barn Tudor. Pylons.

LACKFORD [8], where Icknield Way crosses Lark, and 600 urns at Mill Heath showed that the villagers were cremated until 7c conversion. Church has 13c stone coffin-lids and a beautiful stone female head in top of east gable. Limestone porch with very good moulding. Splendid 14c font. Squints in chancel explained by fact that there was once a central tower, presumably Norman, as may be seen from nave walls. Squint in north aisle a Victorian re-build.

LAKENHEATH [1]. Originally a "hythe" or landing-place in the fen over which it looks to the west. 11,000 acres, 3,000 of them warren, now occupied by one of the largest U.S. air bases in Britain, a different sort of landing-place. A 7c church here was granted to St Ethelreda for her foundation at Ely. The present church is among the ten most beautiful in Suffolk. The headstones and the base of the tower are of limestone: the fabric also contains chalk, a "pan" that looks like ironstone, early Tudor red-brick, and flint (in the building west of the tower, a parvis with old schoolroom above, made of materials from Eriswell's ruined church). Brick floor with some medieval tiles. Norman chancel arch. Best 13c font in Suffolk. 14c wall paintings and window tracery, and an Elizabethan painted text. Bench-ends *c.* 1483, with carved contortionists, etc, a roof probably by the same brilliant carpenter as Mildenhall's. 15c pulpit. Monuments and splendid Charles II royal arms in west room.

LANGHAM [9]. Church, with late-Victorian nave and remains of beautifully traceried screen, stands in park. Hall has pleasant Georgian brick front. Hillwatering Farmhouse, timber-framed and plastered, stands romantically beautiful in open sloping fields below Walsham–Ixworth road.

LAVENHAM [15]. One of the most famous and beautiful of the small local townships that grew to perfection when the clothing industry flourished— between the middle of the 14th and middle of the 16th centuries. Its irregular streets of half-timbered houses and cottages conform with the undulations of the countryside in which they stand, looking as if they grew there: indeed the great oak timbers and the clay and wattle fillings are truly sprung from this ground. Almost as much a part of the surrounding district as of the town stands the massive, magnificent, square-buttressed campanile of flint, 141 ft high, that for all its dignity is not quite finished at the top— a perfect symbol of the whole area's greatest moment of prosperity. Since the 16c, Lavenham has kept going by dint of agriculture and yarn-spinning for the weavers of Norwich. Horsehair weaving introduced 1851. The 1930s were particularly hard, but a Sudbury firm of silk-weavers re-started that industry here, and other small industries including a scent-works. Farming again prospers. So does the tourist industry— another form of yarn-spinning.

That great steeple was endowed jointly by the 13th Earl of Oxford, the very grand lord of the manor, and the less noble but consolingly rich Thos Spring III, one of the leading English clothiers. The site of the Earl's house is marked by a large wooded moat near the top of Park Road. The Hall, with its pond below the church, was his bailiff's house. Spring's headquarters were more in the middle of things, possibly where The Grove (white-brick front *c.* 1750) now stands, half-way up Lady Street, at which point there is certainly a wonderful view: the "Tudor shops", the Wool Hall, Nos. 67–9 Water Street, and in the background the church. The town lies east of Hall, divided from it by High Street along line of old park pales. East of High Street the Market Place stands on eminence, with elaborately carved Corpus Christi Guildhall (*c.* 1520), and Water Street (at right angles to High Street) follows the important line of a swift-running stream (now subterranean) down to the tributary of the Brett that forms east edge of built-up area. Bolton Street (Jn. Bolton's will is dated 1440) and Prentice Street slope steeply down to this tributary from Market Place. The three other streets slope down into Water Street. Shilling Street (Jn. Schylling's will 1476: Isaac Taylor subsequently lived in Shilling Old Grange, where his daughters conceived "Twinkle, twinkle, little star"); Barn Street, named after a manorial barn, removed *c.* 1860; and Lady Street, named after Gild of Our Lady, whose Hall, now known as the Wool Hall, stands at the bottom, restored and now combined with the Swan (Trust House). Impossible here to give detailed account of the wealth of remarkable buildings that line these streets. The great merit of the quaint little guide by F. Lingard Ranson, *Lavenham, Suffolk*, is that it does so. Since he wrote, Nos. 23–6 Water Street have been re-conditioned. Little Hall in Market

Lavenham: former triple Tudor shop window and Wool Hall (*above*) and Late-Georgian re-modelling of timber-framed house in market-place ▷

Leiston Abbey

Place, Suffolk Preservation Society headquarters. In 1961, Donald Insall published a good carefully detailed report for W. Suffolk C.C. Much of it was ignored, and by 1965 the old plaster coat had been stripped from Blaize House (12 Church Street) and a nearby group of cottages was demolished right on the unforgettable bend in that street.

Great tower rather dwarfs rest of church. If 14c chancel had been rebuilt on scale of nave, all would have been well: but Thos Spring II had built vestry east of sanctuary, and it was impossible to extend church east without undoing his work. As one approaches south porch, the Spring or Lady Chapel south of chancel has enough beauty to distract attention from tower. Once through south porch, with fan vault and De Vere emblems, we are inevitably disappointed by lack of length if we have seen Long Melford, and the stained glass is almost all hideous. Interior's most beautiful features are remains of original screenwork all round Branch and Spring chapels, north and south of chancel; and above all, the woodcarving of the two chantry chapels, north and south of nave. The Spring chantry, as distinct from their chapel, is on north side: other chantry usually attributed to De Veres, but is carved prominently with arms of Thos. Spourne. Marble monument of Rev. Hy. Copinger, 1622, in chancel. Admirably designed housing immediately east of church, and good terraced effect from slope of Spring Street.

LAWSHALL [14]. Church has fine exterior, flintwork made attractive by red-brick canopies over windows, and by horizontal courses of bricks along parapets. Mysterious linear earthworks relate to Peddars Way.

LAXFIELD [11]. A number of old scattered farmhouses, broad

village street at centre, with church and half-timbered oversailing guildhall, *c.* 1519, now a lively museum. Curious church has very handsome tower containing unusual abundance of freestone: wills 1444–1463 refer to the building of "the new tower" and contributions continued till 1475. New bell bought 1482. Battlements, comparable with good Somerset work, bear names of Jn. Wingfield and wife, 1460, who got the place its weekly market. As late as 1855 neighbouring farmers were meeting buyers every week at Royal Oak to sell corn by sample. East end of church rebuilt, white brick, 1841. South porch and whole interior physically very broad: nave roof spans 36 ft. Most notable seven-sacrament font, new in 1503. 15c carved benches are mixed up with box-pews containing 16c panels disgustingly speckled. Pews for young men and boys built up at west end. Good Caroline pulpit. Detestable smasher Wm Dowsing born here: Dowsing's Farm is green-moated, cream-plastered, idyllic. Handsome white-brick, blue-pantiled Baptist chapel, 1808.

LAYHAM [21]. Overbury Hall, its memorable portrait by Constable in the V. and A., was thoroughly restored 1871. Church has brick west tower (1742), 13c Purbeck font, painted panel in memory Ann Roane, 1626. Shelley House Farm, brick-nogged. Idyllic watermill approached by Hadleigh sprawl.

LEISTON-CUM-SIZEWELL [18] (pronounced Lace-t'n) stands on good light farmland near a beautiful stretch of coast, with the most extensive monastic remains in Suffolk a mile or so north, and large 19c ironworks, lately gone from its walled site in middle of town. There is an empty anchorite's cell by the shore. Summerhill, the late A. S. Neill's remarkable experiment in self-education, flourishes alongside more orthodox schools. New red-brick school for engineering apprentices, a sort of Sandhurst Georgian, surely uninspiring for young engineers of the '70s? Fine ruins of Premonstratensian abbey are those of a rebuilding in 1388–9, together with those of an octagonal Tudor brick gate-turret, all modified for use lately as diocesan retreat. Penultimate abbot consecrated anchorite 1531 in cell in marshes of Minsmere level, possibly the island site of first abbey, its east end certainly fortified in World War II. Marshes first efficiently drained 1846–50 by Messrs Garrett and Son of Leiston Iron Works. Richard Garrett III, who produced a famous portable steam engine and threshing machine, is represented by bust (Thurlow of Saxmundham, 1866) in church and three of his stove-pipe hats under glass in U.D.C. Council Chamber. Dutch-gabled Hall, beside church, indefensibly neglected. Church, with beautiful 13c font, mostly rebuilt by E. B. Lambe 1854. East window by Kempe 1897: Lambe's roof woodwork defies description. Good external wall-texture, grey flint and rag-stone, with corbel table. Rope family memorials.

Sizewell, a seaside hamlet, chosen in 1958 as site of great new atomic power-station, to which Snape bridge was sacrificed, massive, but less obtrusive from land than sea.

LETHERINGHAM [17]. Beautiful situation on the willowy upper Deben, truncated little church in farmyard, a growth of woodland marking former park, and the sites of three ancient houses: Old Hall, Lodge and "Abbey". A fragment of a brick gatehouse remains beside the church. Old church ruinous *c.* 1770. Sumptuous monuments were deliberately destroyed. Present building with pathetic fragments dates from 1789, on old tower. Watermill, unluckily pink-washed, open to public, near Easton Model Farm.

LEVINGTON [22]. Two pretty brick alms-cottages provided by Sir Robt Hitcham (born here), Hill Cottage thatched Regency Gothick opposite Levington "Ship", where the Orwell estuary provides timeless enchantment in evening sun. Adjacent church admirably restored 1949, tower and window tracery most attractive red brick ?1480s. Terrace of good modern cottages built in 1940s and when Fisons acquired Red House Farm for experimental station (appropriately, for here the 18c discovery was made of value of crag as manure), they erected one of the best-designed groups of modern cottages in Suffolk, 1954–5, and a laboratory by the same Ipswich architects (Johns, Slater and Haward), among the half-dozen best buildings of the decade in Suffolk.

LIDGATE [13]. Church on ridge in bailey of former castle

adapted by Normans. Jn Lidgate the poet-translator born here *c*. 1370: said he preferred as a boy telling cherry-stones to going to church. He would still recognise his church today, though its candle-lit interior has been white-washed. In village, Suffolk House claimed for his birthplace. It has notable Tudor gable, once stepped, and oversailing front, lower half weatherboarded. Street Farm early and late Tudor, by large flag-grown duck-pond.

LINDSEY [21]. Presumably, gave name to Lindsey Wolseys, former cloths. Site of motte-and-bailey castle listed as Ancient Monument. St James's Chapel, a dull barn-like object, is rather over-signposted. Parish church has interesting details: tower fell 1836.

LINSTEAD MAGNA [11]. Remote, much-moated, farm-land. Church fell into ruin early this century.

LINSTEAD PARVA [11]. Admixture of red brick gives chestnut-shaded 13c little church pleasant appearance. Plastered tympanum over rood-beam.

LIVERMERE, GREAT and LITTLE [8]. Red-brick house of Charles II's time demolished 1923. Great mere remains in park, now arable. Handsome gates went to Ampton nearby. Village pleasantly shaded by beeches. Great Livermere

Leiston church. Corn and vines at the altar-rail, part of the rebuilding of 1854 promoted by Lady Rendlesham, of Abbey House

127

church beside decaying 16c cottage has attractive un-restored exterior. Headstone beside porch to "forkner" to Charles I and II and James II. Tympanum in chancel arch, Georgian altar-rails, monuments to Georgian and Victorian rectors. Two eminent antiquaries, "Honest" Tom Martin of Palgrave, and M. R. James of Eton and King's, were brought up in the rectory. Beautiful mere, full of heron and lesser (noisier) waterfowl divides this from Little Livermere's decayed unsafe church, largely rebuilt and furnished with Georgian elegance by Baptist Lee who won £30,000 in state lottery and bought Livermere in 1722.

LOUND [inset]. Base of round tower and rest of church basically 13c: top two-thirds of tower with lovely mixture of dark brick and flints, probably 1470s, when bells re-hung. Later medieval screen and font eclipsed by sumptuous furnishing of 1914—virtuoso work by J. N. Comper: rood loft, Lady Chapel reredos (with hint of Ranworth, Norfolk), font cover and superb organ case. Squint in west wall gives view of altar. Large duck-pond opposite Village Maid.

LOWESTOFT [6]. Borough 1885; modern character acquired since 1847, when arrival of railway made it possible to distribute the fish brought into the new harbour. At same time South Town grew up as holiday resort. Modern industries include coach-building

Mariners Score, **Lowestoft**

and ship-building. Lowestoft became a fishing port of national importance in 14c. The Lowestoft lighthouses are the earliest recorded on the English shores. A Lower Light, on north side of harbour, went back to 1609 (several times rebuilt and made movable). Outer harbour (1827–31) very pleasant scene with moored craft, leading out to south pier and north pier extension each with a light and nicely canopied shelter. Whole terrace of shops and offices along Waveney Road, just north of harbour, cheerfully modernised.

Upper Lighthouse, open to the public on weekdays, marks the north limit of the old town. High Street ran along edge of cliff connected by "scores" (presumably because they resemble gashes in the cliff) with the denes and sea below, and the fish-houses for smoking the herring. Conservation Area designated here, belatedly, 1973. A few old curing-houses survive, and old wooden frames for net-drying: area deplorably dominated by frozen-food factory. High Street, note the Elizabethan house next to Wildes Score, converted to flats 1952, and No. 55, with handsome middle Georgian front. From 2,000 air-raid alerts 1939–45, 178 enemy raids destroyed 266 lives, 500 houses and 78 business premises. In 1964, Planners recognised postwar town centre rebuilding "uninspired", replaced humanscale terraced streets by "St Peter's," isolated and soulless tower of "high-rise" flats!

South Town is connected with north by a swing-bridge. The chief bathing and holiday resort, it contains some monumental terraces, serving as apartment-houses and other seaside lodgings. In piecemeal ownership these great terraces—Marine Parade, Wellington Esplanade and the "Clyffe" (Kirkley) will inevitably deteriorate. Their character is just right for seaside, and public authority should take a lead in conserving. Disintegration of Royal Hotel (1848) is an outrage. The Prince Albert, Tayler and Green, 1960, is among the most effective modern pub designs in Britain. That is in the old town, like Church Green, their superbly well designed neighbourhood for old people.

One gets the best idea of the town's history from St Margaret's church, standing apart from the town: notably from floorslab inscriptions. Roll of naval commanders who fought the wars of the later Stuarts is particularly impressive. The church is a noble building of 1480s (tower and spire, 120 ft, considerably earlier). Elegant pier arcade and roof run right through from east to west, without break, as at Southwold and Blythburgh. Work of restoration in 1580 and 1860s (by local J. L. Clemence, with Teulon's advice) has proved well done. Roof restored and decorated by Bodley, 1899. Eagle lectern, 1504, from famous workshop. Glass in south window of chancel by Robt Allen, 1819, who worked in Lowestoft china factory throughout its existence. Thos Nash (1567–1601) and Benjamin Britten were born here: Joseph Conrad, at twenty, arrived here from Sea of Azov, 1878, served two months on the Lowestoft coaster *The Skimmer of the Seas*. Three-

quarters of a million pounds went on concrete and steel sea defences 1903–49, in a rearguard action. High Water Mark advanced 400 yards at north end of borough, 220 yards opposite Pakefield Church, 1836–1949.

Gunton, beautiful round tower of ancient church almost swamped in suburban tide. "Romanesque" of new C. of E. building eclipsed by new spire of Latter-day Saints. *Kirkley*, a port in 1322, swallowed by Lowestoft, 1907. 15c flint tower of church stands subdued among suburban houses: by 1846 its bell had a "most lugubrious tone". Fabric rebuilt 1750–1 and again 1875–90. Striking reredos and east window and fine iron screen of 1896. *Normanston*, submerged in suburbia, above which St Margaret's and the College of Further Education rise like mirages in a desert. Evergreen Road passes, but look *behind* "The Beeches".

Oulton Broad. Holiday amenities.

Pakefield has nice beach but has lost the rustic look it had. Sea has reached south-east corner of churchyard, and Lowestoft incorporates north part of parish, bulk of the 3,000 inhabitants: old cottages beside the church. Here are not merely two churches in one churchyard (cf. Middleton and Trimley) but both in one building: nave and chancel side by side, divided by common wall that was made into arcade c. 1412–21, later twice bricked up. When two German incendiary bombs landed on thatched roof, 1941, rector and parishioners managed to dislodge only one, and church burnt out. Very pleasantly restored, with decent plain benches, brick floors and several of the old fittings—some of them saved by soaked thatch. Vaulted crypt under south chancel: village stocks north of churchyard.

MARKET WESTON [3]. Pleasant village near source of Little Ouse. No market. Church thoroughly restored by Cottingham, 1846–7.

MARLESFORD [17]. Late Georgian Hall. Church served by Crabbe. Three Norman piers used in early Tudor restoration of south aisle, which has box-pew with nice handle. Monument by Jas Cundy to Lemuel Shuldham, killed at Waterloo.

MARTLESHAM [17]. Creek of Deben, with valley slopes and heathland: tumuli, Roman kiln, vanished settlements, sheepwalks and a large experimental air station from 1917. Massive, towering new Post Office Research Station on airfield 1973, and several small businesses: plans for new village or small town here finally maturing. On A12, Red Lion has well-known sign of crimson ship's figure-head and good Charles II bow window: name goes back to 1620, figure-head traditionally to Sole Bay wreck, 1672. Pleasant church's best feature is the tower, with bequests spread from 1451 to 1472, when perhaps the nice parapet crowned the work.

LONG MELFORD [14] is famous for its beauty, even among medieval manufacturing towns. Beginning at the mill-ford (where a bridge of 1764 is preserved), the houses and shops of the village street flank the Bury–Sudbury road for over half a mile southwards, and the width of this street is as remarkable as its length. North of the bridge the road crosses perhaps the grandest of all village-greens. It is flanked by Long Melford Hall, a great red-brick house of the 1550s with Georgian additions, its fantastic pepper-pot turrets sticking up beyond the tall front wall and octagonal gazebo; while to the north, concealed at first by Victorianised Elizabethan alms-houses, lies the long, grey, flint and glass and freestone church, with the finest body and one of the least satisfying towers of any Suffolk church; and beyond that lies Kentwell Hall, another great Tudor house, completed c. 1564, by the Cloptons, the family to whom the church is in a way a vast memorial chapel. This is to say nothing of the minor ingredients of the beauty of Melford Green—the lesser houses, the group of noble elms, the suggestion of vanished markets and fairs and processions. The west side of the great street occupies the site of one of the largest Romano-British settlements known in England.

The church is the first thing to see, not only in Melford but in Suffolk. Its texture is of elaborate flushwork all over, and of glass. Beneath the battlements are inscribed the names of the donors (field-glasses are a help). The inscription to Richd Loveday, Boteler with Jn Clopton, is dated 1496, the rough date of the "end of the work, to which all the well-disposed men of this town" contributed, under the Cloptons. The outlines of a small classical brick tower, 1725, seem to be perpetuated in the Gothic flintwork of 1903. Within, the first five bays of the nave are those of the previous church, tall perpendicular arches, unusual in a Perpendicular church. On a fine day the effect of light through clerestory is unforgettable. Much of the surviving glass is Norwich work—a gallery of arms and coloured effigies of thirty-two members of Clopton connexion. Clopton chantry, north of Easter sepulchre under which Jn Clopton lies, has verses round its carved wooden frieze. Alabaster panel of Adoration in north aisle. Lady chapel at east end of church, with separate entrance, is singularly beautiful with ambulatory, carved roof, and multiplication table from use as 17c school-room.

Clopton's Kentwell Hall has moated handsome exterior: hall and living-rooms at rear probably go back to Henry VIII's reign. Interior burnt out 1826. Approached along great avenue of pollarded limes planted 1678. The Cordells had Melford Hall: Jn seems to have been in Clopton service, his son Sir Wm was Master of Rolls 1577–81. Elizabeth began her Suffolk visit here, 1578. Turrets have delightful fan-decoration reminiscent of Layer Marney. Wm's Renaissance tomb in church is the most finished of its kind in Suffolk (possibly by Cornelius Cure). His children died and house went to Savage family: it was slighted in Civil War and bought back by Cordells. Distinctive square façades added by Sir Cordell Firebrace who did much redecoration c. 1735. In 1786 it was sold to Sir Hy Parker, son of Vice-Admiral who fought under Rodney and whose portrait by Romney

Topiary and turrets. **Long Melford** Hall

Long Melford

hangs in library, a Regency room with notable rosewood bookcase. His family still lives there, and opens it to public in summer. Bull Hotel has good name and timber-frame going back to 16c, extended in "Trust House Tudor". It is good to see

the Mill House lived in again. Melford is under constant pressure to expand. At *Rodbridge*, south of village, tree-shaded, swan-haunted picnic-site established beside river and flooded gravel pit. Ove Arup Associates have designed single-

storey prospect house on north-west side of Melford.

MELLIS [10]. The most impressive of all the Suffolk Greens, nearly 1,400 acres, stretches nearly two miles east from Pountney Hall: bounded by great ditches, scattered farm-houses and cottages, crossed by London–Norwich railway and warehousing. Scene of Suffolk's most harrowing military experience in entire Civil War: "11 April 1644, Edward Gibes of Thrandeston was slain at a muster, being shot through the bowells, and another of Wortham was shot into the thigh and three others were shot through their clothes." Church on Green nevertheless retains Charles I's arms. Tower fell 1735, never rebuilt: chancel crudely Victorianised. But nave's south windows reveal noble 15c rebuild, which also affected porch (it has Dec. east window, but Perp. south face, lifted to include parvis). Depressing interior includes fine 15c screen, re-daubed *c*. 1900. Needs love and faith.

MELTON [17] became late Georgian suburb north of Woodbridge when grand broad turnpike built—itself now superseded by by-pass of 1930s. Playing-fields, petrol-pumps, pleasant Regency Hall, old shop-fronts, modern farm-implement retailer, charming stucco-fronted cottage, "Plantation Place", 1833, and very well laid-out and gardened council estate on Hall Farm Road, all along one side of the turnpike: on the other stood, till 1963, frame of medieval gaol of the liberty of St Etheldreda—the Ely estates clustered round Alde and Deben valleys. A little way north is St Audrey's mental hospital, originally built 1765 as House of Industry, and early in the 19c one of the first asylums in which modern therapeutic methods were employed (by Dr Jn Kirkman). Parish church

(1867, architect Fredk Barnes), of Kentish rag with Midland broach spire, weathering well. Old church with flowing-traceried window in square tower now remote and used only as mortuary. Delightful millhouse on river alongside.

MENDHAM [5]. Lovely green sloping parish in Waveney valley. Church and main settlement grouped beside bridge: Red House Farm has distinguished red-brick Georgian front. Norman arcading from Cluny cell in marshes removed to Mendham Place and stone quarried for cottages. Curved gable 1698 on Weston House. Middleton Hall is a beauty on the slopes of the Beck, with timber and brick-nogging on the south (garden) front that goes back to the 15c, possibly earlier; named after a 14c sheriff, it has splendid remains of Elizabethan plastered ceilings from Sir Bassingborne Gawdy's day. Walsham Hall, much reduced, still has staircase put in *c*. 1650 when leading Parliamentarian Hobarts lived in it. *Withersdale* church beside the dale is irresistible outside and rewarding in. Fabric and font Norman and delightful: old brick floor and 17c fittings miraculously untouched. Mendham's own church, with timber chancel-arch, is over-restored.

MENDLESHAM [10]. Church tower's crown and battlements displayed proudly over all the fields. Notable north porch, which outside bears carved stone creatures, including two woodwoses in good preservation, and inside has been the town armoury since 1593.

Armour ranging in date from 1470 to 1630. "A note of All the towne Armere" survives from 1588. It is easy to see the villagers trudging off to Mellis Green, a stiff hour's walk, for the eight o'clock parade before the Captain "to be trained and exercised one day" in the late August of 1627. The church also has excellent carpentry, including pulpit and font-cover made by Jn Turner of Mendlesham, 1630. This tradition lasted to the late 18c, when Mendlesham chairs, distinctive but not unlike Windsor chairs, had a high local reputation. They are still known as Dan Day chairs, after Danl Day, a local chair-maker, whose son is reputed to have worked for Sheraton *c*. 1790 and returned to his father's workshop. Near Mendlesham Green, Oak Tree Farm, Ashes Farm and Tan Office Farm are all good old unrestored farmhouses.

METFIELD [5]. Pond and pump at heart of village, where shop-windows have Georgian glazing. Church, beautifully remodelled in 15c, retains painted celure west of chancel-arch, with pulleys—perhaps for rood-veil. Flushwork porch with fine oak bosses. Furnishings and repairs fully described in churchwardens' accounts, 1547–1769. Corner Farm ranges from 15 to 17c.

METTINGHAM [5] has ruins of castle, 1344, built by Sir Jn de Norwich, one of Edward III's captains in the French wars: it must have looked like Wingfield. Ruined flintwork gatehouse remains. Castle converted into well-endowed college, 1394. Present house on site built 1880. Mettingham Hall, with beautiful curved Dutch gables and moat, was built *c.* 1660. Alder Farm: perfect little traditional farmhouse among Waveney willows. Church has round tower and rich Norman doorway.

MICKFIELD [16]. *Great space* implied by pre-Norman place-name. De-hedging has restored sense of this. Ancient church door and knocker, benches and brasses. Distant moated farmsteads. View from top of tower.

MIDDLETON-CUM-FORDLEY [12]. Fordley occupied all southern half of this double parish, united 1620 "because bells and people of one church disturbed those of the other": churches shared churchyard in northern spur over Minsmere river, an odd arrangement for Fordleyites. No trace of their church survives. Middleton's church, with thin lead spire and thatch burnt 1953, now tiled. Lilacs over churchgate. Late 12c features, late-medieval murals and font, a bench-end, holy table and pulpit survived fire, also three nice early Georgian monuments. Pedimented Tudor porch unfortunately stuccoed. Thatched pub, village shop and pump grouped close-by.

MILDEN [15]. Farmland in medieval clothing district. Foxburrow Hill was stronghold of Wm of Milden in Stephen's reign. Wells Hall, with comical red-brick gateway, the *reductio ad absurdum* of the medieval gatehouse, was the troublesome property of Sir Simonds D'Ewes' father. Bare little church has good alabaster effigy

of Jas Alington, 1627, and ledger-slabs.

MILDENHALL [7]. Small market town on the River Lark, at edge of Bedford Level, with magnificent church—its tower (112 ft) looking out over the most extensive Suffolk parish. In the wide fen to the north, the name Drove is common from time (17–19c) when cattle were fed here on last stage of drive from north to London. "Mildenhall Treasure" discovered 1946: engraved and embossed silver dishes and goblets of the late Roman Empire, remarkable for the quality of their workmanship rather than their design, and in a peculiarly perfect state of preservation: now in British Museum.

Mildenhall has pleasant brick buildings, notably No. 2 King Street, silvery Georgian brick. Many roofs have red-and-yellow tiles of Cambridgeshire. Old wooden market cross: lead roof. Four neat orange and terracotta-coloured almshouses, 1722. Church one of the noblest in Suffolk. East window extension early 14c for parson Wm de Wichforde, whose sepulchral slab remains. Chancel 1240–1300, also E.E. chantry-chapel. Nave, five graceful bays, broad aisles and spectacular roofs, date from early 15c: altar tomb of leading benefactor, Sir Hy Barton, in aisle. Lower stage of tower has good internal stone fan vaulting. Beautiful north porch: Lady chapel over. The roofs are the most heavenly features of the church: field-glasses desirable. Construction of nave roof, as masterly as work later in 15c, shows affinity to that at Lakenheath. Whole roof riddled with

buckshot by maniac Puritans: no possibility that they were shooting at birds, as is sometimes stated by their apologists. Luckily the angels' wings took impact of shot without breaking off: the majority of originals survive. Spandrels of north aisle roof, each carved with lively subject, among the most original works of medieval carpentry. Plain chancel roof, 1507, restored. In 1959, £10,000 bequest spent on new benches, carved by Ipswich firm in traditional design. Bad stained glass.

MONEWDEN [16] (pronounced Monna-d'n). Three excellent Elizabethan yeoman farms along road to Otley: Red House, with very nice plaster ceiling, and chimney-stack labelled "G.S. 1592": Mr Francis Martin's Rookery Farm, with chimney-stack labelled "J.S. and M.S. 1593", and between them Mr Wright's Cherry-Tree Farm. Rookery Farm retains exactly almost identical field-pattern shown in map of 1656, also identical farmhouse, though reduced a little from that shown on map: hall in centre, parlour through that to right, kitchen and offices to left. Panelled cupboards with original cock's-head hinges. Initials suggest that George Stebbing built Red House, his son Jn The Rookery. Brasses in church to Elizabethan Reves, one of whom, Fellow of Gonville and Caius, left pension for annual sermon, still remembered once a year. Hall red-brick *c.* Queen Anne.

MOULTON [7]. Newmarket country. Bare cheerful church under chalk hill contains

Sheila - na - gig sculpture. Arched medieval packhorse bridge spans stream of Kennet, dry in summer. "Penny grave" where Chippenham road crosses A45: passers-by insert penny into grave of outcast.

MUTFORD [6]. Ash Farm has great Tudor chimney-stack, much old brickwork, step-gables, window-mouldings and glazed pantiles. Church has very rustic appearance. Round Norman tower with handsome flushwork top. 14c Galilee porch leads in from west. Brick floors. Roof of nave rude, but not that of south aisle. Medieval painted plaster lately renovated away: only 17c Creed and Lord's Prayer left, Boxing Day, 1960. Locked: "Unsafe" 1974.

NACTON [22]. Foreshore sandy, seaweedy, with tree roots exposed by tides, on which the dredger clanks and cargo ships pass silently to and from Ipswich: parkland on both banks, with two historic houses here and a dingy church full of monuments. Broke Hall, down by the water, said to have been rebuilt 1526 and 1767, apparently given its present Georgian Gothick appearance by Jas Wyatt: home of Sir Philip Bowes Vere Broke (1776–1841), who commanded the *Shannon* against the *Chesapeake* in American waters, 1813. Orwell Park, a boys' preparatory school with commanding views of estuary below, is on site of Admiral Vernon's house 1725–9, rebuilt by his nephew after 1757: a square red-brick building that lost elegance in another rebuilding, 1854, by Col Geo Tomline, M.P. His cousin's son has added Orwell Park House

to the pleasant riverside seats (archts: N. and D. Spain, Hanover Square): the Victorian *cottage ornée* below is probably by T. J. Ricauti. Sholland Hill is a very attractive bungalow in the modern glazed manner. Romantic ancient mounds in woods by Police Station.

NAUGHTON [15]. Old scattered farm settlements. Hall preserves noble Elizabethan chimney-stack; Brickhouse Farm, vivid, mature brick and half-timbering; Cooper's Farm a typical Elizabethan yeoman farmhouse at corner of green. Church, rustic outside and in, has 14c king-post roof and organ by Robt Gray, 1777. Churchyard moated.

NAYLAND-WITH-WISSINGTON [21]. Both beside the Stour at the beginning of its most idyllic upper stretch: Nayland a diminutive market and cloth-making town, Wissington (sometimes Wiston), a green, valley-bottom farming parish. An islanded field, just south of Nayland church, is called Court Knoll, and was Norman centre of big Domesday lordship of *Eiland*, including Wissington, Stoke (and the Horkesleys on Essex side). Present name is corruption of "An eiland". Mother church nevertheless up at Stoke: down here St James had "a chapel of Stoke", which in 1429 acquired ½ acre of land for own cemetery. By then Nayland's cloth-making flourished, only to decline in 17c, when Weever recorded many marbles here, richly inlaid with brasses to memory of Jn Ewell, fuller, 1436, Geo. Hamund, *textor*, 1530, etc. Matrixes in church mostly plundered since

Weever's day, but a brass still suggests butterfly headdress of Jn Hamund's daughter, c. 1485. Church porch built by Wm Abel, clothworker, 1525, whose arms are in a north window (his rebus reproduced on keystone of humped Georgian bridge over Stour, and embodied in unhumped replacement, 1959). North door well carved, vine-leaf and linenfold. Decayed linenfold south door preserved Jn Long's name. Superb roof and clerestory run length of nave and chancel. Gallery at west end: 16c screen beneath. Eight 15c screen panels survive, five in good order. Reredos, Christ blessing the Elements, painted by Constable. Tower rebuilt 1834, wrong proportions. But surmounted by new spire, "Essex" proportions, 1966, to great advantage. Georgian obelisk in delightful market-place only 55 miles from London. Among many agreeable lesser buildings, Alston Court (presumably successor to Court Knoll) entered beneath door-hood like Bristol merchant's, is a house mainly c. 1480. Upper room has magnificently carved chestnut roof. Set of glass shields of arms in hall records connexions of Payn family c. 1510.

Wissington. Handsome white weather-boarded water-mill on river. Attractive group of Hall and church. Hall enlarged by Soane 1791, for Saml Beachcroft, Governor of the Bank of England. Church standing timelessly like Iffley or Tixover, perfect small Norman building on tripartite plan, with apsidal chancel and signs of central tower. Now crowned by bellcote. Nave walls covered with faded but remarkable 13c

Wissington

paintings, including a nearly contemporary picture of St Francis and the birds, and a miracle of St Nicholas with 13c sailing-boat: all part of an unusually complete scheme executed *c.* 1250–75, probably by Colchester artists. The Victorians filled the church with "Norman" benches, pulpit, reading desk and communion rails.

NEDGING [15]. The road from Nedging Tye is lined with mainly Elizabethan cottages

and approaching church there is a good prospect up the Brett valley, with Bildeston church in foreground. Church has two Norman doorways, bell founded by Wm Dawe, who made guns for Dover, 1385, and some Victorian epitaphs. Adjoins grounds of delightful mid-Tudor Hall, remodelled *c.* 1920, with small lake and immense oak.

NEEDHAM MARKET [16]. Small "thoroughfare" town originally hamlet of Barking.

Wednesday market said to have died after visitation of plague 1685. Ipswich and Needham Bank, first bank ever established in Ipswich, originated here in 18c ironmongery of Quaker Alexander family. Plenty of old houses, several with Georgian fronts including two notable shops, one a broad bow. No. 111 is especially interesting. "Very handsome red-brick house" noted by traveller in 1777 now offices of District Council, extended in 1965. Famous 15c church was chapel of Barking to 1901, has no churchyard: its buttressed flint walls rise straight out of the street, a rare visual experience in Suffolk. No room for tower. Inscription over priest's door translated reads: "Pray we all for grace. For them that helped this place". Medieval roof by general consent the most ambitious and brilliant performance of its kind in England: "a whole church with nave, aisles and clerestory seemingly in the air" (Pevsner). Furthermore it was largely rebuilt in 1880: certainly everything below present fine arch-braced ties, with their carved spandrels, is late Victorian. At same time fine porch of moulded Tudor brick with step-gables was replaced by present oddity. 2 and 4 High Street built as grammar-school, 1632. Friends' Meeting House at 89, Congregational chapel 1837 goes back to 1662. Hawks Mill, Victorian brickwork, pilastered, dignified, echoes round arches of bridge.

NETTLESTEAD [16]. Folded in little valley of Ipswich hinterland, gave name to a Tudor barony of which nothing remains here at the Hall but a pedimented gateway of the middle of that period. High Hall, Elizabethan, is perhaps one of the new houses described in Ryece's *Suffolk Breviary*: "placed where they may be furthest seen ... best prospects, rooms square, raised high", etc, a delightful brick house with pedimented windows, oak staircase, and at top of house a fretted door of uncertain purpose. Views of distant fields. Church, badly damaged by Germans in Battle of Britain, reopened November 1950. 17c

monument to Saml and Thomassine Sayer well repaired. Red-brick and timber Tudor Grange stands on Offton–Somersham road.

NEWBOURNE [23]. With two brooks running into the Deben was much divided in 1930s into smallholdings for unemployed Yorkshire and Durham miners, replaced now, mostly by Suffolkers. Hall, medieval hall-house: tall Elizabethan extensions at parlour end have delightfully moulded plasterwork inside. Wonderfully unspoilt. White-brick Old Rectory, one of many of the same period, well sited above church and designed, 1856, by Wm Pattisson of Woodbridge. Church has brick body, hammer-beam roof and flint tower-porch with prominent carved pinnacles and graffito of ship inside west jamb of arch, apparently late 15c.

NEWMARKET [7]. A thoroughfare town on one of the most ancient roads in England, and set in a downland heath of famous turf, headquarters of English horse-racing. The surrounding countryside contains the densest concentration of studs in England. Apart from the yearling sales at Doncaster in September, all the sales take place here. The horses are the principal inhabitants: the railway station set aside for their reception is like a grand Ionic orangery.

Newmarket's modern career was suggested early on by the nature of the countryside. The market that gave it its name was set up *c*. 1200 beside the great road where it flanked the ancient manor and half-Hundred of Exning. In the 14c

there were prohibitions against holding tournaments. Three centuries later the court of James I was frequently here, tilting, hawking and harrying the bustard, organising the first recorded horse race in 1619. (The last bustard was seen on the heath in 1840). The great course on the heath lies west of the town, in Cambridgeshire, flanked by a most spectacular earthwork, the Devil's Dyke. The chalky slopes east of the town—Long Hill, Warren Hill and Bury Hill—are landscaped and screened by beech trees with lines as clean and sleek as those of the horses out for their morning walk, ascending and descending in stately file, just as they did when Tillemans painted them.

The great highway itself, the High Street, received a stick of ten bombs as a convoy passed through in 1940: still has ramshackle patches. In 1955 grotesque red lamp standards were erected along it, one of them planted (by somebody who should forfeit the use of his eyes) close beside the Cooper Memorial Fountain of 1909 that for nearly fifty years had formed a perfect termination to the Cambridge end of the town. The Jubilee clock-tower at the other end has merely been turned into a traffic roundabout. James I's lavish palace was sold up by Parliament in 1650. Charles II's red-brick building replaced 1863 by nonconformist chapel lying now over shop on High Street. Jockey Rooms built 1772 from design of Jn Johnson: a single-storey building with triple-sided bay window to north of a round-headed triple arcade, successfully restored and enlarged by Sir Albert Richardson. Rich crag-coloured brick used; nearby post office building caught something of the spirit. At north end of High Street, same side, Rutland Arms has fine Georgian red-brick front, older courtyard behind. All Saints church in rear crudely rebuilt 1876. Magnificent houses look out on to Long Hill from end of Old Station Road, especially Lord Rosebery's Cleveland House. St Mary's Church on other side of High Street has Holy Family by Caracciolo, at home in a resort of Charles II. Good modern iron gates in tower arch: fine Georgian iron gates front modern grammar school. Old outlines survive at Bushel Inn, down Market Street. Modern shapes inevitably sub-Georgian and Cockney. St Mary's Square gives on to Mill Hill, a well-designed square of yellow-brick terraces on two sides of a beautiful lime plantation. Rather lumpy blocks of red-brick flats rise behind. Beyond, on Exning Road (suburban umbilical cord between Exning and its New Market), a delightful Victorian flint pub (The Mount) and long flint-faced terrace (Bakers Row).

Exning is pleasantly watered by a tributary of the Cam. Church, raised behind buttressed valerian-covered wall of Duck Lane. Brick-floored interior, spacious, well-restored and with transepts. 14c "heart-shrine" found in S transept. Georgian pulpit with sounding-board. St Etheldreda born here 630, possibly while Devil's Dyke was building: likely site beside great moat, 250 yards south of church; covered by new motorway, 1973.

NEWTON [21]. Sudbury's golf course by the "Turk's Head" on the Green, overlooked by picturesque Jacobean front of Brook House, other old houses, and clumsy council cottages. Roger's Farm, with good central chimney-stack and timbering, has painted panels, 1623, in ground-floor hall: moulded ceiling in one bedroom. Newton Hall typical unsophisticated old Suffolk farmhouse. Church contains beautiful altar tomb, *c.* 1410, with identity problems. Pleasant textures in porch and in barnlike nave, now sensibly partitioned off from more usable chancel. Pulpit bears name of Richd Modi (presumably Moody) who died 1468.

NEWTON, OLD [9]. Old settlements of Dagworth and Stow (market) very early developed adjacent "new towns": to avoid confusion, these became "Old Newton" and "Gipping Newton" (which is now just "Gipping"). Perfect heavy-clay farm landscape. Church a 14c rebuilding: its splendour still suggested by nave window designs (fragments of glass still in the tracery), by evidence (on tower) of original roof-height, and by recently (1972) uncovered handsome niches in east wall, and sedilia. (A "new" roof mentioned in will, 1444.) Rustic benches under west gallery. Painted arms of George II. Jacobean chimneys at Bush's Farm. At *Dagworth*, a ford, a much-reduced Tudor house, farm buildings and known site of Domesday church half owned by Breme, or Bremere, "a freeman, killed in the battle of Hastings: *in bello hastingensi*".

NORTON [9]. Scattered Tudor farmhouses with red-brick chimney-stacks like Crawley Hall Farm and Fiske's Farm, red-brick step-gables and chimneys like Norton Manor Farm at Norton Little Green, where cottage, too, has red-brick step-gable. Later buildings mainly white brick and flint. Little Haugh Hall, standing emparked beyond a tributary stream of Little Ouse, was tall Tudor or Jacobean red-brick house when it became the home of Cox Macro (1683–1767), antiquarian son of rich grocer of Cupola House, Bury. He modernised it in 1730s and '40s: staircase, ceiling and dome painted for him, 1741, by Fras Hayman—Hayman's only known decorative painting from this period, its style quite different from that of his other surviving works. Much other decoration by Bury carver and painter Thos Ross: rich plasterwork perhaps designed by Sir Jas Burrough, the Cambridge amateur architect. Well-kept church approached through lime avenue stands beside old rectory with good Queen Anne addition. North-west gable of nave "shaped"—very unusual. Eight of best carved misericords in Suffolk include martyrdoms of SS Edmund and Andrew. Carved bench-ends and unusually good font with woodwose and other signs of evangelist. Coloured tomb with emblems of mortality, 1624, anonymous.

NOWTON [14] (pronounced Noat'n). Church extremely restored. Late Norman doorways through which parish bounds of Hawstead pass. Windows filled with Flemish glass "collected" from the monasteries of Brussels at expense of Orbell Ray Oakes, see 1820 tablet. Wife commemorated on monument by Bacon, 1811. Their house, Nowton Court, early Victorian Tudor like so much about here, is boys' preparatory school.

OAKLEY [4] ("oak clearing"). Typical Suffolk church in corn landscape. Porch bears Cornwallis arms. Cornwallis tomb, 1519.

OCCOLD [10] ("oak copse"). Like Oakley, cornland out of forest. Good 1450-ish church tower: pulpit and sounding board usual period, 1620. Brass effigies.

OFFTON [15]. Deep channels drain the rich sloping land. Platform of Wm of Ambli's castle in Stephen's reign impressively sited to command country between Brett and Gipping. Name might well commemorate Offa, bravest and most distinguished of Byrhtnoth's men at the battle of Maldon, 991. Church has 14c wooden porch, simple Norman doorway, king-post nave roof. Tombstone in churchyard bears crude effigy of mourning horse. *Little Bricett*. Talmache Hall home of Capt. Jn Bright of Parliament's army in Civil War.

ONEHOUSE [15] (pronounced Wunnus). Onehouse Lodge a William and Mary house. Stow Hundred House of Industry built 1781 at cost of more than £12,000: "it eclipsed some of the neighbouring mansions". (Rept. of Poor Law Commissioners, 1836.) Are the electricity men at Finborough Hall

mortified by the superior proportions of this palatial old folks' home on the hill?

ORFORD [18]. A disfranchised pocket-borough, with a dissolved corporation, an empty market-place (but with famous small oysterage and smoked fish restaurant), a great 12c royal castle of which the keep alone is standing, a church of which the Romanesque aisled chancel is abandoned to the weather and great 14c tower renovated, an Austin friary of which fragmentary walls remain, a quay filled in and built over, two ancient hospitals vanished, and town lanes like those at Blythburgh, represented now by tracks through vegetable gardens, but perpetuating their former character by the pungency of their recorded names. The river crossing to the ness is now a place for mooring small holiday boats, and Orford comes to life a little at holiday seasons. Coastal defence and trade provided the atmosphere and ancient buildings, and are not altogether forgotten. Castle (1165–71) and rich ruined arcades of chancel erected by Wimar the Chaplain for Henry II. Great septaria keep and flint and freestone body of church still present grey-white seamarks for miles, and walking inland at Capel St Andrew one has the sense of being watched from the top of the keep. Subsidy roll for 1327 suggests population of at least 1,000. Notes of ruin and decay struck in Elizabeth's charter, 1579, when town incorporated free borough. First mayor, Jas Coe, merchant, represented on two brasses in church. Elizabethan map shows moorings reaching up towards

church, along north side of quay street with its fishermen's huts. There were sixteen warehouses. The "Jolly Sailor", despite later sign and front, dates from those days: so do King's Head and Crown-and-Castle up on higher ground: cf. their timbers. Orford's decay, like Blythburgh's, brought on by silting up of river and increasing draught of ships. Decline of population in 17c made town a famous manageable borough in Georgian era: ownership went with manor of Sudbourne Hall. Disfranchisement 1832: dissolution 1886.

Keep built on latest circular internal plan, multi-angular exterior, with three projecting square turrets equally spaced. Porch between keep and south turret on first floor with basement under and chapel over (restored in time of King John). Keep itself has three floors: basement and two halls. One turret has broad spiral stair, others contain chambers (two storeys to each hall). From roof one commands view of whole shoreline Aldeburgh–Bawdsey. Useful look-out in last war. Light stationed on ness since 1634, now automatic, flashes every five seconds at night. On that exposed but secret shingle-spit scientists made first experiments in radar, 1935, before moving to Bawdsey.

Of Romanesque church there remain two four-bay arcades, the two east piers of the crossing and the east wall of north transept. Broad lofty nave and tower built early 14c. Ruined top of tower restored to good sturdy design, 1972. Several brasses inside, including rare representation of Trinity: on beautiful font given

Orford castle before recent excellent restoration

by the Cokerels *c*. 1400, one sees unharmed the kind of subject that brought out the worst in Puritans. Pleasant Stuart wood-work, with 1712 screen in front of organ-chamber. Water-colour shows capitals of graceful nave arcade picked out in black for death of George IV who stayed at Sudbourne. The church is unforgettably associated with first performances of Britten's *Noye's Fludde*, 1958, and *Curlew River*, 1964. As you cross large south porch think of Crabbe's wild father as a young man using it as schoolroom for Orford children.

OTLEY [16]. Rich farmland drains south into cleft of Gull at Otley Bottom, where earth-works of Norman castle stand beside line of Roman road. Hall, High House, Moat Farm and Charity Farm are all Tudor buildings, the first two very notable. Hall, built *c*. 1500 and enlarged 1612, is timber-framed with red-brick nogging, good hall-screen in hall and splendid linenfold panelling in solar. Apart from its Jacobean wing it is almost identical with High House: both have odd stair-turret stuck on at back. Old north door of Hall has initials of Robt Gosnold who built it. High House plastered and coloured a splendid ochre. Monument in church (late 14 and 15c building, with large immersion tank under vestry floor) commemorates Jn Gosnold (1568–1628).

OULTON [inset]. Originally Flixton, with one of the best endowed Norman churches, St Michael's (see stratified flint-work of north wall, and central tower) on early site above reeds

of Waveney. There is said to be ford and footpath across to Burgh St Peter. This part of Flixton took name Oulton only in 14c when long chancel built. Beautiful fragment of glass on north side of choir: rare subject, Christ displaying wounded hands. James II's arms. Georgian red-brick top of tower and urns in churchyard. Borrow's house beside the Broad has gone. "North Landing" designed by Tayler and Green of Lowestoft, whose housing for Loddon R.D.C. (Norfolk) includes some of the most distinguished work of its kind in England.

OUSDEN [130] (first syllable rhymes with cows). Steep valley on Cambridgeshire borders, parkland, large Hall demolished 1955. Stables and kitchen-clocktower converted. Church, a tripartite Norman building with remarkably complete central tower. Georgian monument.

PAKEFIELD, *see* LOWESTOFT.

PAKENHAM [9]. Aerial photography and observation, but not enough excavation, suggest that people lived here long before Romans supplied fort at approach to Ixworth along Peddars Way. Fulmer Bridge retains former descriptive name of Pakenham Fen (fowl-mere). Gentle open country spreads out under tower-windmill worked (under Ancient Monuments Inspectorate) by Bryant family, who show it on request. On site yielding prehistoric finds, large Norman church reflects patronage (from before Conquest) of Bury abbots: Barnack stone, central tower and

later octagon: four Bury monks sit round base of font. Teulon restored south transept, built north one 1849. Before he was killed in Normandy, Rex Whistler painted, in upper window of vicarage, *trompe l'oeil* picture of parson among books. Newe House, handsome, 1622. Working watermill at risk.

PALGRAVE [4] has good plastered and thatched cottages. Headstone to 1787 shows wagoner with wagon, apt beside Bury–Norwich turnpike. "That able and indefatigable antiquary, Thos. Martin, F.A.S." (1697–1771) commemorated in flushwork porch of church. Parish suit of armour hangs inside. Hammerbeam roof with angels sawn off preserves medieval colouring. Mrs Barbauld helped to run a boarding-school here, 1774–85. Pleasant green N. of church.

PARHAM [17] (first syllable short as in parrot, and h silent) lies mostly in valley of upper Alde. Church Farm, a well-preserved Tudor building with late-Stuart improvements: decorative front door, cornice and quoins, and higher middle roof-ridge. 15c flushwork north porch of church retains inner door. Rest of fabric 14c, with tall nave windows: said to be the doing of Wm de Ufford. Walls cream-washed. Remains of simple screen gaudily repainted. Graceful 17c altar-rails have poor-box chained to one end. Hat-hanger inscribed "R.H. 1716". Stone Willoughby armorial shields in north wall of chancel probably brought from Campsey at Dissolution. The famous moated brick house of the Willoughbys, one of the most romantic sights of Suffolk, is now a farmhouse called Moat Hall. The Old Hall is a small farmhouse with pantiles, Tudor chimney-stacks and tarred barn. Of Parham House, only part *c.* 1630 remains, but with beautiful decorated brickwork and (extremely early) giant pilasters: gate-pillars of silvery stone. The house, with which Crabbe is associated in the biography by his son, was called Ducking Hall: site now occupied by Parham Hall, rebuilt from design of R. G. Wetten, 1852, about 400 yds east of church.

PEASENHALL [11]. As one descends from the High Suffolk plateau (150 ft) by the Roman road from Badingham, the Peasenhall drain runs beside main road and along south side of main village street—draining all the fields along its way. Important agricultural Drill Works, founded by Jas Smyth, 1800, beside churchyard, gave church a depressingly urban appearance; effect completed by interior, robbed of all individuality by Victorian restorers and rebuilders. The Ancient House, with early Georgian front, is especially endeared to Suffolk people: here, before the war in which he was killed, Julian Tennyson wrote his fresh, imperishable book *Suffolk Scene*. "Wool Hall", with good crown-post, open hall and timber-framing, has been lately thoroughly restored by Landmark Trust. The village hut is of wood in the Swiss style. Woodlands Farm has a tall Dutch gable-end. Providence House was scene of sensational

murder of Rose Harsant, 1 June 1902.

PETTAUGH [16] (pronounced Petta). Debenham–Ipswich turnpike joined Roman road here, and at the junction in the village a tall post-mill has only lately gone. Farms ditched and moated. Hall has beautiful Caroline parlour with carved beam (vine-pattern). Initials in plaster ceiling presumably those of Anthony Fastolf: Fastolfs owned it *c.* 1524–*c.* 1670.

PETTISTREE [17] reveals unexpected delights as soon as one gets off A12. Pettistree "Greyhound", half-timbered, herringbone-brick pub on south side of churchyard. Early 15c church tower has flushwork chequer-pattern. Nave evidently heightened *c.* Queen Anne, when gently curved plaster ceiling was added, also perhaps the "bottle" glass remaining in nave windows. South-east window of chancel has 13c *grisaille* glass. Brass of 1580 shows a Fras Bacon (of Hessett) with two wives in Paris hats. Church thoroughly restored and plainly refitted 1884, is lit by oil. Bread-cupboard, 1717, resembles Punch-and-Judy stage. "The Laurels" has Gothick windows and glorious topiary peacocks. *Loudham.* Hall, beautiful red-brick house, Elizabethan, modernised 1740. Ruins of well-endowed church long stood in front of it.

PLAYFORD [16]. In the bottom of a steep-sided valley that cuts across parish from west to east. Church stands high above north bank. Moated Hall, middle 16c with additions *c.*

1700, was home of Felton family 1546–1719, and probably stands on site of house of Sir Geo. Felbrigg, an eminent knight: his splendid brass effigy, 1400, is the chief distinction of the church whose tower-porch he built. Church also possesses a most beautiful standing-cup, 1619, and exhibits medallions to Thos Clarkson, 1760–1846, antagonist of slavery, and Geo. Biddell Airy, 1801–92, Astronomer Royal. Airys and Clarksons lie in adjacent iron-framed graves, the Clarksons' hung with honeysuckle.

POLSTEAD [21]. Gathered at junctions of steep wooded tributaries of Box Stream, with a large central pond, and widely known for its cherries and for the murder of Maria Marten in a red barn (later burnt down) near the church. The girl's gravestone at west end of church has been chipped away. Her thatched cottage survives. The Hall, altered and refronted 1816–19 (archt. W. Pilkington) has wall-paintings upstairs in 16c Italian style. Rectory too is an old house given a Georgian front. Church tower alone among Suffolk's medieval towers has its medieval stone spire. It was a fine 12c building, with *façade principale* like Westhall's, its doorway with arch of four orders still visible within tower. The Norman nave arcades, with limestone piers, carved capitals of considerable finish, have brick arches, surmounted furthermore by a brick clerestory. Bricks in the arcades are occasionally interspersed with small blocks of "tufa". Brick alternates with stone in some of the piers. There are remains of round-headed brick windows on all three sides of the chancel. Anglo-Normans made their own bricks here as they did at Coggeshall; Polstead adds to the impressive Coggeshall evidence that this area was abreast of the Low Countries and the Baltic in the revival of brickwork.

POSLINGFORD [14] has a nucleus of cottages on steady slope by the church. Church porch built of pre-Reformation brick. Norman doorway within has beautifully preserved tympanum carved with a sort of carpet pattern. Memorials of Goldings who lived at New House Farm. No significant remains of "Chipley Abbey", a small Austin priory, but dogtooth mouldings in rectory rockery.

PRESTON [15]. Robt Ryece, who projected a history and gazetteer of Suffolk (*A Breviary of Suffolk*) in Elizabeth I's time, born here. During her reign he set up in the church royal arms and commandments and texts arranged on triptychs: these are magnificent. He also set up 167 shields of armorial glass, and the surviving fifty may be checked against his account. It is perhaps the work of Thos Mills of Lavenham, painter and glazier. Church thoroughly restored 1862. Splendid early Norman font and beautiful flushwork south porch. Latin inscription commemorates Nicholas Colman, ejected 1644, restored 1660. Design by Rev. Ernest Geldart, 1903, for restoration of screen. Hall, comfortable and charming, with elaborate chimney-stacks, probably rebuilt by Ryece himself. Rushbrook Farm, now

overlying boundaries of Brettenham and Thorpe, was a separate "vill" like them in 1086.

PURDIS FARM [22]. A few hundred acres of heath, its name curiously derived from ancient church of St Petronilla, of which rubble is still turned up by plough in Chapel Field. Parish contains Bixley Decoy, Ipswich golf club, ribbons of houses delightfully different, and gorse, flaming gold.

RAMSHOLT [23]. The "Ramsholt Arms" nestles in tamarisk down by the river. It was the ferry house when there was a ferry: then, oil-lit and snug in Mrs Nunn's day, it was frequented by everyone with a boat on the Deben, and by the few local inhabitants. Since her death in 1957 it has been crudely enlarged. Between it and church the narrow valley of a tributary stream now blocked by the strengthened river wall, lies waste under sorrel and ragwort, smelling of death when myxomatosis comes. It formerly sheltered the main human settlement. Above stands the church with its unforgettable outline, and, till 1964, a row of cottages beneath. The buttressed septaria tower is round, not elliptical: illusion of ellipse created by ancient buttresses that run up to the top. Early 19c box-pews inside, with nicely curved draught-break at west end.

RATTLESDEN [15]. Main village in valley that winds to Ipswich and gave name to Orwell: given to Ely by widow who died 1007 (all except Clopton Hall, which belonged to Bury abbey).

Lydgate said Caen stone for Bury was brought by water as far as Rattlesden. Cottages thatched and clustered in Lower and Half Moon Streets, below dignified church, which contains more limestone than most Suffolk churches (Ely's influence?) mixed with usual black and grey glint. Buttresses gabled on early 14c tower, which carries small shingled broach spire and is small in proportion to church. Stonepanelled porch and fenestration and embattling of aisles and clerestory Perp., but porch leads into excellent 13c doorway with round window over. Double hammerbeam roof restored, chancel roof covered and arched with wood panels. Bench-end: four-faced man, tongues protruding. *Clopton Hall* on hill-shoulder—early settlement site with natural springs and fishponds descending. Stuccoed north front, 1681, stretched between earlier great chimneys, has original windows as serves as kitchen wing: living-rooms in agreeable Victorian south front with red tile-hung gables, ironwork verandah and Great Exhibition conservatory. North front built by Col Jn Fiske, who had been at siege of Colchester, 1648: south front by Col Windsor Parker, at siege of Bhurtpore, 1825. *Hightown Green* provided little more than roadside grazing. "Friars Hall" is delightful example of small medieval house with crown-post roof, its outer walls clearly plastered all over from the beginning. At *Poystreet Green*, Roman road drained by great ditches either side.

RAYDON [21]. Distinctive and beautiful work of *c.* 1310 in and outside of church: sculptured faces of that age look out from window-stops, buttresses, and east pinnacles. At west end, mellow bell in small cage chimes the hours. In landscape of Sulleys Farm and Lower Raydon "Hills", narrow enchanting lanes.

REDE [14]. High ground. Church uninteresting, its tower propped on crutches and splints.

REDGRAVE [3]. Park of Bury abbey, then of Lord Keeper Bacon, embellished in 1765 for Rowland Holt by Capability Brown when he turned the Tudor house into a quadrangle, mostly pulled down by Holt-Wilson owner, 1950, the rest since. Fine lake remains, and survivors and descendants of St Edmund's oaks. 14c church with impressive chancel window-tracery (and depressing east window glass by Farrow of Diss, 1853) is distinguished by its monuments. Altar tomb of Lord Keeper's son Sir Nicholas, by Bernard Jansen, 1616, with effigies by Nicholas Stone, 1620 (Sir Nicholas died 1624). Stone also did Lady Gawdy's wall tablet, 1621. In chancel, memorial brass to Mrs Anne Butts, one of the best post-Reformation brasses ever made. Superb memorial marble of Chief Justice Holt, 1710, shows him seated: Thos Green of Camberwell's "most impressive work". Many hatchments.

REDISHAM (formerly "Great") [6]. Charmingly seated, modest little un-Tractarian church, with very early chancel walls, and elaborate Norman south

doorway on doll's-house scale. 1619 pulpit.

REDISHAM, LITTLE See RINGSFIELD.

REDLINGFIELD [10]. Flat farmland. Nunnery founded 1120, remains now in farm: infirmary or dormitory in use as barn, standing up well beside church. Prioress in 1427 confessed she went alone with a bailiff *sub heggerowes*. Church has red-brick chancel and brick shows through nave plaster. Stump of a tower, with gabled roof, contains village stocks. Well-carved headstones.

RENDHAM [11]. Attractive village. Offspring of Walpole Congregational chapel established *c.* 1690 via Sweffling. Present chapel built 1750, extended 1834. Monument to Hy Howard, 1788, graces wall beside high pulpit. Pleasant recent redecoration. Manse 1732. Church has brass to Thos King, vicar 1532, fine pulpit "1632. W.P." with back and sounding-board, and Charles II's arms with "God Save the King".

RENDLESHAM [17]. Church, St Gregory's: lofty nave and large chancel. 14c east window has wooden tracery. Monuments. Old Rectory fine. Of old Rendlesham House, two lodges remain, fantastic conceits of the Gothick revival. Repton arranged the park. A new Rendlesham Hall, built close by, and again rebuilt in 1871, was pulled down after the last war. In this parish somewhere lies the site of the royal hall of the Wuffingas, the dynasty whose necropolis was at Sutton Hoo.

REYDON [12]. Mother parish of Southwold. Church well cared for. Reydon Hall, 1692, was much Victorianised. Reydon quay was built 1727 by Sir Jn Players: the present lonely Dutch-gabled house down there was presumably built then or a little earlier.

RICKINGHALL INFERIOR [9]. Easily confused with delightful contiguous thoroughfare-village of Botesdale, its erratic boundary coincides with former East/West county boundary and divides Hamblyn House in two. The church, its greatest treasure, retains Norman round tower (with later delicate octagonal belfry), but is mainly a study in the style of the beginning of the 14c, when Suffolk was moving into perhaps its highest period of prosperity and civilisation. Design of window-tracery and font especially interesting: notice the way the very spandrels outside east window of south aisle have been decorated by the carver. Reredos probably made from former rood loft. Convenient for village, this church nevertheless was almost abandoned (1973) because more expensive to repair than that at

RICKINGHALL SUPERIOR [9] half-a-mile south, whose nave (30 ft wide) would be one of the best examples of late Perpendicular architecture even in Suffolk had it not been scraped clean of almost all character by conscientious Victorians. Flushwork. Mason's mark (square and compass) on south-west buttress. "The Gables" (on south side of thoroughfare) is first example of rescue by Suffolk Building Preservation Trust.

reen de Camberwel

RINGSFIELD [6]. Village in wooded little valley. Name may refer to circular henge monument in clearing. Ridged red step-gables on Old Hall, on one other house, and on the south porch of church. Charming churchyard flanked by serpentine wall. 1883 chancel by Butterfield has excrescent vestry. Roof thatched, tall tower-top decorated with brick and flint. "Père Lachaise" sculpture, 1902, in honour of a great-niece of Napoleon. External wall monuments, including one to Nicholas Gosling, 1663, "preacher of God's word". His pulpit is a fine square one, with sounding-board. Heavily restored church full of Stuart woodwork liberally adorned with texts, possibly Gosling's doing. *Little Redisham.* Air photographs show traces of vanished settlement in pleasant park, north of Hall, and fragments of church remain. Ringsfield monument says Nich. Garnys, 1592, "builded Redsham Hall". Rebuilt on new site mid 18c (see W. dormers), remodelled 1823 (fine Regency front room), entirely faced with red brick and expanded by Victorian squire while Caroline Murat was here, and again remodelled, 1901, for T. de la Garde Grissell, whose *art nouveau* memorial in churchyard displays handsome metal peacock (emblem of eternity).

RINGSHALL [15] (pronounced Rinks'l). Name may refer to vanished circular henge monument. Church, thought to occupy raised, fortified site, has Norman work and 15c tie beams, with great crude pins on outside of wall. Hall, dignified Georgian farmhouse. Its prede-

cessor inherited by Sir Thos Gresham, who came here to arrange for preparation of timber at adjacent Battisford Tye for building of his great Royal Exchange (begun 1566). Chestnuts Farm attractive late 18c weather-boarded box, with part of moat. Chapel Farm, largely devoted to sheep, has 17c carved staircase and panelling. Whole parish subject to annoyance by neighbouring aircraft.

RISBY [8]. On Breckland edge. Much of church 12c, including round tower with arch. Jocelin of Brakelond has tale of surly lord Norman and hospitable lord William of Risby: paintings on north wall of nave executed in their day—upper series devoted to the Nativity and Infancy. In lower series St Margaret is distinctly birching the Devil. Very good screen.

RISHANGLES [10] ("brushwood slope"). Moated farmsteads, one the seat of Elizabethan Grimstons. Dark-featured church, of odd and handsome shape, tower set on south of nave and all set in screen of limes. Charmless inside, and now falling down. The Baptist chapel, with its own graveyard, and a sunnier disposition, is lately done up.

ROUGHAM [9]. Footpaths and hedges mark Peddars Way. Great mound at Eastlow Hill was burial-chamber: traces of important Romano-British building nearby. Fine church, mostly Perpendicular. Robt Tyllot left 50 marks for tower "to be built from new", 1458. Bequests for tower continued till 1478, with last one 1488. Names Tillot and Drury in

flushwork battlements. South porch 14c with 1632 roof. On entering 14c north doorway, see much excellent 14c work: arcading, chancel arch, chancel windows, aisle windows, font, etc. Aisles rebuilt embodying earlier east windows, presumably to keep glass pictures. North aisle buttresses dated 1514. Carved timber roofs and benching. Brass to Sir Roger Drury (will, 1420). Memorial to Sir Jeffery Burwell, Sir Robt Walpole's grandfather.

RUMBURGH [5] (pronounced Rumbra: Ekwall heartlessly suggests "fort where the rūn or council was held"). Priory here, founded 1064–70 and dedicated to St Michael and St Felix: given early in 12c to St Mary at York. Base of west tower has same arrangement of lancets and west door as Byland (on less splendid scale): northern influence unmistakable. On Michaelmas Day there was much offering of money and cheeses here to St Bay, 9c head of a Scottish monastery. Graceful wooden rood-screen unusually complete but coated with horrible graining and varnish. Ledger-slabs to Davy family.

RUSHBROOKE [8]. Great house burnt down during demolition, 1961, tied up with the history of sixteen generations of Jermyns (one of whom built the Jermyn Street area of Piccadilly in Charles II's time), and four of Davers's. Their memorials occupy much of the church, which has the most unusual character: red-brick crow-step gables (will refers to church building 1520), brilliant 16c glass by Thos Wright, the Bury glazier, and extraordinary

Rushbrooke church: the royal arms

re-arrangements by Robt Rushbrooke (1779–1845), who stripped the panelling from the Hall's east wing and would "spend half the night" in the church, fitting it up with these sham "Dec." stalls, arranged sideways like those of a college chapel and surmounted by a bogus painted organ. In place of rood, spectacular Henry VIII arms of painted wood capped by outsize crown, lately thought genuine and thus remarkable, now proves to be more of Col Rushbrooke's handiwork, remarkable in realm of counterfeit. By contrast, the early 16c woodwork of roofs is excellent, the dominant feature of the church. Col Rush-

brooke's wooden font and his monument are the first things you see on entering. Lord Rothschild's model estate (late 1950s) by Llewelyn Davies and Jn Weeks are *still* (1973) the only workmen's cottages built in Suffolk in a wholly contemporary manner; they fit organically into the existing village and its Tudor brick pump even though the colouring (grey slate roofs and whitewashed brick) is more Cumbernauld than East Anglian.

RUSHMERE ST ANDREW [22]. Almost a suburb of Ipswich, retains cricket-field and sense of being in country. Church Victorianised 1861 by E. C.

Hakewill. Tower 1521, modelled on Tuddenham's. Tactful large addition, 1967.

RUSHMERE [6], by Lowestoft, has green look appropriate to name, and rustic church with decaying thatched roof and round tower. Step-gabled brick Hall, *c.* 1600, unluckily whitewashed, retains original great newel staircase, square in plan.

SANTON DOWNHAM [2]. The deep-forest District Office of the Forestry Commission, approached through lime avenues from Brandon or Thetford. Office and Forest Trail centre very well designed, as are all shelters, seats and such notices as "Please take your litter home". Church, in pleasant churchyard, has 12c nave with fork-tailed lion over south door, 13c chancel (see dog-teeth in round-headed priest's doorway and single dog-tooth in tip of lancet window: very unusual) 15c west tower with inscription including names of Jn and Margt Reve, of the family who grappled with the sand-flood, when village overwhelmed, two centuries later. Peninsular War medallion head.

SAPISTON [9]. Church sited beautifully. Norman doorway and font, comic 17c font-cover and complete set of oil lamps. Hole in roof. Redundancy. At ford close by, river shady and pleasant for fishing. Edward Lambert, the original Porcupine Man, a classic figure in the history of genetics, born here 1716.

SAXHAM, GREAT [8]. Hall with fine portico has core leading up to an octagonal room with painted ceiling, designed sometime after 1779 by its owner, Hutchison Mure; the front and wings completed in 1797 by his successor, Thos Mills, from plan of Joseph Patience, junr. Mure abandoned two designs for the Hall by Robt Adam; but, for his earlier expensive embellishment of the grounds, he engaged Capability Brown, whose work is probably to be seen in the handsome "temple" and serpentine waterway. Thos Mills rebuilt the church, apart from doorways, porch and tower, 1798. In 1816 he introduced two windows full of painted glass from France and Switzerland, well worth a de-

tailed inspection. So are the tomb and bust of Jn Eldred, the Turkey merchant, who built Nutmeg Hall and sailed to Aleppo through an eight-day tempest raised by the three witches in *Macbeth*. Nutmeg Hall burnt down, 1779.

SAXHAM, LITTLE [8]. Hall, splendid, pulled down 1773. Distinguished church, the Norman round tower arcaded. Solicitor-Gen. Lucas's Tudor tomb altered to accommodate baroque Crofts monument, fine work of Abraham Storey: Madcap Crofts recumbent in full peer's robes, his wife on a lower plane.

SAXMUNDHAM [11]. A well-built unsophisticated small market-town, mainly on the Ipswich–Yarmouth thoroughfare: market, granted in 1272, occupied seven-acre site, 1311. Pleasant to walk the length of the High Street; the latest building, Post Office and Telephone Exchange (1954: archt T. F. Winterburn) adds to the pleasure. Notable traditional pub, the "Angel". In 1842–6 a company rebuilt Bell Inn (now a Trust House), erected Corn Exchange and Market Hall, with tall stucco arcade and arms of the Longs of Hurts Hall. Hurts Hall, unscreened to south of town, rebuilt 1890 "Jacobean" by architect T. W. Cotman: great dovecote nearby. Their monuments in the much-restored church include works by Nollekens, Westmacott and Thos Thurlow, whose own tombstone lies in churchyard. North aisle roof has 1820-ish character, dark-stained beams and plaster panels. South chancel aisle, 1308, has nine panels

of Flemish glass in pleasant Victorian settings.

SAXTEAD [11]. On the Green the post-mill is the best Mr Rex Wailes ever saw at work, and the subject of the opening section of his book, *The English Windmill*. Now preserved in beautiful order under Ancient Monuments Inspectorate and delights thousands of patient visitors. New suburban dwellings on the marvellous green, despite the threat of stocks and whipping-post in church porch.

SEMER [15]. Takes name from small lake or mere just south of church, which stands in green valley-bottom of the Brett. Mill already at Ash Street (Asce) in Domesday Book. Chancel rebuilt 1873, disastrous restoration 1899. Mural monument, and Georgian Moses and Aaron preserved in chancel. "Old Tiles" has inserted ceiling of moulded plaster-work.

SHADINGFIELD [6]. Undulating farmlands along the Beccles–Blythburgh turnpike, in the neighbourhood of Sotterly Hall. Pleasant pub and church (well-proportioned 1450-ish tower, Tudor brick porch and small 13c doorways) both stand beside main road.

SHELLAND [15]. Small parish with spell-binding long shadowy green, extensive moats and very pretty 18c Gothick church, dedicated to King Charles the Martyr, presumably by the Sulyards of Haughley, stout royalists. Georgian-Perpendicular east window dated 1767 and whole church presumably rebuilt then, though nave has more of an

1820-ish feeling, with grain-stained deal box-pews and triple-decker pulpit with original tassels. Barrel-organ at west end still in use. Whole interior coloured brightly. The font is beautiful 14c work. Fragments of old glass. Handsome marble monument. Pulpit occupies much of chancel. Cupola on west end of roof.

SHELLEY [21]. On steep west slope of Brett valley. 16c brick Hall, where the Tilneys lived and entertained the Queen; stands beside moat of predecessor. Altered and hard to interpret, but embodies panelled buttressed gateway reminiscent on small scale of Cressingham Priory, Norfolk. Tilney chapel in heavily-restored church is now the vestry, north of chancel. Between it and chancel, notable carved wooden panelling. Coloured effigy, Dame Margt Tilney, 1598, in nave.

SHIMPLING [14] lies in valley of Chad Brook. Excellent agricultural college occupies white-brick Georgian house, Chadacre Park, under patronage of Lord Iveagh. Church, approached through lime avenue, a splendid 14c structure drastically restored 1868 through misguided generosity of Helen Hallifax: tomb prominent in churchyard. 14c tracery of five windows contains fragments of worst glass in England. Surviving monument to wife of Jn Plampin of Chadacre, 1771: she instilled in her family "with fascinating persuasion, the precepts of reason and religion".

SHIPMEADOW [5]. Wangford Union Workhouse, 1765–7, dis-used in 1938, now a poultry-farm: turkeys roost on remaining single bedsteads, frame and "mattress" alike of cast iron. Apsidal chapel by G. E. Street, 1866, a hay-store. Extracts from diary of inmate 1837–50 are in print. Church has Tudor west tower and north porch; brick and flint, perfect texture, little interest.

SHOTLEY [22]. From Charity Farm, superb views over sloping fields and the Orwell estuary to Levington, and from HMS *Ganges*, more business-like views across the Stour to Harwich. Since teak-built training-ship *Ganges* stationed off Shotley Gate, 1899, thousands of boys, trained here for sea, climbed rigging of great masts that give blunt nose of peninsula the look of an old man-of-war. Church crouches topless-towered on spur. Black flint clerestory betrays handsome double hammerbeam roof, 1473, over tall light nave. Timber-panelled round chancel arch (on which Lord Bristol's arms usurp royal ones: living belonged to Herveys of Ickworth in 1745 as now) frames beautiful chancel of the age of George II: delicate plaster cherubs float in coved ceiling: fine altar rails and reredos with Commandments and gilded and painted Moses and Aaron: Venetian window above. Old sailors' view of Shotley less favourable:

Shotley church, without a steeple:
Drunken parson, wicked people.

SHOTTISHAM [23]. Church on rise above village has septaria in tower, a well-carved frieze of gargoyles etc round the top. Interior much restored *c.* 1867, but chancel well kept. Pleasant conceit in verse on brass to Rose Glover, on brick floor of nave. Weather-boarded water-mill. Miles of walks and rides through heath: "Brew House" means heath house in Norman French. Two burial mounds among oaks near Bussock woods.

SIBTON [11]. One of the park-like parishes in the valley of the Minsmere river, at junction of two Roman roads, a possible Sitomagus. Poys Street is a cluster of cottages with small 18c brick bridges crossing "the drain" to the road. Two small farms at Rotten End in 1086. Ruins of Sibton Abbey, the only Cistercian house in Suffolk, are close by in the woods: tall arcaded 12c masonry and a fine corbel of the frater arch. The lavatory in the south wall of the cloister remains. What is the medieval font from Darsham church doing here? Sibton House was built out of the ruins, 1610, by Jn Scrivener. Mr Levett Scrivener lives at "Sibton Abbey"—Victorian agent's house with a stone balustrade lately brought from· Henham. Sibton Park, a square late-Georgian house, very handsome from the road, is finished in Parker's cement. Dutch gables on Abbey Farm, and good pargeting on cottages at Hemps Green. Exterior of church unpromising, but good hammerbeam nave roof and most delightful series of monuments: Marianne Scrivener, died at Aix-la-Chapelle, 1781, "to be placed among the angels for whose society she was so early qualified", and her sister married Constable's patron, Bishop Fisher of Salisbury. The

Shotley

most handsome monument has busts of Sir Edmond Barker, Gent. Pentioner in ordinary to "King Charles ye 2nd", and his loving wife, 1676; perhaps the work of Abraham Storey.

SNAPE [17]. Account of uncovering in 1862 of a boat-grave set in the middle of a dense urnfield under the bracken of Church Common reads like one of M. R. James's ghost stories. A local leader was buried here in a 50-ft boat about the time of the great Sutton Hoo burial. Road from Snape church to Aldeburgh runs through the

middle of this cemetery and within a few yards of the boat-grave. Parish church at cross-roads has suitably farouche appearance, and texture of weathered flints patched with brick. Red pantiled roof. Two dragons hiss at one another in spandrels of 15c south doorway. 15c stone carver wrought notable corbels at base of wall-posts of nave roof, also grotesque stops to outside lintels of nave windows—well-lichened. "The Cloisters", an original Italianate house designed by the Edwardian painter Edwin Nicholl, beside blissful shore of estuary. Green Heys nearby designed by Lutyens. The people of Snape now cluster nearer the quay and Snape bridge; the romantic, narrow, red-brick, single-arch humpback of 1802 demolished 1959, first victim of Sizewell atomic power-station. North of the bridge, Abbey Farmhouse has lately been restored in absurdly Sunningdale style. But above that, a windmill, 1668 (the oldest dated mill in Suffolk), converted into a house, became Benjamin Britten's home 1937–9 and 1942–7, and so saw the writing of the operatic masterpiece *Peter Grimes*. Britten's move in '47 to Aldeburgh engendered the Aldeburgh Festival which, in turn, led to the creation within the admirable range of the Maltings (1859, 1885, 1952) beside bridge and quay (and former little railway terminus) of one of the finest, most satisfactory, concert-halls in Europe. The conversion, 1966–7, by Ove Arup Partners: executive architect Derek Sugden, whose special triumph is the acoustics. Destruction of concert-hall by fire, 1969, a

Snape Maltings, Henry Moore and the Alde

mere pause. All renewed 1970, and frequented; near the wind-rustled reeds of the river, a place of exultation, and exaltation, for the musical and for the expressive from all over the world.

SOHAM, EARL [10]. Long (Roman) village street, one-sided, the houses now with their backs to the reedy lake (*sae*) that provided fish for the Old English and medieval villagers: a succession of Georgian-fronted houses and cottages facing the increasingly lorry-ridden thoroughfare, a ditch-drain and sloping fields of allotments being busily tended on the other. The church is at the other end, with its 1450-ish tower standing beside the rectory, a Tudor house fronted by an eccentric trio of shallow Georgian windows, the roofs hung with Victorian bargeboards. Set back from the street, and with an impressive moat, Earl Soham Lodge gives the clue to the village's first name—a lodge of the earl who owned Framlingham. Church with double hammerbeam roof and Charles II arms has puzzling quatrain in flushwork on tower-buttresses. Memorials to Groome, Raven and Abbay families. Rookery has ribbon wall and early Georgian plaster ceiling: Street Farm along Brandeston road has 17c windows with original leaded lights.

SOHAM, MONK [10] shared Earl Soham's lake. Archdeacon Robt Hindes Groome succeeded his father as rector, 1845, and over next forty-four years built rectory-house and school, restored the church, erected the organ, re-hung the bells. Four yews by the church-yard gates were a present to him from Edward FitzGerald, the other subject of *Two Suffolk Friends*, one of the most nostalgic books about Victorian central Suffolk. Church, approached across meadow from north and a fine cornfield from south, has long 14c chancel with beautiful traceried window 14 ft wide. 15c nave with tall windows, hammerbeam roof and great iron-bound medieval chest.

SOMERLEYTON [inset]. Samuel Morton Peto, railway contractor in Buenos Aires, Algiers and Vitebsk as well as East Suffolk, transformer of Lowestoft, and M.P. for Norwich 1847–54, bought Somerleyton, 1844, and by 1851 had transformed it. Twenty-eight "cottage-residences of a highly ornamental character" arranged in a crescent on the "picturesque green" showing "rare attention to the comfort and morality of peasant families", a bizarre-looking school and attractive wooden Union Baptist chapel (Peto's own sect) prepare one for the beautifully timbered park and truly "noble and un-interrupted Domain of nearly 3,300 acres", now open to the public. Peto employed as architect (here and at Lowestoft) Jn Thomas, protégé of Sir Chas Barry and Prince Albert, the incredibly industrious sculptor of stone-work and statuary all over the Houses of Parliament. Here foundations and walls of charming Elizabethan Hall of Jerninghams were re-used: indeed a shapely old gable can be identified beside the east (main) entrance where two stags

exemplify Thomas's statuary. New building red brick and copious dressings of Caen and Aubigny stone. Three-storey stone porch in garden front is "Jacobean"; five-storey tower-smoke-room and observatory "Italian"; and stable-block clock-tower "Wren" or "Vanbrugh". Contemporaries called it Anglo-Italian. It is enough for us to call it very Victorian. Its most famous feature, a gigantic iron and glass winter garden, 126 × 36 ft, was alas pulled down in 1912. Its lofty dome was gas-lit: "a crystal palace with rich and fairy-like appearance". (Thomas's assistant, Hy Parsons, claimed he did most of the work.)

Peto had to sell, the Crossleys of Halifax bought. They became Lords Somerleyton in 1916. Two-storey dining hall, divided horizontally, provides ground floor library-sitting room. "Oak Parlour" beautifully panelled; delicate carved doorcases and overmantel of *c.* 1730 from previous house. Dining-room has pictures by Wright of Derby and Clarkson Stanfield. White, gold and crimson drawing-room (now ballroom) is now the most Victorian room. Staircase Hall, more woodwork from earlier house, and Kneller's portrait of Admiral Sir Thos Allin, one of its most remarkable owners. Outside, notice remains of winter-garden, statuary, and very satisfactory clipped yew maze. Gardens by W. A. Nesfield.

Apart from 15c tower, even the church rebuilt by Peto and Thomas, Cockney Perp., 1854. Chancel later restored to former Dec. proportions. Excellent contents: especially 15c screen, with sixteen very lively painted

panels (St John, for instance, with martyr's palm and poisoned chalice, and Mary Magdalen with ointment): marble bust of Admiral Allin skied: opposite busts, by Anthony Ellis of Parliamentarian Sir Jn and Lady Anne Wentworth, 1651, married fifty-two years, childless.

SOMERSHAM [16]. Steep small valley in Ipswich hinterland. Wooden pegs on roof plate in west end of church thought to have been put there for Maidens' garlands. Brash new settlement.

SOMERTON [14]. Hilly unremarkable farmland above Glem valley. Church contains monument to Montague Blundell, 1733, with good mantling and carving.

SOTHERTON [6]. Scattered farmsteads: Church Farm superbly pantiled, gleaming black. Church, rebuilt with old materials by Benjamin Ferrey, 1853. Very good medieval nave roof survives, and chancel roof retains 15c bosses. Medieval lock and handle on south door. Excellent Jacobean font-cover, 6 ft tall. Two valuable panels from rood-screen. Busts of first three Earls of Stradbroke on loan from Henham, especially fine one of the first Earl, 1811, by Nollekens. The second Earl, present Earl's grandfather, fought in Peninsular War and planted oaks that now form magnificent avenues.

SOTTERLY [6]. Hall, beautifully set in undulating park, is a brick house of *c.* 1744. Central pedimented façade with curved front staircase stands between projecting wings: it has been brought forward in this century to provide a vestibule. Quoins of brick. Plaster now removed. Church in park contains remarkable collection of brasses to Playters family, 1479–1688, and distinguished sculptured monument by Edward Marshall, 1658. Charming recent "temple" beyond lake. Whole village a model of careful maintenance and renewal.

SOUTHOLT [10]. Small village scattered round a green. Church with fragments of 15c glass in a nave window has lost west tower.

SOUTHWOLD [12]. A most distinguished little old borough on the clifftop above the North Sea. Its Georgian pantiled and brick or colour-washed fishermen's and tradesmen's dwellings, together with the equipment of a small Victorian bathing-place, fit it perfectly for its modern role as a residential resort for discriminating persons, though one no longer arrives by Southwold Railway (1879–1929). There is a main street and a few side streets that widen out on to delightful open greens. The wide views out from the town are among its chief excitements and the walks out over the marshes or through the bracken and heath. Gleaming white lighthouse put up on North Green, 1886/7: excellent brewery opposite. Superb 15c church rears its tower in rivalry with that at Walberswick in the middle of the southern view. Lastly, there is a faint but persuasive Dutch tang in the air. At first it may be just the light, or the massing of the town as one

approaches along the only causeway over Buss Creek. It is soon seen in specific buildings—the Dutch-gabled little Museum on Bartholomew Green, and the row of cottages along east side of Church Street where a gable at the north end has been spoilt with roughcast. This flavour owes something to the almost total destruction of the town by fire in 1659, when the Dutch influence was strong in East Anglia, and the community of our interests with them great, despite the most terrible sea-battle fought out there between the English fleet and the Dutch, 28 May 1672: the battle of Sole Bay. The grouping of the town into greens said to derive from an attempt to prevent a recurrence of the disastrous fire, but Gardner (*History of Dunwich*, 1754) shows them here before, and see Walberswick.

As early as Domesday Book, 25,000 herrings a year were contributed to St Edmund's abbey at Bury. Southwold was only a hamlet of Reydon, but a chapel was built c. 1202, when Jocelin of Brakelond was lord of the manor: the forerunner of St Edmund's church here, which became parochial only in 1751. Present church built at one go, 1430–60, porch added in 1480s. First churchyard, 1430, extended south and west 1458. "Hamlet" incorporated as borough 1505, to dispute with Dunwich on equal terms. Mouth of harbour wider then: known as Walberswick Gate, and like a smaller version of Shotley Gate, with Walberswick as peninsula, one estuary running north toward Buss Creek and Southwold, other running south toward Dun-

wich. Years 1560s and '70s very prosperous. In 1590 a cut had to be made through the shingle, the beginning of the struggle to keep the harbour-mouth open.

In 17c Southwold seemed to be in front line of European politics. When Defoe was here he found twenty-seven people attending the church, between 600 and 800 Dissenters. The six eighteen-pounders that grace Gun Hill are said to be a present from Duke of Cumberland, 1746, after Culloden. 1740 saw the beginning of attempt to get the British Fishery established here, with Pelham and Carteret busses arriving from Shetland. Substantial piers were built at harbour mouth, and Blyth Navigation Act passed. Busses sold up at the Old Swan, 1792. Private venture of Southwold Harbour Co., 1906, fared no better. Sea remains in control of that mouth: it is entered only by holiday craft.

Museum, founded 1932, has built up good local collection. Sailors' Reading Room on the cliff has own collection of relics and models (including that of the fine 49-ft beach yawl, *Bittern*, built 1890 for one of the dauntless sea-salvaging beach companies—one of the last of these famous vessels that had so much in common with the Viking ships and that at Sutton Hoo).

Church magnificent. Notice flushwork on buttresses, south porch and west front, lettered imperishably "S. Edmunde Ora Pro Nobis". Linenfold panelled south doors; lightness emphasised by clear glass windows that replaced war-damaged Victorian ones; loftiness of aisle arcades and clerestories with high-pitched ham-

merbeam roof running whole length of nave and choir; celure over chancel—east of the screens; screens themselves, running right across nave and aisles, tall, with much original colouring and gesso work. Look closely at painted figures in all these panels. Pevsner says "Their quality is poor," and south screen is poor indeed. But twelve apostles nothing if not rich, exuding the prosperous feel of contemporary clothes. As to Nine Orders of Angels on north screen, here in medieval paint is Paul's description of "all things visible and invisible", some clad in feathered costumes of Guild actors, all disfigured by Puritans. Jack o' the Clock dates from late 15c. Modern font-cover by F. E. Howard; east window (1954) by Sir Ninian Comper unsatisfactory; north window, engraved with St Edmund by John Hutton, very satisfactory.

SPEXHALL [5] Flat parish of scattered farms. South porch (hung with roses), restored 1733, date of east wall of chancel, pleasantly diapered in brick and flint (Barsham). Tower rebuilt, has yet to mellow. Brasses.

SPROUGHTON [22]. Large parish along Gipping at west edge of Ipswich. Stone Lodge, Strawberry Hill Gothick, stands uneasily at edge of new housing estate: Chantry, an early Georgian house, had been thrice "improved" by 1855. Now a convalescent home, its

◁ **Southwold** water-tower and common

Southwold lighthouse

park made public. Sproughton Hall, church and mill beside river crossing. Church has monuments and bad stained glass. Punning 17c slate tablet to J. Waite: "Behold I come: I waite". Large sugar-beet factory.

STANNINGFIELD [14]. Rookwood family built Coldham Hall, house with projecting wings and tall porch, 1575. Brick dove-house stands in the grounds. Very pretty thatched cottage beside church. Rookwood monuments, and Doom over chancel arch.

STANSFIELD [14]. On slopes of the Wickham brook. Farmhouse with early Tudor middle, just below "The Compasses" in Lower Street. Elm Hall, brick and timber, contains Tudor frescoes. Corrugated iron barn of Stansfield Hall retains medieval frame. Early Tudor roof of fine church has carved spandrels: cf. Cavendish. Chest. Georgian monuments to Kedington and Plume families. Purton Green Farmhouse, timber aisled hall, probably late thirteenth century, restored by Landmark Trust. Cordell Hall, nearby and equally remote, is a handsome 17c timber-framed house rapidly decaying.

STANSTEAD [14]. Church thoroughly restored 1878. Freehand carving of Wm Watkinson's headstone (1813) in churchyard shows view of churchyard.

STANTON [9]. Large parish on Bury–Yarmouth road with "Rose and Crown" looking like some delightful park lodge: oval thatched roof. Roman villa

excavated. Village should be approached by green lane known as Bury Lane. Two parish churches: All Saints, with fine 14c aisle, and good guide, at main corner in village, and St John's, a splendid 14c building with chancel of 1616, abandoned since great 1876 depression except for short time in 1906 when tower of All Saints collapsed. Grundle House's fine 15c timbers have been studied by Dr Oliver Rackham (*Vernacular Architecture*, Vol. 3, 1972): in this comfortable two-storey yeoman farmhouse, he reckons that $332\frac{1}{2}$ trees were used.

STERNFIELD [17]. The Glebe is a very pretty 18c house, visited from time to time by members of the royal family. Basic features of church 14c: after 1362, judging by De la Pole-Wingfield shield of arms on tower. Well-preserved reredos by Benjamin West.

STOKE ASH [10]. Elm predominates. Church mainly early 15c, with original west door.

STOKE-BY-CLARE [19]. Stoke College, now a private school with look of delightful Queen Anne house, incorporates parts of Norman Benedictine priory converted to college of seculars, 1415. Given its present shape and some good panelling by the most notoriously mean family in English history: Sir Hervey Elwes, who had the estate 1705–63, and his nephew and heir, Jn, who would mend the windows with brown paper, and died worth half a million pounds, 1789. Red Tudor dovecote with "portcullis" and other patterns in blue, stands beside entrance

from main road, resembling a gatehouse. Parish church of St Augustine lately accorded to St John on unwarranted assumption that it must have been the collegiate church. Very fine 15c pulpit only 28 in. diameter—inaccessibly narrow for some priests. Doom lately uncovered on east wall of north chapel, one of the latest known, probably from Mary's reign. Pleasant memorial window to Lord Loch (1942). With demise of railway and its inconvenient bridge, the village has regained its pleasant Green. Domesday farm at Boyton End. Marvellous view from Cain's Hill.

STOKE-BY-NAYLAND [21]. On the ridge rising up out of the Stour valley, at its highest point, is the church, the west tower about 120 ft high, surmounted by four stone pinnacles like erect ears, an irresistible landmark for miles around, as Constable found. The tower is of warm, nearly peach-coloured brick. And the detail of the west façade is splendid, with deeply recessed window-jambs, the doorway ornate and with arms of Tendring and Howard, which also appear on south porch and font. Main body of building presumably *c.* 1470. South doors carved with canopied niches that actually contain original figures. Above south porch (14c: oldest part of building) is remarkable 17c library. North porch early Tudor moulded brick. Inside, arcades beautiful, and one always remembers height and beauty of tower-arch seen from east end; especially if west doors are open on to summer evening. Font on stepped stone plinth is carved with figures of monks of

Prittlewell whose church this was. Notable brass effigies: anonymous lady, probably Lady Katherine Tendring in headdress of *c.* 1400, Sir Wm Tendring in armour and forked beard, 1408, Dame Katherine Howard with grand heraldic mantle, 1452, and Dorothy, wife of Sir Fras Mannock, 1632. Fine tombs with alabaster effigies: Lady Ann Windsor, 1615 (rather shattered), and Sir Fras Mannock, 1634. Alec Clifton-Taylor rightly regards the stained glass as an insult to the church.

Only a tree-framed "canal" and a distinguished fishing-lodge survive of the Howards' house Tendring Hall (which was by Soane, replacing a 15c house and one of 1736). Brick and timber boathouse, Bavarian Tudor, 1854.

Giffords Hall was the Mannock house, though named after their predecessors: it was in their family from 1428 to 1880s. Recusants, they held to their faith till end of 18c. Present house mainly work of beginning of Henry VIII's reign: a delightful irregular quad, with most notable features in common with some Cambridge colleges; a red-brick gatehouse on south side, with Dutch-looking panels and corbel-tables and Gothic pinnacles, all of moulded brick; and medieval bell and Georgian clock. House has two-storey hall with hammerbeam roof and carved spandrels. Ancient dovehouse in garden. All most beautifully cared for.

Thorington Hall, smaller house of beginning and end of

Stoke-by-Nayland: west front

17c, with six-shafted chimney-stack towering above roof, contains remarkable early fittings. Close by, Ox's farm is example of unaltered yeoman farmhouse. Thorington Street, like Hadleigh and Lavenham, had own company of actors *c*. 1480. *Leavenheath*, at west end of parish, has small church designed by G. R. French 1836, extended 1883.

STONHAM ASPALL [16]. Old scattered farms. Church, with chapel dedicated to St Lambert, has wooden belfry 1742, and splendid stone clerestory. Recumbent stone effigy in churchyard: Anthony Wingfield of Broughton Hall, 1714, by Fras Bird.

STONHAM, EARL [16]. At Forward Green, it is curiously hard to accept the two large suburban houses along with the old farmhouses round the Green. Deerbolts Hall is a late Georgian house. Church, with handsome tower and clerestory, is distinguished by its singularly beautiful hammerbeam roofs—probably the richest in the county: chancel, nave and transepts all one scheme. There were extensive frescoes. Tablet records loyalty of Thos Goodall, 1614–87, to "martyred sovereign King Charles I". Hourglasses measure sermons by the ¼-hour, ½-hour and the entire hour.

STONHAM PARVA [16]. Hall, now a farm, with tall pediment at once recognisable as old unrestored house of Cranes: echoes remain of their seat at Chilton, now a farm. Church adjoins, and cats and poultry frequent churchyard. Also

down in world, church has excellent flint panelling on tower but corrugated iron over double hammerbeam roof of nave, and much flintwork cemented over. Pleasant porch with oak roof: arms of Crane over traceried west door. Pierced heart and crucifixion surprisingly intact on font. Step-gables on nave and choir: Queen Anne gallery: slate memorial to Gilbert Mouse, 1622. Clock House, along deep-ditched road, has stack of chimney shafts, one a reproduction but others possibly as early as 1500–20 and Elizabethan plaster ceilings. Stonham "Magpie" has a sign across main Roman road to Norwich, and live magpie in cage. Prominent maltings at cross-roads, badly damaged by fire, 1973.

STOVEN [6] (pronounced Stuvv'n). Church rebuilt "Norman" in 1849, retained original fine Norman doorway. Remote farmsteads.

STOWLANGTOFT [9]. Handsome church stands on steep encamped site above village acquiring suburban elements. Spirited gargoyles: flintwork diced with stone. Finely ordered 13c doorway in north wall partly covered by stove-pipe. Nave complete with 15c carved benches: stalls in chancel have early 15c misericords. Whole distinguished rebuilding said to be by Robt Davey de Ashfield, buried in chancel 1401, "a servant to the Black Prince"—like Wingfield, here is another of Suffolk's gains from Hundred Years War. Height of church emphasised by that of windows, which contain panels of 16c Flemish glass and

remains of their original English glazing. Reredos composed of beautifully carved Flemish oak: three scenes of the Passion, the Deposition (very articulate), the Entombment, Resurrection, Ascension. In a niche is a ninth piece: a harrowing of Hell. Fine monument of Paul D'Ewes (died 1631) between two wives, eight children below led by Sir Simonds D'Ewes the eldest, who erected the monument 1624—the only known work of Jan Jansen of St-Martin-in-the-Fields. The D'Ewes house was demolished: present white-brick Victorian-Italian Hall on different site, by J. H. Hakewill, 1859.

STOWMARKET [15]. Small market and shopping centre for prosperous farming district: roads converge, and the A45 from Midlands till lately ran through the main street, which has been remorselessly robbed of character and suburbanised in the last decade. By-pass begun 1973. In 1793 the Gipping was made navigable to Stowmarket, and during the first half of the 19c the town more than doubled its buildings and inhabitants. Violet Hill, a south-west suburb, marks culmination of this Canal Age expansion and still has one long terrace to show for it. Down by Gipping river and railway station (best Elizabethan, by F. Barnes, 1849), old roofs with cones and pyramids of Maltings along Prentice Road need careful conservation. Canal Age Corn Exchange has been replaced, but busy Market Place still has predominantly late Regency character. The Tuscan front of Swain's ironmongery and the rather later fronts of the chemist's and the house over Stead and Simpson's are noticeable: also "The Limes" with well-designed shuttered façade at south end of main street.

Church stands in a delightful close to which four brothers had lately added a second church in 1086 "as the mother church could not hold whole parish." This explains present dedication to Mary as well as Peter and Paul. Its attractive light spire, 1712, replaces earlier more ambitious ones. Iron wigstand, 1675, graces sanctuary wall surviving very severe restorations. North of chancel, chapel has chamber over. Monument to Margt English (née Tyrell), 1604, shows her kneeling with sister-in-law, brother, nieces and nephews: monument to Wm and Dorothy Forth, 1641, alabaster and marble, finely gilded. There is an old portrait of Dr Thos Young, Milton's tutor. Canopied table-tomb. Interior too gloomy.

Back to Buttermarket, now pleasant footway only, and across Market Place to Crowe Street. At head of Crowe Street, *Abbots Hall*, a Queen Anne house amid tall trees, replaces grange from which abbots of St Osyth (Essex) supervised manor and market. Here 70 acres are assigned to *Abbots Hall the Museum of East Anglian Life*, where the collection of objects relating to the region— from farm-wagons and ploughs to laundry-equipment and craft tools—"amongst the best in the country". Open-air section already has magnificent timber-aisled farmhouse of 1340s (Edgar's Farmhouse), a Georgian smithy and (beside the Rattlesden river) a water-

mill with cart-lodge and mill-house all rescued from Tattingstone Reservoir, and all set to be in working order in 1975.

STOWUPLAND [15] sprung, like Old Newton, from Stowmarket. Stately Georgian white-brick Hall. Columbine Hall, now a farmhouse, is an ancient moated manor-house of beauty, standing straight out of the moat, its upper storey oversailing. Church with small spire built 1843: pulpit has Flemish panels carved with scenes from life of Christ, *c.* 1600. Suburbia.

STOW, WEST [8]. Rampart Field, just north of Lackford Bridge (where Icknield Way crosses Lark), now official "picnic site": 400 yards south-east, the County Archaeologist has uncovered traces of large and remarkably early Anglo-Saxon village, settled probably while Romano-British descendants of Iceni still living at Icklingham alongside. "Country Park" being created, and, in 1973, one of over sixty primitive Anglo-Saxon huts has been reconstructed exactly *in situ*. In south-*east* corner of parish, famous Hall is part of large building by Crofts family: remarkable red-brick gatehouse, with tall octagonal corner-turrets bearing arms of Henry VIII's sister Mary, Queen of France and Duchess of Suffolk. Her own house was at Westhorpe. The gatehouse is an essentially Gothic building of Henry VIII's reign, but running back from it is a classical brick colonnade, *c.* 1590. Famous fresco of about same date in upper room depicts four of seven ages of man. Northern exterior of over-

restored church reveals all four styles of medieval architecture. Opposite, Cornwallis Close, with absurd concrete kerb.

STRADBROKE [10]. A village at the heart of a rich cornland parish that had five outlying Greens (enclosed *c.* 1814, their names continue). In Kirby's day, Friday market had "long been disused", but a corn-market was revived in 19c, a Corn Hall built, and though some 200 paupers left for America in the 1830s, the parish reached its peak of 1,800 people in the 1850s, gradually declining to 800 since the depression. This is why Stradbroke's centre today wears a slightly shrunken, undistinguished, but not unprosperous, Victorian face. Victorian street-names, Queen's Head Street, etc. Post-mills, here and at Barley Green, derelict Hepwood Lodge Farm has a striking Strawberry Hill "Dec." porch, and the idea is repeated in pretty window-heads of twin thatched cottages, the Homestead, nearby. The Rookery Farm, Battlesea Green, has straight canal-like ditch 300 yards long. Church has good west tower with arms of Jn de la Pole on west door: his initials on north porch. Interior spoilt in 1871. One good window of Victorian glass. 15c font. School: Lindsay Morgan with county architect.

STRADISHALL [13]. South-east part of sloping parish now devoted to fruit farm, south-west to an aerodrome being converted, with hideous perimeters, into "maximum security" prison (1974). Church not notable. Nice old thatched cottages, one mistakenly stripped of plaster coat.

STRATFORD ST ANDREW [17]. At crossing of broad green Alde valley. Stud Farm has curved Dutch gables, so has cottage beside A12. Church has cream-washed exterior and bright new plate glazing. Fabians fore-gathered at rectory 1896, when indefatigable Webbs took it for a few weeks and Bernard Shaw first made his wife's acquaint-ance "seriously".

STRATFORD ST MARY [21]. Roman settlement Ad Ansam, where their "Pye Road" crosses into Suffolk: it probably forked here to Hadleigh and Bildeston. Village now basking in quiet, relaxed as fine new A12 by-pass takes heavy traffic past. Eliza-bethan yeoman house has painted panelling. "Weavers'" House in Stratford Street was covered with plaster dated 1758 but was meant to be exposed as it is. It now provides a good con-trast with the "Priest's House", exceedingly done up. Church given present harsh flint sur-face at restoration and rebuild-ing of 1876–9 by Hy Woodyer, the most prolific Victorian church-builder in Surrey! Strange porch-tracery (illustra-ting "Perpendicular Church Exteriors" in Pevsner's *Suffolk*) is Woodyer's invention. Origi-nal porch was dated 1499. Flintwork inscriptions survive, recording contributions of Mors family, also the whole alphabet, possibly a reminder of a prayer-ritual. 1530 inscribed on south aisle. Interesting bells and an old bassoon. Beautiful stream beside main road is dominated by ugly pumping-station for Southend waterworks.

STRATTON HALL [22]. Now mainly confined to the Hall Farm, wonderfully set beside the Orwell, with moorings. Name suggests site of Roman road. Site of church still revealed by ploughing.

STUSTON [4]. Flattish Norfolk-border parish with Diss golf-course on common. Church with round tower and octa-gonal top heavily restored 1878. Handsome marble monument, 1727: possibly East Anglian work. Wm Broome (1689–1745), who helped Pope with the Odyssey, occupied this living.

STUTTON [22]. Ridge facing south across Stour estuary pro-vides perfect site for four houses: Stutton Hall, essen-tially Elizabethan, with fine moulded ceilings and an odd little gateway like that at Erwarton; Crow Hall, also probably 16c, with an elaborate ceiling of Charles II's time, all transformed into a Gothick house in early 19c (pargeted cottages at gate); Dovehouse Piece, erected 1952; and Stut-ton House, once the rectory, red-brick *c.* 1750—late for Dutch gables. Behind Stutton House, approached in shade of ilexes, church has tower-porch with great 14c septaria base like Harkstead's. Original door and fragment of Norman carving. Monuments. Alton Hall, on slope of Tattingstone brook, is abandoned to reservoir, though a pleasant 18c (and older) house: excellent panelling and chimney-pieces will be rescued. This was Alsildeston in 1086, a large manor of the Bishop of Bayeux, with a mill whose suc-cessor, with contents and mill-

house, is being re-erected by the river at Abbot's Hall Museum, Stowmarket.

SUDBOURNE [18]. Heathland, parent parish of Orford, for long a famous sporting estate, and H.Q. of experimental 79th Armoured Division in World War II. Hall demolished 1951. It features unforgettably in Stanhope's *Conversations with Wellington* and Kenneth Clark's *Another Part of the Wood*. Church has pleasant west view with flèche above tower. Monument shows Sir Michael Stanhope, who "served at the feet of Queen Elizabeth". Church Farm hand-some with 17c gables. Valley Farm, very early settlement.

SUDBURY [20]. A very ancient borough and clothing and mar-ket town, starting on defensible high ground about St Gregory's in a loop of the Stour; strikingly like Bungay's natural stance in loop of Waveney. St Gregory's stands as a watch-tower as well as a familiar object of beauty. Its name suggests it was founded with the earliest Chris-tian churches in the region by St Felix: it was mentioned by name in Domesday Book. The present main centre, the market hill, has a distinct wedge-shaped outline, but its noblest object, St Peter's church, stand-ing straight up out of the street at one end, is reduced to the in-dignity of redundancy on an island of one-way traffic: much of the market-place is car-covered except on market days and individual façades of sur-rounding shopping premises are nondescript, with only the remains of good Georgian and Victorian fronts on top. Happily H. E. Kendall's splendid 1841 Corn Exchange converted by Jack Digby into Public Library. And start has been made on "Civic Trust" type of improvement. To get the sense of the town's old industrial character walk north along the Melford road or north-west toward St Gregory's to see terraces like Inkerman Row (itself unnecessarily and unforgivably condemned 1973), one of a number of good examples of nineteenth-century silk-weavers' houses with three-storey elevation including a large window to light the loom. Gainsborough's father's cloth business was not a success and he ended up as postmaster. The house now preserved as his birthplace with good gallery and collection was certainly tenanted that year, 1727, by his father, though the fine Georgian front was put on some years later. Statue of the painter on Market Hill, 1913.

Stour navigable to Sudbury by barges 1705–1913. In Sudbury Basin (by the gas-works, part of a group of Georgian buildings), members of the active River Stour Trust raised a sunken Stour barge in 1973 and are now restoring it: the type is immortalised in Constable's pictures.

The best walk to take is down Friars Street past All Saints to the Stour and the transpontine suburb of *Ballingdon*, where cross-piece of original H of the Elizabethan Hall lately transported bodily uphill. Dozens of buildings here reflect cloth-working activity, handy for water for fulling. One day Ballingdon Street may be as prosperous again as Friars Street. Up Stour Street notice "The Chantry": at the corner of Plough Lane and Stour Street, formerly the Castle Inn, and before that the Plough. Next door is an elaborately carved sill, on 15c merchant's house known as Salter's Hall. Ship and Star is a 16c inn. Christopher Lane quiet and walkable.

St Gregory's. Pleasant church-yard above Croft and river. Remarkable font-cover inside: almost as grand as Ufford's: telescopic for convenience. Much of this church rebuilt and north aisle added *c.* 1365. Stalls with carved arm-rests. Monuments, 18 and 19c.

St Peter's, a chapel of St Gregory's, established among houses encroached on market-place. Began to fulfil functions of parish church about time of Reformation: mainly late 15c fabric. Aisled and well-lit: reredos and décor of chancel by G. F. Bodley, 1898. Figures of Moses and Aaron by Robt Cardinall, *c.* 1730.

All Saints church, 15c fabric: very fine proportions: delight especially in splendid 15c wood-work of roofs, north and west doors, pulpit and screens. Rich Kempe glass in west window.

Red-brick R.C. church by Leonard Stokes, 1893, admirably set beside The Croft at St Gregory's. The depressing feature of Sudbury's current expansion from 7,000 to 16,000 is the quality of what has happened so far—the new huddle of shed-like factories out on Newton road, the new massed suburban dwellings at Cornard, the new barrack-like housing near Waldingfield Road roundabout and, perhaps worst of all, the expensive, Surrey or Middlesex middle-class suburb on Melford Road, solemnly called "Chaucer Estate". What do we think we are doing to Suffolk?

SUTTON [23]. Much of it heath, contains the highest land beside the Deben estuary and provides Haddon Hall (1914, "Jacobean" beautifully modernised) with about the best prospect in Suffolk. Doubtless for this reason Sutton was selected as necropolis of East Anglian ruling family in 7c. Discovery of great boat-grave in 1939 at *Sutton Hoo* is probably most momentous single revelation of the Dark Ages ever made. Of perhaps seventeen burials located, most still await scientific excavation. One of the barrows opened the previous year contained a boat and possibly other mounds were erected over boats.

Church tower collapsed 1642. In jamb of south-west chancel windows medieval craftsman outlined small mask while plaster was wet. Beautiful carved figures on font panels: Pevsner sees Burgundian influence. U.S. aerodrome known as RAF Woodbridge starts on Sutton Heath and spreads into Bromeswell and Eyke. But there are miles of heathland walks in Sutton.

SWEFFLING [11]. Good flush-work on church porch. Simple Norman doorway with caps. Commandments, Creed and Lord's Prayer painted on north wall in Anne's reign have lasted well.

SWILLAND [16]. Good corn-land. Mill buildings now studio. Church has had comic appearance since 1897 when, perhaps to mark the Diamond Jubilee, J. S. Corder of Ipswich designed a sort of Swiss cottage to be erected as belfry on top of lower stages of good early Tudor brick tower: in character it belongs to Thorpeness. Rest of building plastered and contains hammerbeam and arch-braced roof. Caroline pulpit and beautifully carved arms of Anne. Delicate stone-carving of west doorway and linenfold panelling of west door both need attention, 1973.

SYLEHAM [4] (pronounced like last part of asylum) in Waveney valley. Henry II encamped here July 1174 with 500 carpenters to prepare siege engines for reduction of Bungay castle. Church with round tower stands in marsh right beside the Waveney, accessible only by quarter-mile causeway. Saxon long-and-short stonework at north-west corner. South porch perhaps built by Alice de la Pole, duchess of Suffolk: it bears arms of her parents and husband. Font has crude Norman base, and cover 1667. Fine altar-rails. Mill houses small clothing factory established 1842. Syleham post-mill is still in working order. Syleham House, Manor Farm and Monks Hall attractive: Monks Hall with red-brick gable and room of late Stuart pine panelling.

TANNINGTON [11]. Hall has two good moulded Elizabethan ceilings. Green on which it stood has been enclosed since the antiquary Davy's gig got stuck in the mud. Braiseworth Hall, small modernised farmhouse with fine lawns and series of moats, is a progressive farm: nearly every hedge, ditch and tree in this flattish parish has been removed. Church dedicated to Ethelbert. Carved bench-ends. Celure over former rood deserves repair. Dades brasses.

TATTINGSTONE [22]. Scattered parish pivoted about a beautiful brook which is the parish's undoing: Hall, a farmhouse of mellow natural growth like the great trees that flank it: buff-coloured plaster and lichen roofs on four different ridge-levels: home of Beaumonts in 17c, who added tallest roof: all about to be sunk as valley becomes reservoir for Ipswich. Grander early 18c Tattingstone Place in fine park with brook widened to lake: Edward White its owner c. 1750 built folly known as Tattingstone Wonder: block of cottages disguised as church; both these will find themselves on the brink by 1975. Workhouse built 1765–6, now converted to St Mary's old folks' home, stands just north of church, with row of thatched half-timbered cottages alongside. Good group of modern cottages west of church, which is over-restored inside. West side of tower 15c with septaria. East side delightfully rebuilt in rich red brick, 1686, when nave re-roofed.

THEBERTON [12]. Romantic coastal village, with hamlet of East Bridge on brink of Minsmere Level. Thatched church, newly reeded (1973), has round tower (octagonal top) and wavy 12c corbel-table under eaves of chancel. Extent of Norman remains led Cottingham in his restoration to give Doughty chapel its lurid Victorian–Norman colouring. 15c pulpit spoilt by modern base and varnish.

Memorial of Germans brought down in Zeppelin, 1917. Hall, reduced, till lately lived in by a Doughty.

THELNETHAM [3] (second syllable pronounced "neeth"). South aisle of over-restored church has splendid 14c windows. (Edmund Gonville, founder of Cambridge college, rector here 1320.) Modern chancel roof of local sweet-chestnut. Remains of medieval preaching cross in slightly unkempt village.

THORINGTON [12]. Church looks across tributary of Blyth to Blackheath in Wenhaston; its low round Norman (or earlier) tower with tall round-headed arcade is crowned by step-gabled octagon in Tudor brick. West tower arch completely restored in rich "Norman". Chancel, largely restored, is a jumble. Monuments and hatchments of Bences from late seventeenth century. Nameless old farmhouse at corner, on Thorington Common, 600 yds west of church, has curiously painted pargeting, red crosses in blue-framed panels, the whole effect German or Swiss: newly painted but apparently based on earlier scheme.

THORNDON [10]. Heavy cornland. Shortt's, named after Tudor owners, half-timbered farmhouse with elaborate step-gable. Unspoilt primitive cottages south of church. Kerrison Approved School founded 1856, taken over by County. Church over-restored 1866. Fine view of village in winter from due east at Thorndon Hill. More delightful houses and cottages on road to Hestley

Timber-framed cottages, Church Lane, **Ufford**. Smooth plaster, decorated thatch and barge-boards

Green, whose perimeter yields archaeological evidence of others now gone.

THORNHAM MAGNA [10]. Whole neighbourhood admirably sylvan, the old houses and cottages in beautiful condition. Seat of Lord Henniker, to whom it descended from Killigrews, in whose time Charles II stayed here. Elizabethan house altered in 1830s by S. Smirke. Since last war reduced to one manageable wing and gutted by fire (1955). New house has agreeable simplicity of a pavilion. One turret of the Smirke

building survives. Church overrestored 1851. Monuments.

THORNHAM PARVA [10]. Church low with unfinished pre-Conquest tower (see splay of round window): early 14c attempt to complete tower on model of Harling Thorp (Norfolk) ended with the new walls fallen "dowen". Grand early 14c painted retable, apparently East Anglian work for a former priory. Discovered 1927 in Lord Henniker's stables having been bought with contents of Rookery Farm, Stradbroke, home of R.C. family. It lately bore sale-

mark on sticky label: *Second Day, lot 171*. There are nine panels. Centre-piece is a crucifixion with Peter and Paul; end panels contain representations of two black friars, Dominic and Peter Martyr. Georgian mahogany bow gallery.

THORPE MORIEUX [15] (pronounced Mroo). White fencing of Strutt-and-Parker farms. Potash Farm utterly idyllic, with old textures, beside pond. Church inexcusably undervalued in earlier edition of this *Guide*. Beautifully proportioned early Perpendicular tower and original carved oak west door. Carved south door, same date, set in fine (re-made) 13c doorway, all within wooden framed and traceried porch of *c.* 1400. The present uncluttered arrangement of pews to suit modern needs means that the architecture (chancel 13c, nave *c.* 1300, both with curious V-shaped buttresses) can be properly appreciated and read, like a good Victorian textbook on the subject. Handsome marbles in chancel to two Georgian rectors, John Fiske, father and son. Across the road, Old Rectory charmingly modified in, presumably, the Fiskes' day. Low signpost at corner incorporates (former) whipping-post.

THORPENESS.
See ALDRINGHAM.

THRANDESTON [10]. Little Green, very pleasant, has one good herringbone-brickwork house. At Great Green, classical stuccoed rectory with Regency Gothick windows. Church: 13c chancel and 14c nave both remodelled "Perp" to match grand new 15c tower—the most handsome feature of the whole building, with shield of arms and "Cornwaleys: Sulyard" set in unusually pretty flushwork. 15c font-cover and screen, choir stalls and a few simple bench-ends (including Peter and John). Two-storeyed vestry with medieval door. 15c glass. Brasses. Arms of V.R. Thos Lee French, rector sixty-four years, died in Mentone in 1909.

THURLOW, GREAT [13] (originally spelt Tritlaw, meaning famous tumulus or assembly-hill) lies in south-west corner of county. Church dull.

Little Thurlow: the Jacobean school

Hall Georgian, in beautiful grounds. From smock mill on ridge fourteen working windmills could be seen at once (some of them in Cambridgeshire).

THURLOW, LITTLE [13] has pleasant domestic architecture, a small Jacobean schoolbuilding and almshouse founded by Sir Stephen Soame (1544–1619). The "canal" in the park remains from his old house here, which was rebuilt 1847. He died here and in 1623 his executors built new aisle on to church, with arabesque work in one arch, to receive his monument, a splendid large affair with effigies, remarkable carving and long inscription. Other Soame memorials. Fine altar-rails. Voluted ace-of-spades bench-ends are modern copies of those at Clare. Norman font.

THURSTON [9]. The railway station, now offices, good Victorian design, owes part of its dignity to height of track above road: contemporary group of buildings on adjacent green blighted by proximity of seed merchant's buildings in cement blocks, corrugated iron and cheap bricks. Church all but demolished 1860 by fall of tower, at once rebuilt on old model, achieving remarkable "Perp" dignity (E. C. Hakewill). Compare Parker's description in 1855. Beautiful 14c font survives, foliage richly carved. Identifiable fragments of 15c glass.

THWAITE [10]. Hall now represented by two small cottages, forty yards apart, each with vast Elizabethan chimney-stack. Church has 15c pulpit. Locally pronounced Twait.

TIMWORTH [8]. Victorianised church disappointing at end of hopeful grass track.

TOSTOCK [9]. Old Hall, among water-meadows, fine over-sailing house, with timbered out-houses. Tostock Place late Georgian white brick, with 1904 additions and minute *cottage ornée* by A45. Church has survived numerous restorations well. Fine 14c font. 15c roof has very original carving, so have all the bench-ends, modern in front, medieval in rear. Beautiful oval tablet to J. G. Tuck, forty-six years rector, died 1933.

TRIMLEY [23]. Two extensive parishes of St Martin and St Mary have their churches in one churchyard beside the main Ipswich–Felixstowe road. The "villages" tend to line this "street", long the busiest route in Suffolk: saved by by-pass, 1973. The character of Trimley is not to be found along old main road, though it is seen from the train and from the new road. It is made up of several farm-settlements on a mixture

of heath and very fertile land stretching from the marshes along the Orwell estuary across to King's Fleet on the Deben. Of the present farmhouses, Grimston Hall has had the most notable career. It stands beside gully leading down to Orwell with 1830-ish brick north wing and south wing that may be Tudor. North chapel of Trimley St Martin church built as chantry by will of Roger Cavendish, 1405. Tower erected 1432, its brick top rebuilt 1949. Trimley St Mary's tower, now accompanied by beech-tree, was also put up *c.* 1430: top long uneven, refurbished 1960: west window and doorway with heraldic shields are well-preserved and beautiful. Arms of Cavendish in spandrels suggest their patronage here too: circumnavigator lived at Grimston. Avenue leads past Searson's Farm to Fagbury Cliff, as romantic a place as "Little Japan" on the Alde, but now adjoined by the hideous warehousing of Felixstowe Dock.

TROSTON [8]. Troston Hall is an Elizabethan house, much altered in 19c. Interesting church with 13c chancel. Behind the altar is the crude front of old rood-loft: a rare survival, apt in view of unpolished behaviour of that Foxite lord of the manor, Capel Lofft (1751–1824). Equally rare royal arms of James I. Suburbia: Capel Close crude beyond words.

TUDDENHAM ST MARTIN [16] (by Ipswich) has village street with 1867 National School, general stores, and cottages straggling out of deep valley of Finn. Finn Lane, "no through road", leads from Fountain Inn

at once into blissful country beyond Waspe's Farm. Steep little climb to church and its vicarage. Top stages of 1460 belfry are a nice mixture of brick and flint. Font 1443. Good bench-ends and roof, and late medieval pulpit: Kempe window, screen well-restored 1946. Hall, on far side of valley, 17c house with Dutch gables.

TUDDENHAM ST MARY [7] (by Mildenhall). Little flinty wayside village, with own horrible RAF station, has fine large 14c church with beautifully traceried windows and plain glass, but suffering from almost fatal attack of Victorian restoration.

TUNSTALL [17]. Edge of heath. West tower of church, its walling and panelling specified as model for Walberswick, is topped by 17c pointed ears. Light interior acquired much of its character—box-pews and gallery—in 1831, then lost a lot of it in 1958 clean-up. Gable Farm, opposite church, Tudor timber-work and brick. Hall has white-brick Regency front, bow-end, earlier back. Box chapel of Particular Baptists, 1805, with addition. *Dunningworth*, a parish down to 16c, is now hamlet of Tunstall. Horse fair till 1912, and hiring fair.

UBBESTON [11]. Hall, red-and-blue Georgian brickwork with silvery sparkle and strawberry-brick 17c barn. Church, unwanted by parish and threatened (1973) with conversion into house, stands possibly on Roman site and has particularly handsome brick tower with blue diaper-work. Thos Cowell, vicar, left 10 marks towards it in 1529. Parker recorded good Perp. stalls here, 1855. Norman south doorway and tall way, in which apse begins. Monument to Fras Legg (1591–1671).

UFFORD [17]. Uffa was founder of Sutton Hoo dynasty, and there are three fords here, also low-arched Georgian red-brick bridge over still stretch of Deben. At first sight, church "Perp", its tower upright like a sentry, beside whipping-post at bottom of lane. But it embodies, visibly, little nave of 11c parent, 32 × 24 ft, with walls of rust-coloured puddingstone. Arcade to south made for 12c chapel of St Leonard, then all extended west at time of 14c oak-and-iron south door, sheltered by porch dated by wills of 1465–75, the last main addition to the fabric.

Roofs, famous tapering font-cover, and seventeen benches deserve close study; defaced screen-painting not negligible, but six fair girl-saints identifiable only by inscriptions. Patches of medieval colour everywhere. M for Mary painted all over roofs. How *did* the carpenters stop these roofs from "doing splits"? Angel in chancel roof bears Willoughby arms, and a Willoughby was rector in 1425. Great finialled font-cover perhaps 1450: 18 ft tall, its equal in wood is not known. Brass effigy of one of Simon Brooke's three wives, 1483, supplies possible date of carved benches: her butterfly headdress rivalled on armrest at west end.

UGGESHALL [6]. Early Georgian red-brick old rectory. All the farmhouses delightful. Thatched church has only bottom stage of tower, capped by thatched belfry. Handsome medieval nave roof-timbers and brick-and-flint east wall of chancel.

WALBERSWICK [12] is approached from Blythburgh across fine empty heaths that were once sheepwalks, or from Southwold across the Blyth by rowing-boat. Fishing and ship-building brought the port great prosperity in the 15 and 16c. Since the 17c it has had all the attraction of a place with a past: two ungrazed little Greens, houses with old walls and chimneys, and a muddy creek that replaces Dunwich haven—the fair-way to a former city-port. The best of what remains is the emptiness, the distance to the horizon, over heath, marsh and sea. Beside the Blyth, old tarred huts of fishermen and painters. The place is truly described in the oils and watercolours of Wilson Steer, who loved it. One physical object of great distinction remains: the ruin of the church of St Andrew, with its proud tower that owes its survival to its utility as a seamark. The present steeple raised on model of Tunstall, with west door stipulated to be "as good as that at Halesworth". Architect: Richd Russell of Dunwich. Steeple finished 1450, with eight gilded vanes, and the whole building must then have looked much as it does today. Complete new building—tower, nave, chancel, two-storied sacristy, porch with parvise, and south aisle—hallowed in 1493: the creation of nearly seventy years. A north aisle was added soon after. Records suggest earlier church on edge of marsh, 600 yds south.

Decline began almost at once. As dependant of Blythburgh Priory, church lost its tithes at Dissolution. Great bell sold 1585. In 1644 Dowsing smashed forty windows, defaced eight tombstones which now floor central passage: a ninth serves as table. "Sacrilegious faction let whole fabric run to ruin," and resorted to meeting-house. Population dwindling: 156 churchgoers in 1634, seldom over forty in 1695, when nave, chancel and north aisle were unroofed, three more bells sold, proceeds to repair of south aisle. Since then, little change. Tower and tall ruined walls of east end splendid. South doors, pulpit, base of rood-screen and a few benches are all the fittings that survive from the 15c, with handsomely incised Tudor ledger-slabs.

WALDINGFIELD, GREAT [20]. A late-medieval clothing village, less industrialised than Little Waldingfield. Babergh Hall, 1840-ish Woolpit-brick, now faces an airfield. House facing church has three good Tudor chimneys and bargeboard carved with vine. Tall chimney-stack at White Hall. Church has splendid tower but outside mostly spoilt by old cement coat. Four devastating 19c restorations. Beautiful carved 17c rails from St Michael's, Cornhill, serve as low chancel screen and as fronts to choir-stalls. Fantastic jumble of mosaics round sanctuary result from fossicking holidays of the Misses Baily in Rome and Egypt, 1867–9.

WALDINGFIELD, LITTLE [21]. "Maltings" Farmhouse has attractive panelled stucco front.

"Priory" has medieval brick vaulted cellar: this manor belonged to Earl's Colne Priory. Headless figure on church tower: tall turret-stairs at east corners of nave. Inside the 15c brick-and-flint porch, the doorway is capped with crude crockets and finials. This curious decoration recurs elsewhere in the fabric. De Vere mullet inset in red-brick north porch: font shows monks from de Vere priory at Earl's Colne minding their book: will 1466 refers to font's "reparation" and to making new north and west doors: well carved. Brasses.

WALDRINGFIELD [23]. Small quay on a quiet and beautiful stretch of the Deben estuary looks over to Ham Woods: beside it the "Maybush" is known to amateur yachtsmen all over England for its cheerful atmosphere, the "locals" mixed up with the holiday-sailors. Tall Georgian brick house opposite. Church, some way off, has elegant cleverly designed diapered red-brick tower. Fine large font with Evangelists round bowl has woodwoses and 15c people round base.

WALPOLE [11]. Famous congregational chapel surviving from the decade of the Civil War was a dwelling-house, gutted and converted for the purpose, some half-a-mile from church, along Halesworth road. Focal pulpit, with sounding-board: scrubbed wooden seating and galleries. Very ancient wall of church above attractive small village contains Norman door-arch, unpleasing Victorian windows and porch, Victorian coconut-pyramid of a spire. Fine chimney-stacks at Old Hall Farm and the Elms House, which has splendid pargeting 1708. Good Dutch gables on Packway Farm and Poplar Farm buildings. Walnut Tree Farm was built for an Elizabethan yeoman.

WALSHAM-LE-WILLOWS [9]. Oblong farming parish all drained by stream which enlivens village centre; unusually varied attractive group of tradesmen's houses and cottages, all periods, watched by friendly face of 1844 classical Congregational church, red-brick with white-brick pilasters, Doric porch. Six Bells at cross-roads, and new "Georgian" house that rudely replaces Elizabethan open-air theatre: "a fayre round place of earth made of purpose for the use of Stage playes". Clerestoried church opposite, with flushwork porch dated 1541, very fine low-pitched roof. Screen with beginnings of vaulting. Alongside, "the Priory" serves as vicarage, as it did when church served by Austin canons from Ixworth: the name of the last of them, "Swr Richard Aldrich", carved in parlour. Elizabethan village minutely detailed in Field Book (Suffolk Records Society). Four Ashes Farmhouse medieval with good Jacobean stair. Cranmer Green Farmhouse: fine Jacobean chimney-stack. Allwood Green, till 1819 broad inter-common for four parishes. Posters Lane, green and delightful, took Walsham people to market at Thetford.

WALTON. See FELIXSTOWE.

WANGFORD [2] near Brandon. Suffolk Naturalists Trust leases Reserve of blown sand, Wangford Warren: these dunes still show wind-action that nearly smothered Santon Downham. Church (St Denis) in macabre wasteland beside enormous American airfield: 12c doorways, a few pretty headstones in churchyard.

WANGFORD [6]. Little thoroughfare village: nice Georgian fronts. Impressive church, much rebuilt in 1860s and '70s. North-east tower. Pulpit and reading-desk made up of rich 17c woodwork. Monuments. Small priory once stood south of church.

WANTISDEN [17]. Sandy parish with church remote on edge of howling U.S. airfield. West tower of local Coralline crag, finer workmanship than Chillesford's, though open now to sky: money for "reparation" 1449. Entering through Norman south doorway one is back in early 19c, before the age of drastic restoration: a melancholy experience, increased by desolation of churchyard where old Mr Gustave Goodwill, buried 1948, has almost the only intact gravestone. Chancel arch broad and Norman, with restrained chevron moulding, melts perfectly into east nave wall: openings each side as at Chillesford. 15c bench-ends made into early 19c benches. Norman font made up of small blocks of stone. Nave wall, flint exterior, lined with crag. Memorials: Mary Wingfield 1582, Robt Hervey of Ickworth 1633. Grey Georgian Creed, Lord's Prayer and Commandments hang high above chancel arch.

WASHBROOK [22] includes former Gt Belstead. Sloping farmland, silent, marvellously secluded so near Ipswich. Church, down beside the brook, has splendid mid-14c six-bay arcading either side of chancel: presumably designed as choirstalls: touched up and not well treated. Adjacent window tracery and other work of same period.

WATTISFIELD [9]. Attractive village of clustered creamwashed cottages. Hy Watson's Potteries have long line of predecessors: bed of fine clay under these fertile fields was being made into pots and bricks in the Middle Ages, and there were potteries on a big industrial scale during the Roman occupation. Site of village on rising ground enabled it to organise its defences during Civil War. Name of village inn, Royal Oak, suggests some royalist sympathy. Independent congregation established c. 1678, but present chapel built 1877. Terracotta arms of De la Pole almost defaced over south church porch. Interior drably Victorian. Post Office has pleasant Georgian shop-front. Wattisfield Hall probably built in 1590s, with fine chimneys outside main frame of house. Walnut Tree Cottage is a small medieval house into which chimney later inserted.

WATTISHAM [15]. Sloping fields, with aerodrome full of shrieking demons. "The Castle", a fruit-farm, has quadrangular arrangement of farmhouse and barns, castellated and with dummy Gothick tracery. Series of moats at Hall—remarkable even in High Suf-

folk. Church has 14c doorhandle.

WELNETHAM, GREAT [14]. Name means "*ham* frequented by swans": presumably at *Sicklesmere*, where cottages are approached over little bridges across the drain, and Hawstead Lane runs beside pastures of former large mere. On rising ground, church roughcast, with distinguished painted wooden belfry, 1749. Inside, white walls, alabaster and marble memorial, 1660. Old Rectory with charming late Georgian and recent improvements severely burnt and happily restored, 1974.

WELNETHAM, LITTLE [14]. Priory of Crutched Friars converted into romantic-looking house with red-brick step-gables and chimneys at Dissolution. Church also has step-gabled porch, good nave hammerbeam roof; window tracery; some carved benchends. Mysterious foundations east of chancel. Roman road.

WENHAM, GREAT [21]. Tudor farmhouse on Wenham Hill, a spur near main London road. Church has good tower and funeral armour. Adjacent well-grouped council housing. Half-timbering at Old Rectory and tall, thatched cottage nearby. This parish is eclipsed by

WENHAM, LITTLE [21]. Despite suburban sprawl of Capel, there is an unforgettably romantic (preferably evening) approach from Gipsy Row to the famous castellated Hall (unoccupied on lawn below modern house), the best preserved of the English 13c houses

and the earliest built in brick. The lower 5 ft of walls are of rubble and septaria: the rest, apart from stone buttresses and dressings, is of pink and pale yellow brick, pale yellow predominant. Bricks probably made on site. Extensive stretches of moats. Building c. 1270–80: plan L-shaped. Long side occupied by hall, short by chapel (dedicated to St Petronilla). Both are on first floor, above brick vaulted undercrofts. Chamber above chapel gives that wing extra height: turret-stair in corner of L goes higher still, and top commands extensive views over level neighbourhood. Walls crenellated. Brewse monuments in church, which has black-tinted flint texture: low tower has rich red-brick top. (Church saved from demolition in 19c by refusal of one man, Jn Keeble, to concur with wishes of parish meeting.) Medieval wooden porch with 17c balusters. Main body of church contemporary with Hall. Lower half of stone screen. 14c murals. 15c stone canopy with plaster coat-of-arms and headdress above. Coloured monument 1585. 16c red-brick and timber barn completes incomparable group with Hall and church.

WENHASTON [12]. Expanding village on high ground above Blyth river. Church has one great treasure. Rood-loft survived till 1811, but rood presumably destroyed at Reformation. However, the tympanum (boarded filling of chancel-arch) on which the Doom had been painted, as background to rood, was plastered and white-washed over, and black-lettered with text to accompany royal arms: "The powers that be are ordained of God." Thrown out into churchyard 1892, it was washed by miraculous fall of rain: to horror of sexton, Doom revealed! Now conveniently placed for seeing: Christ in Glory with sun, Mary and John intercede under moon, St Michael weighing good soul against bad deeds, Peter receiving into castellated heavenly mansion princes of church and state clad only in hats. Two handsome marbles in chancel: one, 1757, signed "P.L. *fecit*", Philippa Leman's own initials. Grange and Old Hall are delightful old houses. *Mells chapel*, a small neglected early Norman ruin.

WESTERFIELD. *See* IPSWICH.

WESTHALL [6]. In remote, secluded valley, graveyard with Victorian trees and thatched church of splendid surprises. Norman nave represented by present south aisle: its chancel was apsidal, and traces may be seen of its arch. At west end of this aisle, masked by tower of *c.* 1300, stands richly decorated Norman *façade principale*.

To this, north aisle added in 13c. Present fine chancel added in 14, and old one taken down (blocking light from south). Lovely reticulated windows. In 15c, walls of nave and aisle heightened, roofs fitted over, large Perp. windows inserted, seven sacrament font procured, retaining colour and even gessowork. Central boss in chancel roof movingly carved with figures of Trinity, patron of Westhall guild (binoculars needed). Four sections of screen remain, late Norfolk paintwork, with names of donors. Unusual

triple panel depicts *Transfiguration*. Hall entirely rebuilt 1872, *looks c.* 1690. Home of Edmund Bohun, 1645–99, "non-resisting Williamite", Chief Justice of Carolina, whose interesting diary published 1853.

WESTHORPE [9]. Hall a farmhouse, replacing old Hall pulled down 1764. One moat is still spanned by medieval three-arched bridge.

Church of beautifully unrestored appearance. Fabric is sounder than it looks. Apart from faded royal arms, 1765, interior might never have been touched since erection of superb monument to Maurice Barrow for which he left £500 in 1666. (Wm Barrow, 1613, has pleasant little monument north of altar, two wives in stiff hats.) You get inklings of the pleasures of the interior from uneven brick floor and original door and roof of the porch. Then down two steps on to the uneven brick and stone floor from which all monumental brasses have been stripped, and there you see it all: 14c nave, early 15c aisles (1419: two aisles of the church and the steeple to be "performed" at my cost and to make bells of said steeple: Elizabeth, wife of Sir Wm Elmham), the chancel lit through 14c window tracery, the soft lights falling on innumerable patches of colour in medieval floor-tiles, in the wooded screen of the south chapel and in a few green remains of damp.

WESTLETON [12]. Coastal heath and farmland. The Grange is a strikingly pretty white-brick house of *c.* 1810. Post-mill down 1962. Moor House has Elizabethan gables

and pink-washed bricks: several other nice buildings. At bottom of village green, delightfully shady duck-pond unluckily has White Horse car-park alongside. Brickwork of "Crown" is a mellow red, almost orange: Henry James called in for a glass of shandy in the course of a bike-ride in August 1897, and described its "polished passage" and "little dusky back parlour which held a windowful of the choked light of a small green garden". The church, opposite, is a large thatched barn of a building. A week's fair is held on the Green every summer, with races and other festivities. Well-established clematis nursery. Marvellous heathland walks and Nature Reserve leading to Minsmere bird sanctuary. Scotts Hall has tall Jacobean chimney-stack at edge of woods.

WESTLEY [8]. West of Bury, on steep slope of Linnet, has 1835 "Early-English" church by W. Ranger. A good contemporary verdict was: tower and spire "not inelegant; but the proportions and architectural details of the building altogether are objectionable, and patent cement is used in the place of stone". Some ruins of its predecessor survive.

WESTON [6]. Hall stands back from road, delightful step-gabled remnant of Rede family's Elizabethan house. Opposite stands their engaging "prospect" Cottage, also Elizabethan, with initials of Thos Rede, and moulded ceilings: lately modernised. Hall Farmhouse also step-gabled Tudor. Church Victorianised tunnel, with double squad of poppy-heads, well-carved (one with picture of post-mill). Seven-sacrament font. Quotations from Geneva Bible, 1560, painted up over medieval view of Christ's entry into Jerusalem. James II's royal arms. Two members of Clowes family held living 1870–1947.

WETHERDEN [9]. Central Suffolk farming parish: church beside a stream of the Gipping, amid limes said to have been planted in 1750 by Rev. Richd Ray. Fine east front and very handsome features inside, especially nave hammerbeam roof (faultily constructed for taking thrust). Small stone-vaulted chapel north of sanctuary. South aisle built by Sir Jn Sulyard, a Chief Justice in time of Richard III: c 1625 they built Haughley Park. Heraldry on front of south porch suggests aisle extended west and porch built by his widow, Anne Bourchier, who died 1520. Founder's tomb with an Elizabethan Sulyard crowded in on top is in two sorts of limestone, Purbeck and alabaster, with helmet and crest above: sculpture crude. Final words of inscription referring to the soul, defaced by Dowsing, together with nineteen superstitious brass inscriptions weighing 65 lb: he also claimed he broke 100 pictures (in glass) and ordered destruction of sixty more. Nice decapitated figures in chancel roof. Pews, monuments and hatchments.

WETHERINGSETT - CUM - BROCKFORD [10]. Heavy farmland with well-built church in tree-shaded village: one of the cottages built up over stream.

Brames Hall is farmhouse of 1590s: Shrubland House over three centuries farmhouse home of branch of Revett family, has frescoes of birds in one room. Church has noble arch leading into west side of tower, largely 15c clerestory, and a fine arcade, 13c, heightened in the 15c. An egregious Gothic organ stands at east end of south aisle. In the rectory next door Hakluyt collected the narrative for his *Principal Navigations of the English Nation*. In 1959, Anglia Television erected a mast here, 1,000 ft high. Brockford's boundary with Mickfield was made in the 10c.

WEYBREAD [5]. Church, with lovely tapering cylindrical tower, good flint wall, clerestory and timber roof, totally Victorianised (by R. M. Phipson). West wall covered by painting. Much colourful glass. Church seems packed with poppy-head benches and *art-nouveau* oil-lamp standards. Chancel occupied by huge organ. House opposite is pargeted. Glazed pantiles on cottage roofs. Instead Hall, Jacobean, has contemporary over-mantels.

WHATFIELD [15]. A Domesday holding, Barrard's Hall, moated, was refronted and remodelled 1704: retains Jacobean plaster ceiling in room over hall and has wonderful view over Brett valley to Kersey. Moated Old Rectory built in 1657 by rector Saml Backler (ejected 1662): has charm left it by the 18c rectors, Geo and Jn Clubbe, father and son: bay window either side of front door, each with small round-headed window in gable above: pleasant plaster ceilings.

Well-carved ceiling beams in Hill House and Church Farm. Clubbe monument in church refers to Jn (1703–73), "respected and beloved": he published *History and Antiquities of the Ancient Villa of Wheatfield* (1758), satire on contemporary antiquarianism, especially on Morant's *Colchester*. Register says Jn Clubbe made the gardens and canals in the pleasure garden: presumably out of the moats. Church, like Old Rectory, has pleasant plastered exterior, and is well looked after. Nave and tower c. 1300. Some sign that chancel c. 1300 too. Roof of chancel a very beautiful wagon vault, panelled with moulded ribs, flowers, lions, human faces: surely 14c woodwork, with Edward II, his queen and St Margaret of Antioch? Village and church feature delightfully in Simon Dewes' *A Suffolk Childhood* (1959).

WHEPSTEAD [14]. Fine rolling country. Church, only parish church dedicated to Petronilla, has large "Norman" chancel arch to replace a Georgian one that collapsed in 1926. Best glass in church, modern copy of Chartres work in west window, was presented by J. S. Austen, who carved the church door. Monument. Two of Cromwell's brothers-in-law lived at Plumpton Hall. Its external character (French of the English Regency) has been strengthened by modern brick additions and the creation of a courtyard in the same style. The great sweeping drive through the wooded park is as fine as anything of its kind in Suffolk. Doveden Hall (pronounced Duffin) is moated and with

Tudor chimneys. Manston Hall is an oversailing Tudor red-brick and half-timber farmhouse with fine chimneys. Pretty Baptist chapel, 1844, of white brick and flint with barley-sugar finials.

WHERSTEAD [22]. Park is area H.Q. of Eastern Electricity Board: a plain white-brick house with fine stone staircase, designed for Sir Robt Harland by Wyatville, 1792, his earliest known design. In 1819 the Harlands, living across the river, let Wherstead for the shooting to Lord Granville for £1,000 a year: here he entertained Huskisson, Canning, the Duke of York, Lieven, Greville and Wellington. Wonderful gossip survives. Edward FitzGerald's parents were tenants 1825–37: at sixteen he read the newly published *Redgauntlet* in a skiff on the fishpond below the church. Wm Scrope succeeded them: he wrote *Days and Nights of Salmon Fishing in the Tweed* (1843) here, and was driven away by the great work of railway-cutting, 1846, when the liberal old Sir Robt Harland came back here to die. H. Repton landscaped the park. Church tower of flint, septaria and brick, was long surmounted by black ball as leading mark up river. Vicarage designed 1880 by vicar and historian of Wherstead, F. Barham Zincke. Bourne Hall has fine Tudor brick and timber barn beside road.

WHITTON-CUM-THURLESTON. *See* IPSWICH.

WICKHAM MARKET [17] had market only in 14 and 15c centuries, but keeps name to distinguish it from two other Wickhams. Roman site nearby. Thoroughfare township on A12, though originally an early settlement beside the transverse Roman road from Coddenham. Potsford Gibbet was erected beside this old road, its decayed main post still standing. Wickham also had early part in administration of area round Alde and Deben belonging to Ely, but lost this, together with her market, to Woodbridge.

Main square, presumably owing its shape to the medieval market, is now a car-park and bus-stop: flanked by pleasant late Georgian white-brick façades, by the ancient White Hart Inn, and at the east end of north side by old manorial buildings with beautifully weathered roofs. Church with graceful octagonal tower and familiar landmark spire stands in a small close just off the square. From this high ground (*c.* 100 ft) the main Lowestoft road descends to the river, past the buildings of Victorian mill-wrights and engineers to mill and mill-race.

Church mainly building of *c.* 1299 with 15c north chapel and north aisle added in late 19c when the whole was drastically restored. Money for making of tower 1384. Beautiful spire rebuilt in 1790s: re-leaded 1968.

WICKHAM SKEITH [10] (pronounced Skeeth: Old Norse for a race-course). Heavy farmland. Church stands aloof from village, a regular 15c building, lit now by plain plate-glass. Base of tower unusually massive. Two large porches. As lately as 1825 they swam an old man here for witchcraft.

WICKHAMBROOK [14]. Adrian Bell country. Parish scattered about seven Greens and over comparatively hilly country. Giffords Hall, Clopton Hall, Wickham Street and the church lie in south-east corner: Aldersfield Hall is farther north, and Badmondisfield Hall stands in own park on north-west boundary. *Giffords Hall*, like that at Stoke-by-Nayland, derives name from 13c owner. Present large timber-framed house begun by a Higham *c.* 1485–90, including the single-storey hall with great chamber over, and present dining-room wing running at right-angles. Great chamber is one of the most splendid living-rooms in Suffolk. Jacobean staircase. *Badmondisfield Hall* was until lately "very much as it was when Sir Geo. Somerset took up residence in 1541", though upper stage of great panelled hall had been reconstructed in the 18c. Recent owner's ambition has been to restore it to its hypothetical condition in fourteenth century. Old men in 1591 remembered a chapel of St Edward standing within moat of Badmondisfield Hall, probably the church recorded here in 1086. *Aldersfield Hall* has a number of 17c features. *Clopton Hall*, once in possession of the Cloptons of Melford, seems to be an early Tudor house dismantled, shifted and rebuilt in 17c. Lofty spacious church, with 13c doorway within 14c porch. Chief contents, the brasses to Thos Burrough and two wives, 1597, and the Nicholas Stone monument to an Elizabethan soldier. Small, possibly Anglo-Saxon, stone figure with shield, lately uncovered outside south aisle.

WILBY [11]. Small brick cottage opposite church newly thatched with Eclipse wheat-straw by Mr G. Whatling of Wilby Green: "it should last 40 years". Some reader may be in a position to check in 1999. Manor House with beautiful old tiles and white plaster was home of Thos Green, whose interesting monument, 1730, is in the church. Oppste the Manor House is a willowed cow-pasture of the kind that typified this High Suffolk district from Defoe's day to Arthur Young's, giving way almost wholly to cornland in the 19c. Wilby is Old English for "ring of willows". Beautiful little church dates almost entirely from middle of 15c: full of ingeniously carved bench-ends. Three leading themes of the Wilby carvers were the sacraments, the acts of mercy and seven deadly sins. Some heads have been lopped off, some carving is modern. Flushwork clerestory. Remains of lovely 15c glass. Early 17c pulpit is elaborately carved. Tower "new" 1459.

WILLINGHAM [6]. A dozen flints remain of the church of this parish, their position marked by a young oak. Across the narrow valley stands the imperilled parish church of Ellough, a hamlet of Willingham in 1086.

WILLISHAM [15]. Sloping corn-fields and small towerless church, rebuilt c. 1878.

WINGFIELD [10]. Collegiate church, adjacent house, and nearby castle owe their richness first to Sir Jn Wingfield, Chief of the Black Prince's Council.

His executors, 1362, rebuilt the church "sumptuoso", and founded college of secular chaplains. College's original timbers still embedded in College Farm (behind handsome new front of c. 1700). Wingfield's only daughter married Michael de la Pole, licensed to build the castle on the edge of the Green, 1382, after Peasants' Revolt. His son Michael died at Harfleur with Henry V in 1415, and was commemorated with wife (wooden effigies) on magnificent tomb for which church extended eastwards about 1430 by son William, Duke of Suffolk, who spent £75 8s 4d on the extension, and brought thirty-eight tons of Lincolnshire stone for it. (Old east windows rebuilt in the extended aisles—presumably to preserve their glass.) William's elder brother killed plying battle-axe at Agincourt. Himself outsoldiered by Joan of Arc, 1429, became leading dove, married widow of old commander (she was Alice Chaucer, the poet's grand-daughter), and had son John, Duke of Suffolk, who shares tomb north of altar with wife Elizabeth of York, sister of Richard III and Edward IV.

Church best approached from south. 1362 window-tracery easier to admire than more mechanical Perp. of c. 1430, now lacking its glass pictures: carved heads of Jn and Eleanor Wingfield's contemporaries on the earlier window-hoods, and of themselves one each side of south doorway: he lies by himself north of chancel. Screens and stalls (candle-holders on stalls, 1911, by Comper). Medieval paint still in Trinity chapel, north of chancel, and original colour on Duke John's

tomb. His head rests on helmet matching funeral armour above the crest, a Saracen's head.

Castle now mostly Tudor timber-work, but 1384 south front complete and impressive: central gatehouse (with original door and carved wicket-gate) linked by walls to corner turrets. Beautifully gardened and furnished but not open to the public. The College, on the other hand, is shown to students of vernacular building by appointment (Mr and Mrs Ian Chance). Another house, of similar structure and antiquity, has come to light in the parish: White House.

WINSTON [16]. Church has early Tudor brick porch and a few carved bench-ends in chancel.

WISSETT [5] along stream of Blyth above Halesworth, with a number of interesting-looking farmhouses. Wissett Lodge, Elizabethan, with remains of patterned frescoes, glazed pantile roof and modern front, rented by Duncan Grant for fruit-farming with David Garnett during summer of Somme. What did Wissett make of their visitors? Lytton Strachey was one. Ashtree Farm looks charmingly unspoilt. Grange restored and converted out of three cottages by Seymour Lucas: king-post in hall roof "no later than 1450". Elizabethan alterations included parlour with shields bearing emblems of Passion, as on 15c south porch of church. Church has 11c round tower and Norman doorways, from time when it belonged to the twelve monks of Rumburgh priory. Font primed and painted 1491–2.

Shire Hall, **Woodbridge**

tall walls containing 13c lower windows and 15c clerestory, as though 15c aisle was planned but never built. Entrance through tower porch. Interior very pleasant with plastered walls and ceiling, brick floors and fine font set up opposite the entrance. Precepts freshly painted on walls. Interesting monuments to King family, early 19c.

WIXOE [19]. Above Stour valley. Church restored, reseated and tiled 1898, contains one pretty grey and white monument, 1751.

WOODBRIDGE [17]. The most attractive small town in Suffolk, contains hardly an ugly building, and more beautiful ones than will be particularised here. Approached by half-a-dozen roads, each delightful: best of all by rail from London, down the Finn valley to alight at the salt-water's edge of the Deben. One chief artery of the town leads from the station and the quayside (with its 16c houses and inns, its tall ancient newly weatherboarded tide-mill and sheds and beautiful old tiled roofs); the other artery, the old London–Yarmouth thoroughfare crosses, but is now led up to the ridge of the Market Hill. Overlook miserable "One Way Traffic" discs—our age's characteristic contribution to the scene: we have also contributed good paving and tree-planting on the market enclosure. The massive, aloof, grey flint steeple of St Mary's stands to the south, guarded by a plane-tree and beautiful wrought-iron gates, and

WISSINGTON, or WISTON. *See* Nayland.

WITHERSDALE. *See* MENDHAM.

WITHERSFIELD [13]. Very pleasant valley with good ancient farmhouses. Ditch, fifteen feet deep, forms parish boundary at Hanchet Hall, successor to Domesday freeman's farm, spelt Haningehet by the French. Handsome apricot-brick parsonage, *c.* 1720. Church has north aisle roof with carved bosses, excellent carved bench-ends in nave, but lost its character in the 1867 restoration, when south aisle erected and chancel rebuilt. Late 17c cherubs and flower-ornaments have been let into 15c screen, recently daubed red and green. Awful glass in east window.

WITNESHAM [16]. In steep little valley of Finn, north of Ipswich. Red House Farm has an old cider-press. Hall added-to 1845–6, in the Dutch manner. North wall of church looks odd with

crowned by a flushwork parapet. In the middle of Market Hill stands the red-brick Shire Hall, basically Elizabethan (where there are stone quoins and the bricks are dark) but given its elegant double staircases, tall hipped roof and Dutch gables curved almost to the degree of an oriental temple, presumably *c*. 1700. Examples all round of that familiar combination: 16c dwellings with Georgian shop and housefronts. Near northeast corner "E.F.G. 1860–73" marks house where FitzGerald lodged with Berry the gunsmith, whom he had reason to admonish as "Goose-berry". Across the corner is the plastered and painted Bull, where he put Tennyson up. Higher up on north side is entrance to Glovers' Yard, with 16c black and white cottages and view, the scene of former glove-making. Higher up, Angel Lane drops down to the right in the Tudor suburb along Bredfield Street, now distinguished by John Penn's Felbridge Court, 1966. Continuing north up Theatre Street, shell of Georgian theatre is now a school: opposite, good building rising in 1974 beside portals of yard bearing remarkable Tudor woodwork. Red row of cottages still labelled CORRECTION. Further along, Woodbridge Grammar School, red-brick 1862, has modern timber chapel in colonial style and good open grounds. Further on, two noble disused tower-mills (of former four) on left, and very well laid-out sub-

St Mary's, **Woodbridge**.
Geoffrey Pitman above wives and sons

urban housing on right (Fitz-Gerald Court, by A. D. Cooke, 1966). Further still, Farlingaye Hall, where FitzGerald was staying when he entertained Carlyle. New housing estate flanks by-pass.

Leaving Market Hill by Seckford Street we pass plastered half-timbered over-sailing fish-shop with medieval carved wooden heads in the original frame: contrasts beautifully with red Dutch-looking Shire Hall seen out of corner of eye. Opposite, serried fronts of houses that have lovely rear views over valley. Along on right is site of former cattle-market and then the fine red-brick range of Seckford alms-houses, which would do credit to a Cambridge college: based on designs of C. R. Cockerell by Jas Noble, 1835–40: lodge and gates by Noble, 1841–2.

New Street was new in the late Middle Ages. Its weigh-house or steelyard (a lever machine for weighing cart-loads) dates probably from middle 17c: last used 1880, tried out 1959. To north of New Street, signalled by stump of pale brick church tower of St John (1842), lies small 19c extension of Woodbridge, much of it now demolished and rebuilding, along south facing slope of narrow gully. St John's, designed by J. M. Clark, built by Alfred Lockwood, whose father built an adjacent white, stuccoed, crenellated "Castle". He employed plasterer and modeller Jas Pulham, whose early models, masks and comic faces look down in medieval tradition from so many early 19c Woodbridge housefronts. Running at right-angles to bottom of New Street and Church

Street is the Thoroughfare, known beyond the Crown as Cumberland Street, and containing fine houses. Despite density of modern traffic and narrowness of this delightful thoroughfare, there are fewer pleasanter places to go shopping for everyday provisions. Old cobbled streets (for pedestrians) run down to quay. Down to railway age, almost to our own time, Woodbridge had maritime, seaport character, which can only be recaptured by looking closely at the old quayside buildings and soaking oneself in Edward FitzGerald's letters and George Arnott's *Suffolk Estuary*. Best view of Woodbridge is from river, next best from top of St Mary's steeple (108 ft above its hill) where you see down the twisting channel to Waldringfield and—straight down below—the pattern of the town's old red roofs, so many of them high-pitched in 17 and early 18c. Great tower, fine north porch and whole fabric were built in the middle years of 15c. Only north chancel aisle is of another period, built by Thos Seckford, 1587. Seven-sacrament font, and remains of rood-screen are contemporary with main fabric: there is a notable three-storied monument, 1627. *Kyson Hill*, four acres of National Trust parkland overlooking the Deben, takes name from Kingston, ancient manor of East Anglian kings who were buried just across river. Kingston Farm is a tall Georgian red-brick farmhouse: once remote, now surrounded by modern housing and school.

WOOLPIT [9]. Village of several late medieval and Tudor buildings at junction of former

south–north Roman road with A45, main east–west Stowmarket–Bury road, which now mercifully by-passes the village. Woolpit had important annual cattle-fair down to the 19c, and a famous manufactory of white bricks from at least the 17c: the kilns and sheds now derelict. Most of Woolpit's own buildings are half-timbered or else of old *red* brick: the yard of the Swan provides fine view of old roofs and chimneys. Cottage opposite has Elizabethan frescoes. Noble church. Stone porch (1439–51) has parapet-coronet of pierced tracery and a chequered flushwork east wall: five images were willed to be placed in those five elegant front niches in 1473. (Anything over to be spent glazing the windows.) Tower and Nene valley spire rebuilt 1853 to replace traditional 15c Suffolk tower and 42 ft pinnacle of 1708: the text-book hand of R. M. Phipson, diocesan architect, is revealed in the 1853 work, as at Tower church, Ipswich. Interior drab yet compensates for tower: there are Caroline chancel-gates, monuments and famous roof, canopy of honour, rood-screen and benches with traceried ends. To these "stolys", Jn Aubry left 40s in 1494. There was a bequest to the making of the north aisle in 1500, to lengthening it in 1501. Dowsing destroyed windows. A well-known image of Mary stood in separate chapel, presumably in S. churchyard: "Lady's Well" was long reputed good for bad eyes.

WOOLVERSTONE [22]. Orwell estuary. Hall has view out along its wooded slopes. Now part of a G.L.C. boarding-school, with

Woodbridge: the restored tide-mill ▷

distinctly modern additions, 1959. Main building designed by Jn Johnson and built of Woolpit-brick, 1776–7. Best room, central drawing-room, with double bows and fireplace with Egyptian *motifs*. Front hall has medallions by Rossi: landing-ceiling coved like half an egg. Ceilings variously designed and delicately coloured. "Cat House" down at water's edge is very pretty Georgian Gothick cottage associated with smuggling and baptism. Church in park, largely rebuilt by Gilbert Scott, 1862. Woolverstone House is by Lutyens. Home Farm is an example of first-class early Victorian "Tudor" brickwork.

WORDWELL [8]. Light land parish: stream wells up near church and runs *under* the Lark. Small church: very interesting Norman features, a few medieval benches and a monument to Booty Harvey, a farmer's son, who went to sea at ten, rose to be captain under Jervis, and distinguished himself off Dieppe, 1812.

WORLINGHAM [6]. Waveney valley. Hall, one of the most beautiful houses of manageable size in Suffolk, remodelled *c.* 1800 from designs of Fras Sandys: "grand octagon hall", colonnades, and square pavilion on west side for picture-gallery (now squash-court). Ravishing double staircase in hall. Library with curved walls and partly coved ceiling. Handsome ceilings and fireplaces. Castle Farm, flint and brick, Georgian "Norman" folly on Beccles boundary, till lately neglected in hideously sprawling suburb. Church largely Victorian rebuilding contains the

Timber-framing revealed at Southolt Green, near **Worlingworth**

earliest known monument by Chantrey, sculpted with weeping old gent, Robt Sparrow, builder of Hall and folly.

WORLINGTON [7], at junction of breck and fen, boasts Royal Worlington and Newmarket Golf Course. One or two pleasant Georgian houses. Church, mainly 14c, has west doorway beautifully recessed. Fine open nave has simple steep-pitched roof, now protected by red and yellow Cambridgeshire tiles.

WORLINGWORTH [10]. In ownership of Bury abbey all through Middle Ages, church

differs in scale and dating from its more secular neighbours. Chancel *c.* 1300 ("E.E." at moment of becoming "Dec", see change in south windows). Nave, tower and flushwork porch 15c, on very grand scale: notice fine detail on porch, including the desirable sun. Nave 100 ft long, 45 ft high, no less than 30 ft wide, tremendous span for the double hammer-beam roof (no simple tie-beams could have made it). Sublime conception of roof best seen from chancel, also that of soaring font-cover, *surely* designed to go with roof? Inscription on font for Nicholas Moor's soul.

Surviving lights of medieval glass lately restored. Screen needs ridding of chocolate paint. Caroline pews. Graceful sounding-board over pulpit: collecting shoe and poor-box. Fire engine of 1760, supplied with water from rector's great moat. Five of the six bells cast 1804: fund-raiser Jn Jessop's headstone, south of chancel, refers. Extraordinary picture in tower records Worlingworth's celebration of George III's jubilee, 1810. Brasses. Monuments include Duchess of Chandos's by Jn Bacon, jun., 1817. Oak Farm's 17c woodwork under eaves sheltered by Victorian bargeboards. Reed thatch said once to have lasted seventy years in good order on this roof.

WORTHAM [10]. Large parish beside upper Waveney: formerly in two medieties, Eastgate and Southmore, it is now roughly grouped into five main settlements, one of them well named Long Green. Oldest parts of Manor House near river go back to 1480 when Betts family first lived at Wortham: it was their home from 1480 to 1905, small gentry and squarsons, protestant in 16c, and staunchly Tory from late 17c onwards. The fabric remains intact, plan basically early-Tudor, fenestration Georgian on all three floors—the home of the East Anglian writer Doreen Wallace. The Dick Inn celebrates the fall of Tumble-down Dick, Oliver Cromwell's son. A plaque commemorates the tithe war—seizure of pigs and cattle to value of £702 in 1934. Church has great ruined round tower, 29 ft across. Good 14c font, and fine royal arms of

Charles I. North aisle built 1731. Much restored. 1893 bench-ends well carved. Rev. Richd Cobbold, rector fifty years, 1827–77, wrote verses for many headstones in churchyard, as well as parish history and *Margaret Catchpole*.

WRATTING, GREAT [13]. Village strung out across shallow Stour valley near its source. Several cottages substantially built for successful founder of W. H. Smith and Sons, who also paid for disastrous restoration of church, 1887. Only 13c sedilia interesting in this melancholy fabric.

WRATTING, LITTLE [13]. Small church here has oak-framed bell-turret, essentially an "Essex" feature. Fine situation on brow of low hill. Nave thought to be late Anglo-Saxon, from structure of doorways. Baffling inscription on lintel. Early ironwork. Jacobean chimney-stack at Wash Farm. Large Sainsbury factory at cross-roads. Firm's founder lived at Broadlands.

WRENTHAM [6]. A large thoroughfare village on A12, with inn, petrol pumps and usual accessories. Several pantiled roofs, the local glossy blue-black. Along Southwold road on seaward side, lodge of Wrentham House embodies Palladian doorcase in façade. Heart of ancient parish, Church Street, lies west of A12, past tall red-brick congregational chapel, built in 1778. The Brewsters, who built Wrentham Hall *c*. 1550 (demolished 1810), made this one of the most influential English centres of Puritanism. It began in parish

church with ministry of Richd Mowse, 1597. Old Meeting House Farm is site of chapel of 1710. Church has impressive west tower, with flushwork decorations and a command of countryside and coast: used as signal tower, 1804. Lancet windows: 13c chancel. Notice timber construction of inner piers of south aisle wall. Brass effigies include Humphrye Brewster, armoured, 1593. Dowsing left them alone, though he smashed windows. Pleasant surviving glass-fragments depict St Nicholas.

WYVERSTONE [9]. Scattered farming parish. Church more interesting than at first appears. Good 15c nave roof. Remains of 15c glass in north nave windows include touching fragment showing Magi, piping shepherd, and old man seated with stick. This subject also occurs on remarkable base of rood-screen, which, with Gislingham, has its subjects carved, not merely painted. Disastrous overcoat of chocolate paint being gradually removed, 1974.

YAXLEY [10] (means cuckoo-clearing). Anglo-Saxon kink in Roman road about to be by-passed. Hall, fine middle-Tudor building, given Gothick front 1772, slimmed, restored, 1963. Church retains some of the richest features of any in Suffolk, despite barbarous restoration of 1868. Stands beside main Norwich road. North porch is of a most superior 15c design, with a pair of windows to the chamber over. 1635 pulpit, declared "the best in Suffolk", is certainly the most elaborately carved, even after Victorian dismantling and

Wortham round tower, the biggest of its kind. Entrance at ▷ first floor level emphasises their original defensive purpose.

amputation of legs. Central opening of screen gives some idea of original splendour. Mary Magdalen's is the richest surviving panel: in dark green robe, pink hat and skirt, she stands on a tiled floor with ornate casket in one hand, the lid in the other, every inch the wealthy lady of a Flemish burgher. Rood itself was replaced by Elizabethan commandments and royal arms. One aisle window has good Victorian glass. East window has all the surviving medieval glass—a glittering patchwork-quilt, and enough at least to suggest the original scheme of glazing. Hour-glass has survived, and "sexton's wheel" for determining fast-days.

YOXFORD [11] deserves its local name: "the garden of Suffolk". Surrounded by the parkland of three country-houses—Cockfield Hall, Grove Park, Rookery Park—it was lucky in building its village street along minor Roman road and stream of the Minsmere "drain" instead of the roadside of A12, which passes it by. Unluckily lorry drivers have learnt merits of even minor Roman roads. The very long Street has a wholly charming appearance, with colour-washed cottages, Trafalgar-balconies, bow-windows, a Victorian lodge of Cockfield Hall. At west end, it begins with Beech House, plain late 18c brick villa, a very attractive old cottage, and 1856 Primitive Methodist chapel, with specially nice glazing. Wisbech's keeps name of owner in 1562. Grove Park and Rookery Park are pleasant Georgian houses. Cockfield Hall is one of the most interesting houses in Suffolk. During Henry VIII's reign, a beautifully designed red-brick step-gabled gatehouse, with moulded brick chimneys, was built by Sir Arthur Hopton. He probably also built the north wing, with its three step-gables and moulded brick dripstones, and the splendid red two-storey stables and coach-house in the same manner along one side of the courtyard. The north wing is the only part of the living-quarters remaining from time when Lady Jane Grey's sister Katherine was kept here at Queen Elizabeth's orders. The estate was bought in 1597 by Robt Brooke of Aspall, alderman of London, whose son Sir Robt rebuilt the central block c. 1613, which then had only two storeys, and dormer windows in roof. His daughter Martha married a Blois of Grundisburgh, with which family the house remains. Jacobean part altered in 1650s, 1840s, and in 1896, when the spectacular "Stuart" great hall was designed by Ipswich architect, E. F. Bishopp. Back part rebuilt and modernised since fall of bomb, 1941. Church signalled by tall, slender lead-covered spire. The many delights inside are much impaired by reredos and pews and other dreary wooden furnishings, New Zealand pine 1868, oak 1922. Monuments.

INDEX

Charles II, *see* Barking, Brundish, Cretingham, Hopton, Ipswich, Lakenheath, Livermere, Newmarket, Rendham, Sibton, Soham, Thornham
Chateaubriand, vicomte de, *see* Bungay
Chesterton, M., *see* Homersfield
Chillesford, *see* p. 29
Christmas, G., *see* Chilton, Hawstead
Christmas, J. & M., *see* Ampton, Denham
Clark, J. M., *see* Ipswich, Woodbridge
Clark, Kenneth, *see* Sudbourne
Clarke, Joseph, *see* Ipswich
Clarkson, Thomas, *see* Playford
Clay & Son, Printers, *see* Bungay
Claydon, *see* p. 35
Clemence, J. L., *see* Lowestoft
Clench family, *see* Bealings
Clevely, John, *see* Ipswich
Clifton-Taylor, Alec, *see* Stoke-by-Nayland
Clowes, William, Printers, *see* Beccles
Clowes family, *see* Weston
Clubbe family, *see* Whatfield
Coade, *see* Ickworth
Cobbold, Rev. Richard, *see* Wortham
Cockerell, C. R., *see* Woodbridge
Coddenham, *see* p. 32
Coke family, *see* Bramfield
Colvin family, *see* Bealings
Comper, Sir Ninian, *see* Eye, Ipswich, Lound, Southwold, Ufford, Wingfield
Congregationalism, *see* p. 17
Conrad, Joseph, *see* Lowestoft
Constable, John, *see* pp. 17, 22, Bergholt, Brantham, Ipswich, Layham, Nayland, Sibton, Stoke-by-Nayland
Cooke, A. D., *see* Woodbridge
Copinger family, *see* Buxhall, Lavenham
Coppyng, R., *see* Brockley
Corbet family, *see* Assington
Corder, J. S., *see* Swilland
Cornard, *see* p. 22, 32
Cornwallis family, *see* Brome, Oakley, Thrandeston
Cotman, J. S., *see* Barsham, Bungay, Covehithe, Ixworth Thorpe
Cotman, T. W., *see* Felixstowe, Saxmundham
Cottingham, L. N., *see* Market Weston, Theberton
Cowlinge, *see* p. 35
Crabbe, George, *see* p. 22, Aldeburgh, Bredfield, Clopton, Glemham, Marlesford, Orford, Parham
crag, *see* p. 29
Crane family, *see* Chilton, Stonham Parva
crinkle crankles, *see* ribbon walls
Crisp, Thomas, *see* Butley
Crossley family, *see* Somerleyton
Cullum, Sir John, *see* Hawstead
Cundy, James, *see* Marlesford
Cure, Cornelius, *see* Melford

Cure, William, II, *see* Framlingham

Dades family, *see* Tannington
Davers family, *see* Rushbrooke
Davey, Robert, de Ashfield, *see* Stowlangtoft
Davis, Rev. G., *see* Kelsale
Davy, D. E., *see* Tannington
Davy family, *see* Rumburgh
Davy, Henry, *see* Athelington
Day, Cachemaille, *see* Ipswich
Day, Daniel, *see* Mendlesham
Daye, John, *see* Bradley
Defoe, Daniel, *see* Southwold
de la Pole family, *see* Fressingfield, Sternfield, Stradbroke, Syleham, Wattisfield, Wingfield
Denmark, *see* Boxted
D'Ewes family, *see* Milden, Stowlangtoft
Dewes, Simon (John Muriel), *see* Whatfield
Digby, Jack, *see* Sudbury
Donne, Jn, *see* Hawstead
Doughty, Charles, *see* p. 22
Doughty family, *see* Theberton
Dowsing, William, iconoclast, *see* Barking, Bildeston, Bramford, Clare, Laxfield, Wetherden, Woolpit, Wrentham
Dowson, Philip, *see* Eleigh
Drake, Francis, *see* Dalham
Drapers' Company, *see* Bungay
Drury, Rev. G., *see* Claydon
Drury family, *see* Hawstead, Rougham
Drinkstone, *see* 35
Duke family, *see* Benhall
Dunwich, *see* 35
Dutchness, *see* pp. 35, 37, Aldeburgh, Ashby, Badwell Ash, Barsham, Baylham, Beccles, Bedingfield, Belstead, Blythburgh, Bradfield Combust, Bredfield, Claydon, Cookley, Eleigh, Gedgrave, Hengrave, Herringfleet, Holton St Peter, Ipswich (and Westerfield), Leiston, Mendham, Mettingham, Norton, Polstead, Reydon, Rickinghall, Ringsfield, Rushmere, Southwold, Stowlangtoft, Stratford St Andrew, Stutton, Sudbourne, Walpole, Weston, Witnesham, Woodbridge, Yoxford

Eastawe, Jn, *see* Hengrave
Eden, F. C., *see* Barsham, Capel St Mary, Clare
Edmund, king and martyr, *see* Bures, Bury, Hoxne
Eldred, Thomas, *see* Ipswich
Eldred, John, *see* Saxham
Eley, C. C., *see* Bergholt
Elizabeth I, *see* Bures, Ipswich, Hengrave, Melford, Shelley, Sudbourne
Ellis, Anthony, *see* Somerleyton
Elmham, Elizabeth, *see* Westhorpe
Erith, Raymond, *see* Felixstowe, Friston

190

White, Gilbert, *see* Hawstead
White, John, *see* Hacheston
Whitefield, G., *see* Bildeston
Whittingham, A. B., *see* Bury St Edmunds
Wightman, Robert, *see* Dennington
Wilby, *see* p. 37
Wilbye, John, *see* Hengrave
Wilkins, William, *see* Bury St Edmunds
Willis, Faber & Dumas, *see* Ipswich
Willoughby family, *see* Parham, Ufford
Wilson, W. G., *see* Aldringham
Wimar the Chaplain, *see* Orford
Wimbish, Richard of, *see* Bradley
windmills, *see* p. 16, Aldringham, Dalham, Drinkstone, Elmham, Framsden, Friston, Holton, Pakenham, Saxstead, Syleham, Thurlow, Woodbridge
Wingfield, *see* p. 16
Wingfield family, *see* Dennington, Fressingfield, Hacheston, Laxfield, Sternfield, Stonham Aspall, Wantisden
Winterburn, T. F., *see* Saxmundham
Winthrop, John, *see* Groton
Wolsey, Cardinal, *see* Bergholt, Ipswich

Woodbridge, *see* p. 29
'Woodlands', *see* p. 10
Woodyer, Henry, *see* Creeting St Mary, Stratford St Mary
Woolnough, Constantine, *see* Dennington
Woolpit, *see* p. 37
Worlingworth, *see* p. 37
Wright, Charles, *see* Beccles
Wright, S., *see* Ipswich
Wright, Thomas, *see* Rushbrooke
Wyatt, James, *see* Henham, Heveningham, Nacton
Wyatville, Sir Jeffry, *see* Wherstead
Wythe family, *see* Framsden

Yale, Elihu, *see* Glemham
Yarmouth, *see* p. 37
Yaxley, *see* p. 33
Yorks influence, *see* Halesworth, Rumburgh
Young, Arthur, *see* Ampton, Bradfield Combust
Young, William, *see* Elveden

Zincke, Rev. F. B., *see* Wherstead

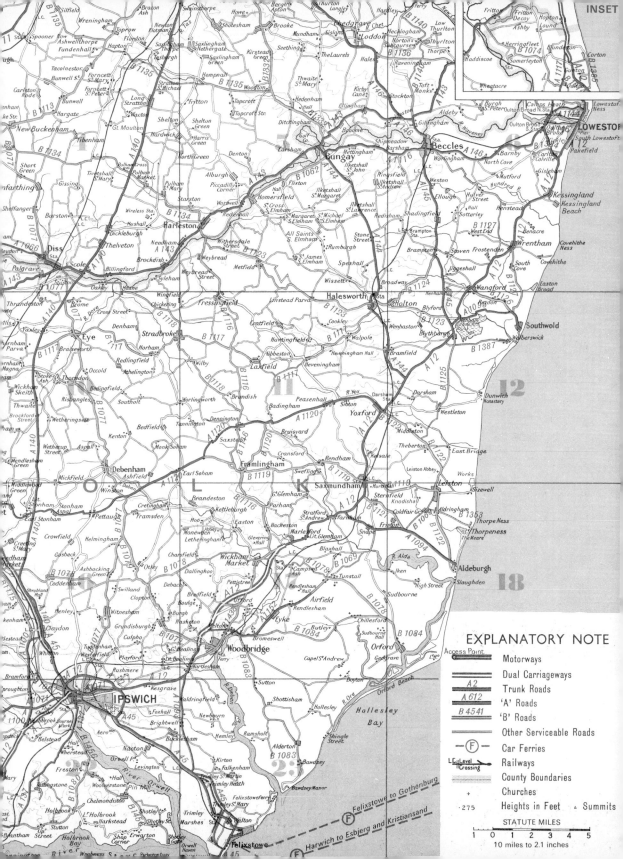

INSET

EXPLANATORY NOTE

	Motorways
	Dual Carriageways
A 2	Trunk Roads
A 612	'A' Roads
B 4541	'B' Roads
	Other Serviceable Roads
Access Point	
—(F)—	Car Ferries
LC Level Crossing	Railways
	County Boundaries
+	Churches
·275	Heights in Feet ▲ Summits

STATUTE MILES

1 0 1 2 3 4 5

10 miles to 2.1 inches